MW00390310

The publisher gratefully acknowledges the generous support of the Humanities Endowment Fund of the University of California Press Foundation.

The publisher gratefully acknowledges the generous support of the Barbara S. Isgur Public Affairs Endowment Fund of the University of California Press Foundation.

America's Social Arsonist

America's Social Arsonist

FRED ROSS AND GRASSROOTS ORGANIZING
IN THE TWENTIETH CENTURY

Gabriel Thompson

UNIVERSITY OF CALIFORNIA PRESS

University of California Press, one of the most distinguished university
presses in the United States, enriches lives around the world by advancing
scholarship in the humanities, social sciences, and natural sciences. Its
activities are supported by the UC Press Foundation and by philanthropic
contributions from individuals and institutions. For more information, visit
www.ucpress.edu.

University of California Press
Oakland, California

Library of Congress Cataloging-in-Publication Data

Thompson, Gabriel.
    America's social arsonist : Fred Ross and grassroots organizing in the
twentieth century / Gabriel Thompson.
        p.   cm.
    Includes bibliographical references and index.
    ISBN 978-0-520-28083-0 (cloth : alk. paper)—ISBN 0-520-28083-0 (cloth :
alk. paper)—ISBN 978-0-520-96417-4 (ebook)—ISBN 0-520-96417-9 (ebook)
    1. Ross, Fred, 1910–1992.   2. Community Service Organization—
History.   3. Community activists—California—Biography.   4. Community
organization—California—History—20th century.   5. Immigrants—Civil
rights—California—History—20th century.   I. Title.
    HN79.C23C684   2016
    307.1′409794—dc23   2015031924

Manufactured in the United States of America

25 24 23 22 21 20 19 18 17 16
10 9 8 7 6 5 4 3 2 1

In keeping with a commitment to support environmentally responsible and
sustainable printing practices, UC Press has printed this book on Natures
Natural, a fiber that contains 30% post-consumer waste and meets the
minimum requirements of ANSI/NISO Z39.48–1992 (R 1997) (*Permanence
of Paper*).

To Rafi

CONTENTS

ILLUSTRATIONS

ACKNOWLEDGMENTS

This is my first attempt at writing history and biography. Having never set foot inside an archive, I knew I would need plenty of help. As it turned out, I needed a lot more than I imagined. Fortunately, I got it.

Fred Ross Jr. provided enthusiastic cooperation from the very beginning. Over the course of six years, he spoke with me countless times and connected me to many former members of the Community Service Organization and United Farm Workers. He dug up boxes of old letters and photographs and reviewed a draft of the book, offering suggestions, corrections, and clarifications. His support was critical, and I am grateful for it. Ross's two other children, Julia and Bob, were also unfailingly generous with their time, sharing documents and memories—some quite painful—that helped fill in little-known aspects of their father's life.

Several colleagues shared valuable research, observations, and writerly advice. Miriam Pawel went out of her way, many times, to answer obscure questions and track down bits of information. She also read and commented on the book, improving it greatly. Thanks as well to my other reader, Frank Bardacke, who pointed out a number of gaps and raised important questions to grapple with. Both have written groundbreaking histories of Cesar Chavez and the UFW that informed this book. Jeff Miller of Utica College, who is completing a book about Syracuse's War on Poverty project, also provided documents critical to my understanding of that period.

The bibliography lists the people I interviewed, and I extend heartfelt thanks to each. LeRoy Chatfield deserves special mention, as he has labored for years to create the Farmworker Movement Documentation Project, an invaluable online archive that I relied on extensively. Thanks also to Gretchen Laue, whose book about the CSO I eagerly await. And, of course, thanks to the librarians at each archive I visited; they were, without exception, helpful and patient. I made especially heavy use of Stanford's Special Collections and University Archives, where the Fred Ross Papers are deposited, and often relied on the expertise of librarian Tim Noakes.

I completed this book while a Steinbeck Fellow in Creative Writing at San Jose State University, which provided much needed financial support at exactly the right moment. I was also extremely fortunate to have the backing of 150 individuals through a Kickstarter campaign, whose contributions allowed me to visit several archives and enjoy protected time to write. An especially hearty thanks to Kickstarter backers Tom Cassutt, Joni and Billy Greenfield, Don Greif, and Jim and Elana Ponet. (And, of course, Budd and Ruth Rockower, who have made so many dreams possible.)

Peter Dreier introduced me to Fred Ross Jr., a connection that got the ball rolling. And Peter Richardson connected me to Niels Hooper at the University of California Press, which turned out to be a perfect publishing home for the book. At UC Press I am also indebted to Bradley Depew for keeping me on track and to Julie Van Pelt for skilled copyediting. Thanks also to my agent, Michael Bourret, who always has my back.

My parents, Jim Thompson and Sandra Hietala, have been unabashed supporters of my earlier projects. This time was no different. I also received regular bouts of inspiration from my ninety-four-year-old grandfather, Ralph Hietala, who continues to spin out amazing poetry. My wife, Daniella Ponet, has patiently lived with this book for many years, including a few in which it was not at all clear where it was heading. She even agreed to move across the country so I could work on it—before I had so much as a contract. (Yes, I'm lucky.) As with my previous books, she has been a supportive partner and extraordinary editor. And who could forget our exuberant son, five-year-old Rafi, who already knows quite a bit about Fred Ross, and our daughter, Laylah, who was born two days after I turned in the manuscript. Whatever they end up doing, may they do it with the kind of passion that Ross brought to the world.

Introduction

ON A WARM JUNE EVENING in 1952, two figures approached the front door of a small, wood-framed house in East San Jose. The first, Alicia Hernandez, was a young nurse who ran a well-baby clinic out of a nearby church. Accompanying Hernandez was a tall, square-jawed man named Fred Ross, whose erect bearing made him appear taller still. Ross was new to San Jose and learning his way around this neighborhood, which locals called Sal Si Puedes.

Sal si puedes is Spanish for "get out if you can." And there was plenty to get away from. Many streets were without lights, sidewalks, or sewers. A nearby packinghouse dumped refuse into a creek, and when it rained the creek overflowed, flooding the neighborhood with toxins. Afterward, stagnant cesspools glistened in the sun for weeks, littered with the occasional drowned and decomposing rat. Two years earlier, residents had gathered signatures asking the city to pave the east side's dirt roads. Nothing had happened. Mexicans were meant to pick and pack the valley's fruits and vegetables, and stay quiet. Sal Si Puedes was the embodiment of what author Michael Harrington would call, in a decade's time, the other America: separate, unequal, invisible.

Hernandez was a familiar figure, but many must have looked at Ross with a sense of puzzlement. White and wiry, with movie-star looks and a poor grasp of Spanish, he seemed in need of directions back to the freeway. The forty-one-year-old had recently moved to the Bay Area from East Los Angeles, where he had helped form the Community Service Organization (CSO). In five years, the group with an innocent name had turned the city's growing Mexican American population into a political force. They registered thousands of new voters, elected a Spanish speaker to the city council, and waged a high-profile campaign against police brutality that helped put cops behind bars. "New England–style Town Hall with a touch of old Mexico has mushroomed in the socially bypassed hills, hollows and flats of Los Angeles, and the back streets will never be the same," reported the *Los Angeles Daily News*.[1]

After the successful experiment in Los Angeles, Ross dreamed of expanding the CSO into a statewide organization. San Jose was his first stop. Soon after landing in the city, he had linked up with Hernandez, who was enthusiastic about the project and had agreed to introduce Ross to families she thought might want to get involved. Tonight, she had brought Ross to meet a young man named Cesar Chavez.

In time, Chavez would rise to international fame as the public face of the farmworker struggle. He would march until his feet were blistered and fast until he was faint. Millions of people would rally to the cause, refusing to eat grapes. But on June 9, 1952, when Ross showed up at his door, Chavez was still an anonymous twenty-five-year-old struggling to support his growing family. The young man knew little about organizing and was suspicious when he heard that "this gringo," as he later put it, wanted to talk to him.[2]

Two hours later, Chavez's skepticism had transformed into wide-eyed enthusiasm. In his short life, Chavez had seen plenty that wasn't right. His father had lost their ranch during the Depression, and much of Chavez's boyhood was spent on the road, picking crops under a scorching sun. The problems seemed vast, the only solution to buckle down, work harder, and rise above. That night, Ross presented another option: Mexican Americans rising together. And he somehow made progress feel not just possible, but inevitable. "Fred did such a good job of explaining how poor people could build power that I could even taste it," Chavez recalled. "I could really feel it. I thought, gee, it's like digging a hole. There's nothing complicated about it."[3]

When they met, Chavez would later say, Ross had been "about the last person I wanted to see. Then he started talking—and changed my life."[4]

"A good organizer," wrote Ross, "is a social arsonist who goes around setting people on fire."[5] He began organizing after World War II, when he was in his midthirties, and he pursued this calling—and for Ross, it was indeed a calling—over the next four decades, until Alzheimer's forced him to stop in the late 1980s. During those forty years he directed groundbreaking campaigns and pioneered tactics that are widely used today. But his greatest legacy is in the people he inspired and mentored, who went on to shape California and US history.

Ross shaped history too, of course. But he did so as an organizer who worked behind the scenes, and he was easy to miss. As far as I can tell, only five articles were written about Ross while he was alive. That he largely escaped public notice isn't surprising. For Ross, an organizer was supposed to fade into the crowd as others stepped forward. As he wrote, "An organizer is a leader who does not lead but gets behind the people and pushes."[6] He spent his life pushing people to lead—in living rooms, in union halls, on picket lines—and in so doing, he pushed himself right out of the spotlight. That he is both an obscure figure *and* one of the most influential organizers in American history is not as paradoxical as it may seem. These dual facts are what caused me to write this book.

Ross was an unlikely radical. Born in 1910 to conservative parents, his turn to the political left occurred during the Depression. After graduating from the University of Southern California, he spent a decade working for the government, engaged in projects that he considered interesting and meaningful. But his life shifted into another gear when he discovered organizing, like an artist who has found his medium. His first campaign involved black and Mexican American parents who were protesting segregated schools. He spent many weeks away from his family, living out of motels. He worked so hard that he frequently made himself sick. Still, he was hooked. He was fascinated by the nitty-gritty of the craft, the daily efforts that were needed, as he once put it, to pull people "over the edge of their life grooves" into taking public action.[7] This involved a lot of grunt work, like making endless house calls in neighborhoods like Sal Si Puedes. Some people, including Saul Alinsky—who worked closely with Ross for nearly twenty years—considered such work tedious. Ross found it exhilarating. When Ross was seventy-four, a young man asked whether he had ever felt like quitting. "Hell no," Ross replied.[8] When I came across this recording, early in my research, I took the statement as bravado. Now I think he was telling the truth.

Ross did his most important work during the McCarthy era, when he crisscrossed the state to organize chapters of the CSO, occasionally tracked by the FBI and investigators from California's Un-American Activities Committee. Historians have largely overlooked the CSO, perhaps in part due to its boring name. (Alinsky once complained to Ross that it made even "the Junior League sound militant.")[9] There is little doubt, however, that the organization altered the political landscape of California in ways that reverberate to this day. People could arrive at the CSO curious but skeptical. They often left, years later, as seasoned political actors who had tasted some measure of victory and wanted more. This confidence seeped into the following decades, when CSO leaders like Chavez and Dolores Huerta—whom Ross also recruited and mentored—founded what became the United Farm Workers (UFW). And when Chavez went about organizing the union, he did so using tactics he had learned from Ross.

That Ross felt his proper place was in the background is not to suggest that he was an especially modest man. He held a high opinion of his work and tended to be dismissive of people who proposed other organizing strategies. In the last quarter of his life, in which he trained thousands of organizers, he would often respond to suggestions by saying something along the lines of, "Sure, you could try it that way ... but it won't work."

He also believed that only a select few—the word he used was "fanatic"—were cut out for organizing. An organizer had to be ready to shove aside all other priorities, no matter the personal consequences. (Ross practiced what he preached: twice divorced, he spent his later years living alone in a primitive one-room cabin.) And if someone burned out, he or she was a "loser" who was "just not committed enough."[10] This almost gladiatorial attitude inspired some people to become organizers, but it also led others to drop out. "Injustice never takes a vacation," Ross liked to repeat, underscoring the need to push through without rest. But plenty of people found that they needed time to rest, relax, and pursue interests outside of work. Ross was an organizing fanatic, and this served his career—if not his family—well. But it shouldn't be held up as the only model to emulate.

His ferocious internal drive meant that, aside from a few breaks to focus on writing, he was nearly always in motion. Fortunately, he left behind a rich archival record. Reports and other documents from his time as a government employee—when he worked with Dust Bowl migrants and Japanese Americans—have been preserved, as has significant material from his years with the CSO and the UFW. I have also been able to draw from the extensive correspondence between Ross and Alinsky, most of which hasn't been seen by scholars, thanks to his son, Fred Ross Jr. Another important source of information was Ross's own writings, along with his vast audiotape collection, which includes interviews he gave and trainings he conducted. Both can be found in his papers at Stanford University. Even short-lived projects—

such as his one-year stint at Syracuse University, where he trained students in a controversial "War on Poverty" organizing initiative—generated boxes of archival material.

It took me four years to research and write this book. Along with examining archives in six states, I interviewed dozens of people, read widely in relevant fields, and scoured newspapers and census data for glimpses of Ross. But biography is a strange and obsessive creature, and I kept coming up with more questions, many of them ultimately unanswerable. Ross was a private person who rarely divulged details of his personal life, and there are gaps that I would like to fill in but can't. Still, one doesn't need to know everything about a person to know something important about that person. While trying to track down countless documents, I was often reminded that it is sometimes the small detail, or the story told as an aside, that can capture an essential characteristic, without which an individual doesn't entirely make sense. So before diving into the narrative, let me share one story about Ross.

It is the second week of January in 1945. Ross is driving from Cleveland to California, accompanied by two Japanese American men. The US government had evacuated ethnic Japanese from the West Coast during World War II, and Ross's two companions are among the first to legally return. They cross into Southern California on Highway 10 and stop for the night in Indio, a dusty desert city near Palm Springs. When they walk into a crowded restaurant, the room falls silent. After they take their seats, several burly men stand up and walk over, staring with hatred. Another man picks up the phone and calls the police, loudly reporting that "a couple of Japs" have walked through the door and predicting trouble. Ross hurries the men outside.

Back at the motel, Ross gathers what he calls his "propaganda"— pamphlets and flyers that document the bravery of Japanese Americans who have volunteered for the army. He returns to the restaurant alone, armed with these papers, and proceeds to explain to the men, not all of whom are sober, that the Japanese are now welcome on the West Coast and that many fought honorably for their country. He stays until the men seem to agree with him. Then he picks up three meals and returns to the motel.

What struck me about this story? First, of course, was the measure of bravery involved in the act of returning to the restaurant. I would not have done so. Much easier to cut my losses and go somewhere else, especially since no one was there to judge. But more fundamental was what the decision to return revealed about how Ross thought about people. It only made sense to return if he believed that men threatening violence in one moment could be convinced that they were wrong in the next.

Ross had that kind of faith. His belief in the decency and potential of ordinary people ran deep, even though, as he had many chances to witness in his life—indeed, as he had just witnessed—ordinary people often behaved badly. They could be moved and transformed; they could act in ways that would surprise themselves. This conviction inoculated Ross against cynicism and probably goes a long way toward explaining why, unlike his onetime student Chavez, he never gave up on organizing. It didn't matter how bad things had become or how many defeats had been suffered. An organizer could always go looking for the next person, because one never knew what the next person might be capable of.

PART ONE

The Education of an Organizer
(1910–1947)

ONE

_____

All That You Do, Do with Your Might

BEFORE HE BECAME AN ORGANIZER, Fred Ross wanted to be a writer. He wasn't a particularly good writer, and his penmanship was often illegible. But throughout his life he would fill countless yellow notebooks with his left-handed scrawl, working on various versions of an autobiography that was never published.

In his writings he tended to repeat the same stories. There was the college party he attended, where he passionately argued in support of striking citrus workers until a woman boldly interrupted. "All you do is blab, blab, blab," she said. "When are you going to do something about it?"[1] There was the episode, several years later, when he experienced the misery that can be farm work, spending twelve hours in the carrot fields and coming home, exhausted, with eighty-four cents to show for it. There was the Depression, when Ross took a job as a relief worker and visited his first client, an older man who had spent most of his life working in a cement quarry. The company had fired the man just days before he was to earn his pension. He now sat mute, staring at a blank wall in the corner while his wife sobbed. And there was, of course, the evening when Ross first crossed paths with a young Cesar Chavez, an encounter that would eventually be told so many times, by so many people, that it took on the power of a myth.

For Ross, these were the stories that explained who he was and how he had become that way. About his childhood he had less to stay, though it would also leave a mark.

Ross described his childhood home as located on a hill that also served as a status marker: the wealthier you were, the higher you lived. "We lived fairly close to the bottom," he remembered, "but not so close that we couldn't look down on other people."[2] Above the Ross household lived lawyers and doctors; below, construction and service workers. When his parents sent him out to play with neighborhood kids, they always encouraged him to travel uphill.

The hill was in Echo Park, a middle-class neighborhood of Los Angeles kept entirely white by the restrictive racial covenants that forbid people of color and Jews from buying properties. To his parents, this homogeneity was both natural and desirable, but the effect on the youngster was a budding fascination with those kept out. The only person of color who entered the neighborhood was an African American woman who cleaned a neighbor's house, and the young Ross would press his face to the window when she passed. On occasions when the family drove through the city's east side, Ross recalled his father cursing the "goddamn dirty greasers" who clogged the streets with wedding processions, while Ross peered out at the forbidden territory, "launching dangerous exploratory expeditions from the carefully protected confines of the back seat."[3]

His parents, Daisy and Frederick, did not share their son's curiosity. Ross's father was born in Evansville, Indiana, and had inherited the region's racial prejudices. The son of a postmaster, Frederick worked as a steamboat pilot on the Mississippi River before moving to Los Angeles in his early twenties and meeting Daisy Crowell. They married on March 23, 1908, with the *Los Angeles Herald* noting that the guest list was kept low despite the fact that "the bride is a popular young society woman." After the wedding, they left for San Francisco, where Frederick had found work in the advertising department of the *San Francisco Examiner*. Two years later, on August 23, 1910, the couple celebrated the birth of their first son, Frederick Williams Ross Jr.

The marriage of Daisy and Frederick wasn't without controversy. Daisy's parents, industrious owners of a modest hotel, had prepared their daughter for a life beyond the limited roles open to women. In 1905, Daisy had graduated from the prestigious Girls' Collegiate School, located in the West End neighborhood of Los Angeles. One private-school directory noted that the institution sent girls "to the leading colleges East and West," and Daisy had continued on to Stanford University, whose tuition was free. But to the chagrin of her parents, she dropped out of school to marry Frederick and became a housewife. (Daisy's brother attended MIT and would become a respected chemistry professor at UCLA.)

Soon after Ross's birth, the family returned to Los Angeles, where Frederick had landed a position managing automobile advertising for the *Los*

Angeles Times. His politics meshed with the conservative paper, whose larger-than-life publisher, Harrison Gray Otis, waged an around-the-clock campaign to keep organized labor out of Los Angeles, calling unions "leeches upon honest labor."[4] In 1910, after Otis spearheaded efforts to break a strike of metal workers, two union employees dynamited the *Times* headquarters, killing twenty-one people. The brazen attack, which occurred just before Frederick started his job, underscored the dangers represented by radicals and likely did little to soften the senior Ross's attitude to the working-class. Ross remembered both parents referring to poor people as "trash."[5]

There is little to indicate that much tenderness—or even much of a relationship—existed between father and son. If Ross had any happy memories of his father, they went unrecorded. Daisy was the nurturer and the protector. One year, the boundaries of her son's elementary school district changed. On the first day of school, Daisy marched Ross to his new school and demanded a transfer. Her complaint? The new school taught both black and white children. She stomped into the principal's office and announced, according to Ross's childhood memories, that her son "didn't get along well with Negro children." Ross was embarrassed—he didn't even *know* any black children—but remained silent. When the principal refused to budge, Daisy put her foot down. "That's not the way my son's been raised," she exclaimed. "I've brought him up to stay with his own kind and that's the way it's going to be."[6] The statement was racist, but it also took courage to make such a public stand. The principal eventually gave in and sent Ross back to the all-white school. Her son would later prove wildly disobedient: staying "with his own kind" was precisely the opposite of what the adult Ross would do.

The most formative event of Ross's youth was the divorce of his parents in 1921, when he was ten. After the divorce, Frederick dropped out of his son's life, remarried, and eventually moved to New York City, where he worked for the National Association of Manufacturers. After Frederick died in 1961, Saul Alinsky, who was estranged from his own father, mentioned the passing in a letter. "Knowing your relationship with him somewhat paralleled the relationship I had with my father, I am not going to engage in a lot of conventional condolences."[7]

Ross never wrote in detail about the divorce, though it appears that his father was cheating on Daisy and that Daisy initiated the proceedings. More certain is that Daisy was suddenly responsible for raising two boys

FIGURE I. Fred Ross as a toddler, circa 1912, holding his father's hands; his mother, Daisy, is to his right. Courtesy of Bob Ross.

alone—Ross by now had a brother, Bob, younger by four years—and was forced to take a secretarial job in the office of the county assessor to make ends meet. She returned home from work exhausted and, in the eyes of her oldest son, paid far too much attention to little Bob. The divorce was a confusing affair for Ross, and he acted out, teasing and tormenting his brother. Daisy, overwhelmed, tried to discipline Ross, but nothing seemed to work. Finally, she began sending him across town to San Pedro, where her parents lived and ran their small hotel, called the Esterbrooke.

From then on, Ross arrived home from school every Friday afternoon to find his bag packed for the weekend. He would set off alone through a small African American neighborhood—a route Daisy expressly forbid him to take—and catch a streetcar that took him to his grandparents. Soon he was passing his summers at the Esterbrooke as well. Ross took the forced exodus hard. His father had disappeared, and now his mother was sending him away, while Bob stayed home and soaked up all of Daisy's affection. When he was home, Ross would sometimes retreat to his room, screaming hysterically and pounding his pillow. "I was so sad . . . total rejection," Ross later remembered, convinced—as he would be for many years—that his mother loved his brother best.[8]

In an attempt to win her affection, Ross wrote poems to Daisy. During high school, one of those poems, "I Love Her," was published in a local paper, whose editors noted that it had "attracted wide attention among Los Angeles literary people." An illustration of a stern-looking woman staring down at her child accompanied the verse. The two middle stanzas capture both the turbulence of the relationship and Ross's feelings of guilt:

> She rants an' rages 'round the place,
> An' swears by saints above 'er,
> An' makes a terrible lookin' face;
> But just the same, I love 'er.
>
> Sometimes I pull a little trick.
> An' thin I run fer cover.
> 'Cuz I ain't hankerin' for no stick;
> But just the same, I love 'er.[9]

Ross's doubts about his mother's love were mitigated by the affection displayed by his maternal grandparents, Lillie and Hiland Crowell, whom he called Nanny and Boppy. The Crowells had moved from Massachusetts to California shortly after Daisy's birth, settling in the small town of Santa Paula in Ventura County. Here they ran the general store, and after several years they had saved enough to purchase the San Pedro hotel, located near the water at 810 Beacon Street, where they lived and rented out half a dozen rooms. The Crowells were deeply religious Congregationalists, influenced by "a very strong Puritan and Calvinist strain," Ross recalled, who "put a lot of stock in such things as total and complete honesty, perseverance, tenacity."[10] While Daisy could become hysterical at Ross's outbursts, his grandparents considered him "just a nervous little tyke" in need of the discipline only religion could instill.[11] They also made it clear that he was special. His grandmother Lillie, in particular, drilled into the young boy the notion that he was a gifted child, with the makings of a great writer.

FIGURE 2. A young Ross stands in front of the Esterbrooke Hotel in San Pedro, circa 1922, next to his maternal grandmother, Lillie Crowell. Courtesy of Bob Ross.

At the Esterbrooke, every night after dinner Ross happily wedged between his grandparents, listening to stories from an illustrated children's Bible. The young boy loved the tales, finding the pictures of a "jealous, wrathful, vindictive God" both unforgettable and a bit terrifying.[12] One year, for his birthday, his grandparents gave him a new Bible, demanding that he commit verses to memory. He took up the challenge with gusto, eventually memorizing so many psalms that he became the junior pastor at his grandparent's Methodist church. This would later amuse Alinsky, as by adulthood Ross had completely shrugged off any interest in religion. But the stress his grandparents placed on values like perseverance and commitment grew deep roots. His grandmother drilled countless rhymes into Ross's head, each with a simple moral. Don't procrastinate. Don't complain. Don't give up. And don't *ever* do something halfway.

Sixty years later, Ross could recite many of the rhymes from memory, including one of his favorites: "All that you do, do with your might / Things done by halves are never done right." Although he never published a book on organizing, he did eventually write up a series of pithy statements, called *Axioms for Organizers,* where the lasting influence of his grandparents is obvious. Here's Ross, for example, on an organizer's need for total commitment: "In any kind of work if you do a half-assed job at least you get some of the work done; in organizing you don't get anything done." His grandparents had Ross baptized, turned him into a junior pastor, drilled Bible verses into his head, and taught him to meet life's challenges with religious fervor. He would do so, eventually, but the religion he found was organizing.

Ross lived two very different lives as a youth. On the weekends and during the summer, while living on Beacon Street with his grandparents, he was a studious and serious young man. But at home in Echo Park, he was a slacker and a rebel. He flunked classes, spent days on end in the principal's office, even tossed fireworks into his elementary school graduation rehearsal. By the time he reached high school, teachers complained about constant classroom disruptions, and his mother had had enough. For the second semester of his freshmen year, she sent Ross off to the San Diego Army and Navy Academy, a school of several hundred students that overlooked the harbor. It was a financial stretch that attested to her desperation: the school cost eight hundred dollars a year, more than half of Daisy's annual salary. (At this time, Ross's father was also providing twenty-five dollars a week in child support.) But the military discipline didn't take. In one memorable event, during a chapel service that hosted a visiting dignitary, Ross got into trouble after "screeching out some weird, ungodly noise."[13] His stay at the school was cut short by a bout of rheumatic fever, and he returned to Los Angeles thoroughly unreformed, taking from the experience only the words of a few new dirty songs.

The teenage Ross returned to a city that was still relatively homogenous. In 1926, the year he turned sixteen, more than 90 percent of Los Angeles residents were white, the vast majority Protestants. For boosters, the result was a "city without slums" and "the last purely American city in the nation." One article in the *Los Angeles Times* described the city as "more Anglo-Saxon than the mother country today."[14] But such claims masked an anxiety. The rapidly growing city, whose population would triple to nearly 1.5 million from 1920 to 1930, was becoming increasingly diverse.[15] Ethnic Mexicans began to expand beyond the downtown plaza into various neighborhoods of the east side; by 1930, Los Angeles was the largest home to Mexican Americans in the country. This growth sparked a nativist backlash. One reporter, in the *Saturday Evening Post,* described a city filled with "endless streets crowded with the shacks of illiterate, diseased, pauperized Mexicans, taking no interest whatever in the community, living constantly on the ragged edge of starvation, bringing countless numbers of American citizens into the world with the reckless prodigality of rabbits."[16]

Daisy sought to shield her oldest son from what she viewed as dangerous influences. But after the divorce, Ross had more freedom to explore the city, and there were two exceptions to his "lily white" upbringing that, in his adult years, he would recall as formative. On his southbound walks to the H Line streetcar, en route to his grandparents, he often stopped in the small black enclave along Temple Avenue known as Dinge Town—at least by whites— to play basketball. On one occasion he stuck around until it was late, with the game interrupted by the calls of mothers to come in for dinner. Rushing to the streetcar, he passed the lit-up houses. After all of the warnings about staying away from the neighborhood, with the implied dangers he would face from the exotic people within, the scenes looked ordinary and familiar: fathers, mothers, and children were gathered around tables, preparing to eat.

The second experience he often recounted occurred on the banks of the Los Angeles River. Today the river is paved and usually dry, but at the time it ran along a muddy track and created swimming holes, serving as a natural barrier between the city's west (white) and east (Mexican) sides, with youth from both groups coveting the holes. Usually an unspoken system governed the charged territory: whichever group arrived first had the right to the whole spot, until others showed up, at which point you pulled back to your side. But on "a particular summer's day," as Ross recalled, "I didn't drift back quite soon enough, a shouting match ensued, and all of a sudden a little Chicano about half my size sort of exploded across the river and charged me." Ross slapped him away, but the boy was determined and charged again, cheered on by his friends. This time Ross hit him hard enough to make him cry. While Ross watched the boy wipe tears from his face as he waded across the river in retreat, he became overcome with feelings of guilt and nausea. But those only lasted so long: before dropping from sight, the boy turned back to Ross, raised his fist, and let out "the worst string of obscenities" he had ever heard. Ross would later jokingly refer to the episode as his first "contact" with Mexican Americans.[17]

In 1929 Ross completed his unspectacular high school career, graduating from the recently opened Belmont High School just west of downtown. His surviving report cards show that he maintained a C average, though he earned a D in civics and failed chemistry and physical education. (Not that he seemed to care; on the back of one report card, he modified the grading

FIGURE 3. Ross as a young man, circa 1930, heavily muscled and deeply tan, the result of countless hours spent lifting weights at the beach. Courtesy of Bob Ross.

system so that A meant "awful" and D equaled "darned good.")[18] He made one close friend at the school, an aspiring gay actor named Allen Douglas. The two remained close until Douglas died in his fifties, and Ross would celebrate his friend's occasional roles on television, which never quite panned out into a career. (To make ends meet, Douglas drove a bookmobile.)

Other than his friendship with Douglas, Ross seems to have been little affected by his high school years. They certainly didn't stoke his curiosity. The census of 1930 lists the nineteen-year-old living at home with his brother and mother—Daisy described herself as widowed—and working as a clerk at an electrical appliance store. He spent the next three years aimless and drifting: menial jobs, some math classes at Los Angeles Junior College. If Ross had a passion at the time, it was traveling to the beach to lift weights with his brother. A photo from the period shows a tanned and shirtless man flexing for onlookers, his shoulders and arms swelling. Looking at the image, one can imagine a number of potential futures awaiting this burly and cocky young man—football captain, fraternity brother, perhaps a business executive—but there is not, yet, any hint of a radical stirring beneath the muscle.

TWO

Dealing Firsthand with the Rotten System

ROSS ENROLLED AT THE UNIVERSITY of Southern California (USC) in 1932. One in four Americans were out of work. The stock market dipped to its lowest point of the Depression, having lost nearly 90 percent of its value in less than three years. Thousands of banks failed; millions of Americans lost their homes; shantytowns named after the president—Hoovervilles—multiplied across the country. Protests against poverty were met by violence. In Michigan, thousands of unemployed workers marched on the Ford Motor Company, greeted with bullets from police and private security, with four protesters shot dead. A ragged crew of World War I veterans, dubbed the Bonus Army, journeyed to Washington, DC, to demand early payment of their war bonuses, swelling to crowds of more than twenty thousand before their tents were burned to the ground by federal troops. The drama and heartbreak played out against the backdrop of a presidential campaign, in which Franklin Delano Roosevelt walloped Herbert Hoover. "We are in the midst of an emergency at least equal to that of war," Roosevelt declared, promising to focus on "the forgotten man at the bottom of the economic pyramid."[1]

For Ross, unaware that "there was anything much wrong with anything," the drama of the Depression barely registered.[2] It's not that he lived large or was particularly privileged. Heading into USC, he had delivered newspapers, worked in retail, and mowed lawns. He lived at home with his mother, who earned the modest salary of a secretary. He later wrote that he made it into college on "some miraculous dispensation," without elaborating.[3] In fact, paying for college was beyond his means, made possible only with the financial contributions from a judge, who was having an affair with Daisy and agreed to bankroll her eldest son's education.

If the Ross who entered USC—muscle-bound, academically unambitious, thoroughly apolitical—was an unlikely radical, the campus of USC was an equally unlikely place to become radicalized. As one critic acidly observed in the 1920s, the school had become "the darling of patriotic Angeleanos, and is exactly what the darling of such a race might be expected to be: large, sprawling, noisy and vulgar, and if it has any intellectual significance, that fact has not as yet become generally known, even to people living near it."[4] This was harsh—probably too harsh a description by the time Ross enrolled—but it captured a degree of truth about the rapidly growing university, which in 1924 had been barred from the Pacific Coast Conference due to lax scholarly standards. (That Ross chose to attend USC was likely due to his poor high school grades.) Football ruled the campus, followed closely by Greek organizations. There was a cheering squad mentality about the place, not unlike the general boosterism driving the growth of Los Angeles, and it often had a reactionary edge. On campus, well-bred WASPs dominated student life, and the dividing lines were strictly policed. Even Gilbert Kuhn, an all-American center on the football team, was barred from a fraternity because he was partially of Mexican descent.[5]

Although Ross was a WASP, his modest economic background still cast him as an outsider. "I was just barely able to scrape by, and I certainly didn't have any money to join expensive fraternities," he remembered. "I was not impressed by the caliber of kids—the jock type, the wealthy type."[6] He fell in with fellow outsiders, becoming especially close to a Jewish student he met in a philosophy class. Eugene Wolman was from Mount Vernon, a suburb north of New York City, and was two years younger than Ross. The East Coast transplant mesmerized Ross, who found him "so loaded with charm you were drawn to him the second he turned it on."[7] Wolman introduced Ross to radical politics and labor organizing, and his passion, along with his tragic death, would have a lasting influence.

The pair initially bonded over the fact that neither wore a fraternity pin (Jews were prohibited from joining fraternities). At Wolman's urging, Ross became involved in a budding student movement to organize those shut out from fraternities, dubbed the "non-orgs." They distributed antifraternity leaflets at Los Angeles City College, while City College students dropped off literature at USC—the groups switching campuses to avoid academic punishment. Before meeting Wolman, Ross hadn't given much thought to anti-Semitism. There were a fair number of Jewish students at Belmont High School, and he'd even had a brief fling with a Jewish girl. But it was a relationship Ross had kept under wraps: as he recalled, his neighborhood wasn't the kind where you took Jewish girls home to meet the parents. While his parents didn't expressly forbid him from playing with Jews—as they did with blacks or Latinos—he remembered "the way they talked about the Jews made it clear they were not the most popular group of people in society, by a long shot." When neighborhood kids talked about "those damn little kikes," Ross joined in.[8] Wolman helped Ross reassess the anti-Semitism he had passively accepted.

Ross entered USC with the vague notion of becoming a lawyer, but as his studies progressed, he was increasingly drawn to history, politics, and literature. His most memorable course, which he took at Wolman's insistence, was called "The Economic Interpretation of History," taught by Professor Bruce Anthony, whom Ross dubbed the "showcase Socialist." It was the sort of class that, for a sheltered student like Ross, instantly made the world much more interesting. "He knew all about the profit system and had marvelous Marxian categories, which he could fit into every process of capitalism," recalled Ross. "You could annihilate people by just memorizing those arguments, which I did."[9] Soon he was supplementing his assigned reading with James Farrell's *Studs Lonigan,* a best-selling trilogy that pinned the blame for social evils on the capitalist system, and browsing through issues of the *New Masses,* a Communist weekly. Wolman also helped form a local chapter of the National Student League, a Communist-led group, and arranged for Ross to become president. Ross was aware that Wolman was hoping to convert him to the Communist Party, but his friend evidently had little success. While Ross would admire many Communists he met during the Depression, including militant union organizers he later befriended in the San Joaquin Valley, it is extremely unlikely that he ever joined the party. In 1951, when applying for a federal civil defense position, he marked that he had never been a member of the Communist Party, and index cards kept on Ross by members of California's Un-American Activities Committee, which closely tracked Ross's movements in the early 1950s, make no mention of Communist ties. In his FBI file, the only link is a reference to an agent's list of party members in 1937, which includes a "Fred Ross" but doesn't provide any other identifying information.[10] As Ross was a government employee in 1937, it is hard to imagine that this file, if it has the correct name, refers to the same person. (Elsewhere, the file is riddled with errors.)

For the more reserved Ross, the voluble Wolman was a study of contradictions. He came from a relatively prosperous family yet incessantly vowed that he would someday help destroy the upper class. He was by turns spoiled, arrogant, dedicated, and sensitive. As Ross wrote, "Over coffee at a restaurant, right in the midst of a rhapsody to the working-class, he'll suddenly turn on the waiter and really ream his ass out over a minor oversight—solemnly indicting me as a hopeless Romantic when I call him on it."[11]

While college can sometimes shrink the world, with students buried in texts and preparing for tests, it had the opposite effect on Ross. The outside world he had thus far ignored came bursting into view, full of color and conflict. The campus was abuzz over 1934 gubernatorial candidate Upton Sinclair, muckraking author of *The Jungle,* whose campaign to End Poverty in California—EPIC—rallied the poor and nearly catapulted the dedicated Socialist into the most powerful seat in the state. Class discussions served as springboards into the streets. After one conversation in an economics class about the ongoing raids targeting Mexican immigrants, Wolman and Ross went down to the depot, where they watched deportees being loaded onto trains. On another occasion, Ross accompanied Wolman to Pershing Square, a frequent rallying place for radicals of all stripes. Suddenly, members of Los Angeles's notorious "Red Squad," under the command of police captain William Hynes, charged into the crowd. Ross retreated, but not fast enough to avoid getting kicked in the crotch. He limped out of the park leaning on Wolman, "off to a flying start in the cause of hating cops."[12]

The most dramatic college excursion happened in the summer of 1936. Some twenty-five hundred Mexican citrus workers were on strike in Orange County orchards, seeking a raise from twenty-five to forty cents an hour. In response, the sheriff deputized four hundred men and issued a "shoot to kill" order, arresting people on the flimsiest of charges. Journalist Carey McWilliams, who would become the country's most incisive critic of big agriculture, was astonished by "how quickly social power could crystallize into an expression of arrogant brutality in these lovely, seemingly placid, outwardly Christian communities."[13] When Ross and Wolman drove to the region, they were stopped at a checkpoint. Football players from USC, wielding baseball bats, demanded they open their trunk; the deputized guards were making sure outsiders weren't bringing in food for strikers. When the pair arrived in Santa Ana, they saw strikers penned in by an open-air corral: so many had been arrested on trumped-up charges that the jails were overflowing. The strikers, covered in bloody bandages, struggled to communicate with their wives through the barricade. "That was my introduction to what a strike is," noted Ross.[14]

Ross and Wolman both graduated from USC in 1936. Ross stayed at USC an additional semester to earn his teaching credential, while Wolman took a job at the Los Angeles factory of the American Can Company, with the intent to organize the workers into the Steel Workers Organizing Committee. It was this experience that introduced Ross to union organizing and all its challenges. During the drive, Ross rarely saw Wolman; when their paths did cross, he found his friend "in a state of super-euphoria about the progress he was making."[15] Wolman invited Ross to the group's first organizing meeting, held in a large room at a Los Angeles hotel. Wolman could barely contain his excitement. He had spent weeks talking union during lunch breaks and received numerous commitments from workers to attend. After the many long college debates about the coming revolution, here was Wolman's chance—finally—to help usher it along.

The big meeting was a complete bust. Three people showed up: Wolman, Ross, and one worker. As the minutes ticked by, Wolman grew frantic, pacing in circles around the empty folding chairs he had so carefully arranged. "Where are they?" he shouted, finally sinking into one of the chairs, despondent.[16] For Ross, it wasn't the most inspiring introduction to organizing. But it did offer a useful lesson: to organize, you needed energy and passion, which Wolman had in abundance, but you also needed a solid plan. Heart wasn't enough.

More than a year later, the American Can Company would sign a contract with the union, after striking workers shut down the plant. But Wolman, who was determined to make an immediate dent in the events swirling around the world, left Los Angeles soon after the disappointing meeting. "This is one of the toughest letters I ever expect to have to write, but I feel sure you will understand," he wrote to his father on March 13, 1937. "As you know, ever since hostilities commenced I have wanted to go over there but my Union activity was such that I felt it my duty to remain here. Now things have reached that point where I feel free to go." The place Wolman wanted to go was Spain; the cause was the fight against the Fascist uprising of General Francisco Franco, who was being supported by Germany and Italy. Wolman signed up with the Abraham Lincoln Brigade, a volunteer group dedicated to supporting Spanish democracy. "Unless these forces are stopped," he wrote, "we are sure to have another war."[17]

Ross shared Wolman's belief that the United States wasn't doing enough to resist the rise of fascism. In his senior year, Ross had written a long letter, published in the school paper, which criticized an editorial in support of US participation in the 1936 Olympics, held in Nazi Germany. While acknowledging that it would be a "blow to our young track stars to be denied the privilege of representing our country," he argued that the United States had a duty to protest a country where "discrimination against minorities runs rampant." If the United States and its allies refused to travel to Germany, argued Ross, "there will be no games and a heavy blow will be struck at the heart of Fascism."[18]

Wolman arrived in Spain in the late spring of 1937. By the summer he was on the front lines. On July 15 he wrote to his parents that his company had been "shot at, shelled, machine-gunned, bombed from the sky, peppered with rifle shots & grenades, cut apart with trench mortars, and knocked off by snipers." But he was holding up well, he assured them, and promised to "really begin to appreciate life" when the fighting was over.[19] By the time the letter arrived, Wolman was dead, killed under heavy shelling on the outskirts of Madrid. "TROJAN GRADUATE KILLED IN SPAIN," read the front page of the school paper, noting that the twenty-four-year-old had endured "days of continuous fighting without food and water."[20]

Ross took the news hard. Not long after the death, Wolman's grief-stricken younger brother, Elmer, traveled from New York to visit Wolman's friends in California. He found Ross, who was by now working in Indio and handing out food to Dust Bowl migrants, and asked a single question. *Had his brother's life meant anything at all?* Ross explained to Elmer that, were it not for Wolman, he would have never found himself out in the desert, helping the poor. Wolman would serve as a sort of moral lodestar for Ross for the rest of his life, an example of how, no matter what sacrifices he might make as an organizer—the long hours, the low pay, the constant travel—others had sacrificed much more. During an interview in his seventies, Ross admitted that although Wolman hadn't asked him to come along, he still felt guilty that he "didn't have the guts to go to Spain."[21]

During high school Ross had acted in several plays, including as a Jacobin in a production about the French Revolution. At USC he joined a drama group and continued acting, which is how he met, during his senior year, a fellow drama enthusiast named Yvonne Gregg. Vivacious, bright, and attractive, Gregg had recently graduated from UCLA, where she had acted in and directed several award-winning plays and served as the president of Zeta Phi Eta, an acting fraternity. She was at USC to earn her teaching

FIGURE 4. Eugene Wolman, July 1937, days before he was killed in Spain. Courtesy of Tamiment Library/Robert F. Wagner Labor Archives, New York University.

credential. Like Ross, she had grown up in Los Angeles and was from a relatively modest background, her father a carpenter who had been unemployed for much of the Depression.

Gregg wasn't particularly political, but she shared Ross's interest in film, theater, and literature, and soon the pair was frequently hanging out together at parties, discussing the newest crop of books over glasses of wine. In 1936,

FIGURE 5. Yvonne Gregg, 1942. Bright and outgoing, she and Ross married in 1937. Courtesy of Bob Ross.

she and Ross were both members of a five-person cast that performed *The Revealing Moment,* a one-act play about Anton Chekhov that won a regional award and was covered in the *Santa Ana Register.* Gregg played Chekhov's wife and Ross played a servant. By now they were likely a couple. In 1937, despite disapproval from Ross's mother, they married.

Soon after the wedding, Gregg landed a job as a high school drama teacher in Fillmore, a small town outside of Ventura. Ross stayed put in Los Angeles and searched for work teaching social studies. But such jobs were hard to come by during the Depression, and with all the excitement in the air—the breadlines, the labor unrest, the waves of Dust Bowl migrants pouring into California—he wasn't particularly eager to spend his days with "a bunch of mooning teen-agers."[22] During one visit to the employment office, he applied for a position as a caseworker with the State Relief Administration (SRA) in Riverside County, about an hour's drive east of Los Angeles. A few days later, he found himself sitting through the SRA's daylong orientation, "learning all the road blocks a guy out of work has to butt through before he can get barely enough dough to keep him and his family alive."[23]

The SRA that Ross joined in March 1937 was hardly a progressive force. Its director, Harold Pomeroy, did everything in his power to turn the agency—established to provide relief during the Depression—into a tool to help the state's powerful agricultural landowners, or growers. If any kind of farm work was available, no matter how little it paid or how far away it might be, Pomeroy ordered a purge of the relief rolls. If farmworkers struck, they lost their benefits; if farmworkers refused to break the strike and scab, they lost their benefits too. While the relief payments certainly provided a vital lifeline for the destitute, the SRA's policies also ensured that growers had access to a steady stream of people who would work for low wages. (Pomeroy's ultimate loyalties were later revealed when he left the SRA for a position at the Associated Farmers, the most powerful—and reactionary—agricultural organization in California.)

Initially, Ross was little affected by the SRA's atmosphere. Venturing down Riverside's skid row, lined with boarding houses and crumbling apartments, he found an army of desperate people whose lives had been completely upended by the Depression. It was here he learned his first Spanish phrase. "Donde está el señor? Trabajando?" he would ask. Almost always, his inquiries about work were met with the same refrain: "No hay trabajo"— there isn't any work. After studying Marx, Ross was now, as he put it, "dealing first hand with the end-product of the recent collapse of the 'rotten system.'"[24]

His habit of diving headfirst into assignments began in Riverside. "It was all a wild pell-mell," Ross wrote. "Rushing to a family, signing them up for all the law would allow, and rushing on to the next. And when you quit at the end of the day, it was always with a frustrated sense of having seen too few, 'given' far too little."[25] Although he was a simple caseworker earning just twelve hundred dollars a year—less than twenty thousand dollars today—the job evoked both a deep sense of satisfaction and a desire to do more. He felt *useful.* And it wasn't just being able to offer some minimal amount of aid, which he recognized was insufficient. The deeper satisfaction came from providing a sympathetic ear, listening carefully to people without interruption and nodding along as they recounted their recent misfortunes.

But back at the SRA office, Ross heard a counternarrative from his coworkers. The problem wasn't a lack of work—it was the lack of a work ethic among the poor. Generous relief policies were creating "chronic dependents" too lazy to go out and earn a living. Worse, easy checks were attracting migrants from other states. In 1936, acting on such fears, the Los Angeles Police Department had attempted to seal off the state from the rest of the country, setting up border checkpoints and turning back anyone who had no proof of employment. The campaign, dubbed the Bum Blockade, was mild compared to another proposal floated by the City of Los Angeles that sought to place poor people in "Vagrancy Penal Camps," letting them out only to perform hard labor. The idea that people flocked to California for instant welfare didn't hold up: one had to be in the state for a year before even qualifying. But such was the mood of the land.

A year later, as Ross went about visiting clients, the antirelief mood had only deepened. Nearly a decade into the Depression, the *Bakersfield Californian* editorialized that workers had begun to "look upon relief as a right." This might have made sense earlier, the paper admitted, but now "the emergency had passed." Having announced the Depression officially over—editors at the paper clearly hadn't spent much time in the squatter encampments that littered their fine city—providing relief posed "a menace to the agricultural industry."[26] Sensitive to the desires of growers, Republican governor Frank Merriam, who had defeated Sinclair in 1934, initiated a "no work, no eat" policy. All but the disabled had to get into the fields, with Merriam ordering a "complete purge" of SRA caseworkers who didn't follow the directive.[27]

Working closely with the poor certainly nudged the twenty-seven-year-old Ross down an activist path, but at this point his political sympathies and worldview were still very much in formation. He had been transferred from Riverside to Indio, a city southeast of Palm Springs in the Coachella Valley, where most of his clients were unemployed farmworkers. Driving past a field one day, he noticed several familiar faces and slammed on the brakes. The faces belonged to clients who had told him that, despite their best efforts, they hadn't been able to find work. Ross, outraged at their lies, rushed into the field and announced that he was striking them from the relief rolls. He spent the rest of the afternoon checking the payroll records of local growers, discovering that fifteen other clients were also padding their wages with relief checks. The people he had assumed were poor victims were actually gaming the system! He dropped them all from the rolls. The tenor of his client visits changed as he began what he called his "Calvinist kick." While before he had expressed sympathy as people chronicled their fruitless search for work, he now dragged anyone who showed "the slightest sign of life" into his car and dropped them off at the carrot fields, where Ross knew an extra hand was always needed. "I turned my attention to those who were losing ambition," he wrote, consumed with the prospect that, in coddling his clients, he was creating the "chronic dependents" his coworkers had warned him about.[28]

But even transporting clients to the fields didn't completely solve the problem of dependency. The paychecks from tying carrots—where workers kneeled in the dirt under a harsh desert sun—were so puny that many still qualified for relief. Ross, distrustful of his clients, suspected that they were loafing. Workers were paid by the piece, and surely a dedicated individual could bring home a decent wage. One Saturday morning, disguised in a cap and sunglasses, he went into the fields to prove it. The shift started at 6:00 A.M. Twelve long hours later, Ross, dusty and sore, had earned only eighty-four cents. The episode, which he recounted years later, caused him to drop any talk of "chronic dependency." You could "work your guts out," he wrote, and come home with next to nothing to show for it.[29]

The winter of 1938 brought heavy rains to the San Joaquin Valley, making clear that "the emergency" of the Depression was far from over. Cotton workers huddled together, hoping in vain that the clouds would part. For sixteen days the rain came down in sheets, spilling out of the rivers and lakes and roaring through squatter encampments, leaving families on the brink of starvation. "The water is a foot deep in the tents and the children are up on the beds and there is no food and no fire," wrote a visiting thirty-seven-year-old writer named John Steinbeck.[30] Seeing the catastrophe up close, Steinbeck ditched his pen and notebook, rolled up his sleeves, and worked around the clock to rescue stranded families, at times "dropping in the mud from exhaustion."[31] Steinbeck would end *The Grapes of Wrath* with a biblical flood inspired by his experience.

The floods were catastrophic, but they were nothing new. As Devra Weber notes in her incisive history of cotton workers in California, *Dark Sweat, White Gold,* Mexican laborers had endured similar conditions for years. But the mass deportation of Mexicans and the arrival of Dust Bowl migrants had caused a demographic shift in the fields. The faces of California's farmworkers were now white, and their hardships could no longer be so easily ignored. The public outcry was such that, in the wake of the floods, the federal Farm Security Administration (FSA)—a New Deal agency—pledged more than a million dollars in aid for migrants who, due to their recent arrival, were ineligible for state relief.

The federal government's decision to provide additional welfare proved to be fortunate for Ross, who had unwisely shared his undercover carrot-tying experiment with his supervisor at the SRA. Aghast at such "unprofessional" behavior, she transferred Ross back to the Riverside office for a refresher course on proper work etiquette. Ross instead resigned and was quickly hired for a newly created position with the FSA in Indio, managing a warehouse of dry goods.

By now, Yvonne was living with Ross. For nearly a year, the newlyweds had spent their weekdays apart, with Ross driving to visit her each Friday night in Fillmore. "From then until Sunday night, we partied, movied, drama'd, drank, and made mad love, trying to make up for all the lost days of the week just past, cramming into a few hours a week's build up of wanting, tenderness and love," he wrote years later.[32] But the weekly two-hundred-mile round-trip journey was tiring, and Yvonne soon quit her teaching job and joined Ross in Indio, where she worked in the SRA office. It proved to be a brief reunion. When Ross was disciplined, the same supervisor transferred Yvonne to the office in Redlands, where she shared an apartment with an old theater friend from college. She and Ross still saw each other on weekends, but he could feel the distance between them begin to grow.

Not that he spent much time worrying about the relationship. He was focused on his new warehouse job and the colorful characters who streamed into the building looking for help. Ross was especially drawn to one Dust Bowl migrant whom, like Eugene Wolman, he would credit with having a lasting impact on his political worldview. Ross had first come across Milligan on a 110-degree summer day, where the sixty-two-year-old was picking cotton and, growing purple in the face, seemed ready to keel over. Ross offered Milligan a job inside the cool warehouse, where he filled bags with beans, corn meal, and sugar. The bald-headed old-timer had fled Oklahoma after his land dried up and his wife deserted him, bouncing around California to pick cotton and fruit, dreaming of someday again owning a piece of land. At his lowest point, desperate for steady meals and a roof over his head, he had even tried, unsuccessfully, to get arrested, displaying a bottle of liquor for a federal agent during Prohibition. Having seen the reality of farm work in California, where large armies of migrants shuffled from one poor-paying job to the next, he had given up any notion of landownership, and each night he sucked on Bull Durham cigarettes while regaling Ross with colorful stories from his life.

Ross harbored thoughts of being a writer, and he sat alongside Milligan—whose first name he never mentions—with a sheet of paper in hand, taking notes for what he imagined might become the "Great American Depression Novel." Those notes are lost, but while they never found their way into fiction, the long bull sessions marked the beginning of an important shift in how Ross thought about the poor. No longer were they political abstractions, neither the right's lazy creatures prone to "chronic dependency" nor the left's flawless victims who deserved, as Ross put it, "peppermint-candy glorification." The poor were complicatedly human, as three-dimensional as anyone else; they just happened to have more roadblocks thrown up in their way. Milligan "straightened me out," Ross wrote. "There was a man, just a plain ordinary guy who wasn't shiftless and wasn't stupid, and he gave it his best shot for his whole pain-filled life, and still he couldn't make it. I've thought of him often over the years and of how much I owe him for giving me that chance to come close enough to a plain, ordinary, working stiff to get to know a little bit about him."[33]

THREE

Witness to The Grapes of Wrath

RELIEF WORK SUITED ROSS. SOME college graduates might have looked upon the job as depressing, or at least a dead-end: he spent his days hanging around poor farmworkers, tracking warehouse inventory, handing out food, earning a modest living. But Ross, who was eternally curious about the migrants and had little interest in money, relished the chance to hold long and rambling conversations, and it gave him a deep sense of satisfaction—once those conversations had concluded—to hand over a bag of dry beans or cornmeal. "It wasn't Spain," he acknowledged, referring to the Spanish Civil War and the American volunteers, like Eugene Wolman, who had risked it all.[1] But the work was interesting and meaningful. At the end of each day he had learned something new and given something to someone in need. Still, handing out food and checks wasn't organizing. It was a bow-tie-wearing bear of a man named Robert Hardie who would nudge Ross down that path.

In February 1939, Ross and Yvonne moved north to Visalia, a small city in the San Joaquin Valley, where Ross had been transferred to work in the Farm Security Administration's relief office. In Visalia—which had been hit hard by the floods of the previous winter—the FSA also operated a migrant camp, one of nineteen the agency built throughout California. Although modest, these federal camps were meant to serve as models, proof that with a relatively small investment, safe housing could be provided for the migrants streaming into California. (Growers, whose private camps were often barely habitable, would fail to follow the government's lead.) The camps were also intended to be incubators of democracy. Each camp had an elected council that made many of the day-to-day decisions, and camp managers emphasized community events to strengthen bonds among people considered to be rugged individualists. "Our purpose," wrote one FSA administrator, "is to encourage democracy and development of self-government among the campers."[2] The camps were to be places of dignity, safe havens where Dust Bowl migrants could begin rebuilding shattered lives and slip back into mainstream society.

Robert Hardie managed the Visalia camp. He and Ross crossed paths at the relief office, and Ross was immediately drawn to the burly man from Nebraska. And for good reason: even among the many New Dealers in the FSA, Hardie stood out for his idealism and enthusiasm. Some had grown disillusioned with the camp council structure—democracy could be slow and messy. But Hardie, who had managed two other camps prior to Visalia, remained passionate about the project. Ross had considered the camps little more than places for farmworkers to bed down for the night. Hardie placed the camps in a broader social context. Hundreds of new migrants arrived every day, certain to be exploited by growers and demonized by politicians; the camps were the best shot the workers had to learn to work together. Ross hadn't been hunting for a new job, but he immediately applied to be Hardie's assistant.

Ross would only work with Hardie at the Visalia camp for a short period before being promoted, but he gained two valuable lessons from the experience. At council meetings, he noted how the manager gave camp residents the opportunity to, as he put it, "thrash out" the issues without interference. When Hardie did interject, it was usually in the form of a question. Although the manager ultimately had the power to veto any council decision, he served as a moderator and didn't think a row between campers was necessarily a bad thing. Learning to solve conflict was a key step in self-government, after all.

Then there were the two commandments that Hardie drilled into Ross's head. After one council meeting, where a circular argument over whether to hold dances in the community hall had turned into a multihour affair, Hardie pulled Ross aside. Hardie had remained quiet through most of the session, which ended with the council's deciding in favor of dances. "There's no mystery," Ross recalled Hardie saying. "It's getting to know people. Really know them. And, of course, putting in the time it takes to get it done."[3]

So there it was. Listen. Take the time to really get to know people. Hardie had just demonstrated two fundamental skills of a good organizer.

In June 1939, after a four-month mentorship under Hardie, Ross was promoted to manage the Arvin Migratory Labor Camp. The camp, soon to be famous as the model for the fictional Weedpatch in *The Grapes of Wrath*, wasn't much to look at. Located in Kern County, on a lonely country road fifteen miles southeast of Bakersfield, the camp consisted of little more than a collection of tents thrown up in a field, along with a first-aid station, laundry facility, manager's quarters, and bathrooms. (By the fall, some tents were replaced with tin sheds.) Life at the camp wasn't for the delicate. The summer heat burned; the winter rains turned the ground to mud. When powerful winds swept through the valley, one camp resident recalled, they "blew away our washtub and everything else."[4]

But living conditions certainly beat the alternative. During the 1930s, between 300,000 and 400,000 "southwesterners"—the polite term for Okies—came to California from Oklahoma, Arkansas, Texas, and Missouri.[5] They fled drought, foreclosure, and economic collapse, with many dreaming, as captured in this verse, that California represented a lucky break just around the corner:

> When I first came to California,
> Was in the year of thirty-seven,
> From what I read in papers,
> I thought it was poor man's heaven.[6]

Entering California along Highway 66, "heaven" quickly came into view. Clusters of tumbledown shacks and lean-tos dotted the landscape, built by migrants with whatever materials they could scavenge. Squatters took refuge along the banks of irrigation ditches, living beneath shredded tarps and tents. Tuberculosis and pneumonia were endemic; children frequently went hungry; some people likely starved to death. Alarmed public health workers tore down many of the settlements. Without other options, families just found new ditches and started over. Migrants were soon changing their tune:

> I'd rather drink muddy water
> Sleep out in a hollow log
> Than be in California
> Treated like a dirty dog.[7]

While public opinion turned hard against the Dust Bowlers, nowhere was the backlash as strong as Kern County, whose population jumped by 60 percent in the second half of the 1930s. The California Citizens Association floated a statewide petition seeking the removal of Okies; their secretary, a Bakersfield businessman, claimed that "no greater invasion by the destitute has ever been recorded in the history of mankind."[8] Others cited Okies' supposed tendency to commit "sordid, depraved acts."[9] One doctor called them "shiftless trash who live like hogs."[10] Another likened them to "a different race" who "don't seem to know anything."[11] Even sophisticates piled on, with H. L. Mencken expressing bluntly, "They are simply, by God's inscrutable will, inferior men."[12]

The Arvin camp was modest. But in a hard land, it offered clean drinking water, hot showers, free medical care, and even a library—all for only a quarter a week. It would be the place Ross and Yvonne called home for the next two years.

On his first day Ross was shown around the camp by departing manager Harold Tefft. When a drunk resident approached and let loose with a string of curses, Tefft shoved the man to the ground and began pummeling him in the face.

Ross had unknowingly walked into a firestorm. Several weeks earlier, more than a hundred residents had signed a handwritten petition requesting the removal of Tefft and sent it to the FSA headquarters in San Francisco. They accused him of entering the women's bathroom without warning, ignoring decisions made by the camp council, and "beating the Osborne child with a handsaw."[13]

It was an ironic turn of events at what had been considered the crown jewel of the migrant camps. The first manager of Arvin was the brilliant Tom Collins, a slight man with a square jaw and finely trimmed mustache who took the Okies' cause as his own. Raised in an orphanage, Collins had trained for the priesthood, managed a school system in Guam, and aspired to write novels (one of his unfinished books was titled "Oklatopia"). "He is one of the most unusual persons I have ever met," wrote one FSA director, "with infinite capacity for good work and at his best when he is nearly killed with work."[14]

When John Steinbeck visited the camp while gathering material for *The Grapes of Wrath,* he was impressed by what Collins had accomplished. "I want to thank you for one of the very fine experiences of a life," he wrote. "I hope I can be of some help."[15] Collins became Steinbeck's "migrant liaison," with the pair traveling the valley to visit and assist desperate farmworkers. (It was while traveling with Collins that Steinbeck helped families who had been washed out during the tremendous floods of 1938.) Steinbeck would partially dedicate *The Grapes of Wrath* "to Tom who lived it," and he portrayed the Arvin camp as a utopian paradise. In the book, the Joads have fled a squatter camp to arrive at Weedpatch in the middle of the night, exhausted and filthy. A security guard welcomes them and explains the basics: the camp has running water and toilets; police aren't allowed inside without a warrant; an elected committee of workers makes the rules. The Joads, who have thus far suffered one misfortune after another, are incredulous. Tom asks the guard, "You mean to say the fellas that run the camp is jus' fellas—camping here?" The guard replies, "Sure. And it works."[16]

That utopia, no doubt idealized by Steinbeck, was in shambles when Ross arrived. The elected council was moribund and most of the recreational events, which Collins believed so central to creating a sense of community, had been scrapped. In his last report, Tefft did hit one positive note, writing that he had been warmly received after addressing a group of farmers, who appreciated his efforts "to cooperate with them in furnishing labor at the established wage scale."[17] The established wage scale was miserly. Tefft, essentially, was being thanked by growers for convincing camp residents to work for low wages without complaint.

Ross set out to repair the damage done by Tefft. Although the manager held ultimate power at the camp, on both a personal and professional level Ross needed the residents to like him. "I wouldn't have been happy if even one person had been against me," he later said.[18] After moving into the manager's quarters, he began to visit residents at the crack of dawn, before they headed out to the fields, moving from tent to tent, making small talk, and drinking huge amounts of coffee. It was the perfect training ground for an organizer. The camp had its share of stubborn folks—it took a certain amount of stubbornness to keep going after the hardships they'd endured—and while they appreciated good company as much as the next person, they were weary of patronizing attitudes. "Hypocrisy, pretense, insincerity, lack of interest in their problems and in them—these evils we can never hide from them," wrote Collins, who wasn't immune from occasionally striking patronizing tones himself. While sympathetic to the plight of the migrants, some in the FSA viewed them as stunted creatures unable to grasp basic concepts, or mounds of so much clay that reformers needed to reshape in their image. The buzzword of the day was "rehabilitate," which captured the arrogance of this position. One supervisor, visiting Arvin in 1936, wrote that the migrants "seem almost child-like at times, as indeed they are."[20] They weren't childlike, of course. They were poor.

Like Collins, Ross was fascinated by the migrants. "What started out as a way to win them [over]," Ross later said, "almost immediately became a driving interest to be around them, learn about them, pick up their stories. If you are really interested, listening comes naturally."[21] As he had with Milligan, Ross chatted for hours, soon becoming a member of what he called the "spit and argue" club, an informal group that held long, rambling discussions. His curiosity and sympathy won many over. One resident called the previous managers at Arvin "educated men, who have never done any real work," and likened them to "dictators." He considered Ross, on the other hand, "an educated man but when he came here he acted as one of the boys. . . . He didn't act one bit better than his staff or the people in the camp. And he's always got time to say a few words to you."[22]

Within months, the visits were bearing fruit. "Practically all traces of the recent difficulties at Arvin Camp have disappeared," wrote a supervisor after visiting. "Mr. Ross is doing an excellent job of promoting camper recreation and activities."[23] By the fall, communal events were held every night of the week, a new council was elected, a co-op store was formed, and a camp newspaper, the *Tow Sack Tattler,* was being published.

Luke Hinman showed up at Arvin in early September, just as the cotton harvest was getting under way. Tall and skinny, wearing a ragged leather jacket and driving a junk heap of a car, he looked every bit the hardened radical he was. Five years older than Ross, the ex-Wobbly had joined the Communist Party, volunteered for the Abraham Lincoln Brigade, and returned from Spain to fight on behalf of farmworkers. He was coming off a weeklong stint in jail, the result of supporting striking workers in Marysville, and asked Ross if the camp's community hall was available.

Hinman was the statewide director of the United Cannery, Agricultural, Packing and Allied Workers of America (UCAPAWA). Established in 1937 and affiliated with the upstart Congress of Industrial Organizations (CIO), the union sought to organize the "unskilled" field workers long ignored by the American Federation of Labor (AFL). Had he arrived earlier in the year, Hinman would have been sent packing: under Tefft, the camp council had banned union meetings and forbidden the posting of union material on the bulletin board. But the arrival of Ross signaled a change in politics. When growers publicly burned *The Grapes of Wrath* and Kern County pulled it from libraries and schools, residents at the camp sent a letter of protest, while passing a well-worn copy of the banned book from tent to tent. The editor of the new camp paper was a CIO activist, and he filled the pages with militant slogans—"An Injury to One Is an Injury to All"—and poems with unsubtle titles like "Join the Union." The council voted to allow the CIO inside, and soon Hinman and another organizer, Wyman Hicks, were spending their nights talking union with residents in their tents. Ross often poked his head in to listen, amazed at the audacity of their project: two broke but fearless organizers, responsible for the entire state, were itching for a fight against the powerful growers. When it got late, Hinman and Hicks bedded down on the patch of grass beneath Ross's window.

The battle lines being drawn were over what constituted a "fair wage" for cotton pickers. California's newly elected liberal governor, Culbert Olson, had pegged muckraking journalist Carey McWilliams to be the state's commissioner of immigration and housing. McWilliams, no friend of big growers, moved quickly, tripling the number of labor inspectors and hosting a public hearing in Fresno, where he determined that a fair cotton rate for the season was $1.25 per hundred pounds picked. The growers balked, offering 80 cents. While the state couldn't enforce the higher wage, McWilliams promised that any worker who refused to work for less wouldn't be cut from the relief rolls. Big growers "screamed like banshees," but McWilliams didn't back down.[24] It was such policies, and his hard-hitting exposé of big agriculture, *Factories in the Field,* that would cause the Associated Farmers to label McWilliams "Agricultural Pest No. 1 in California, outranking pear blight and boll weevil."[25] In the coming years, the paths of Ross and McWilliams would frequently intersect, with Ross coming away deeply influenced by McWilliams's analysis of farm labor. Decades later, Ross would insist that United Farm Workers volunteers read *Factories in the Field* to better appreciate the nature of the beast they were up against.

UCAPAWA launched a strike in Kern County on October 9, 1939, calling for the $1.25 wage rate.[26] The strike, coming soon after publication of *The Grapes of Wrath,* caught the attention of the John Steinbeck Committee to Aid Agricultural Organization, which was chaired by Helen Gahagan Douglas, a future congresswoman and wife of movie star Melvyn Douglas. Members of the committee raised money for UCAPAWA and traveled to the Arvin camp to hand out clothing and shoes. Also visiting was a frizzy-haired, guitar-toting Woody Guthrie, who, along with movie star Will Geer, became a frequent guest at the camp. Guthrie was coming off a stint as the "hobo correspondent" for a newspaper called the *Light,* for which he had traveled the state to visit migrant camps. Many of the migrants knew him from his radio program in Los Angeles, *The Oklahoma and Woody Show,* and at Arvin he stood in front of a crowd, strummed his guitar and belted out, "I ain't gonna pick your 80 cent cotton / Ain't gonna starve myself that way."[27]

Before long, Geer and Guthrie were sleeping on the grass under Ross's window, alongside the two union organizers. Ross was enthralled with Guthrie, admiring his natural ease with the campers and the way he used his songs to stiffen the backbones of the strikers. That fall, when Ross began writing a weekly segment in the camp paper, he titled it "The Feller Sez," taking inspiration from Guthrie's "Woody Sez" column published in the *People's Daily World,* a Communist paper out of San Francisco.* During the strike, Ross asked Guthrie to write a letter for the camp paper. "Go tell the Ass Farmers and the vigilantes I said go take a long, tall, flying suck at a sunflower," wrote Guthrie, with characteristic bravado. "Tell 'em I said go ahead and pay you guys that $1.25."[28]

In Arvin, the walkout began promisingly, with workers shutting down a number of fields. It was an exhilarating experience for Ross, who reported that nearly every camp resident refused to scab. Relief work had been eye-opening but ultimately frustrating: Ross had witnessed the grinding poverty of his clients, but there was little to do but express sympathy and make sure their meager checks arrived on time. But in the strike people were fighting back. Ross ignored orders from the West Coast director of the FSA, Laurence Hewes, to remain neutral. In the camp paper, Ross used his column to stress the need for cooperation, criticizing the "man who'll work for less wages than all of his neighbors."[29] The *Tow Sack Tattler* announced that a picket line would be thrown up around every cotton field, reminding readers of the "very unpleasant word for those who cross the line."[30] Ross woke early each morning to watch caravans of strikers leave the camp and chase scabs from the fields. His partisanship was so overt that one resident would pen a letter to Ross's supervisor complaining that the camp was "practically run" by the union, that Ross was a "strong member" of the CIO, and that the camp was no longer a place "for us honest and non-communists to live in."[31]

Hewes, the FSA director, didn't consider the strike a "legitimate labor dispute" but instead saw it as a "put-up job" by Communists, whose only goal

---

* As was the fashion of the day, Ross attempted to adopt the colloquialisms of the migrants in his columns, with unfortunate results, such as: "Well, feller that may git sumpin' fixed in jig-time."

was violence.[32] But Ross had no such cynicism. He had been to the fields and watched growers cheat workers out of their already pitiful wages, claiming the cotton they picked wasn't "clean." He knew many went hungry, and he heard reports of frustrated parents who, driven mad by the constant whimpering of their malnourished children, beat them into silence. This was no manufactured crisis, and the Communists who helped organize the strike were heroes to Ross. Yvonne, too, became swept up in the cause, serving as the secretary of the Bakersfield chapter of the Steinbeck Committee.

But Hewes was certainly right about one thing—attempts at organizing farmworkers were often met by violence. The strike centered around five cotton-growing areas: Arvin, Corcoran, Pixley, Visalia, and Madera. In the Arvin region, strikes were called at 150 ranches, but growers had little problem finding replacement workers, and the strike was effectively broken within two weeks. The same pattern played out elsewhere, with the notable exception of Madera, north of Fresno, where 90 percent of the workers struck. In response, two hundred growers attacked unarmed strikers at the city park, swinging pick handles and clubs.[33] With strike leaders bloodied and Governor Olson refusing to intervene, the union put on a brave face. "Clubbed, But Still We Strike" ran a leaflet headline, promising more action.[34] But the crackdown had done the trick.

Although unsuccessful, the strike left a deep impression on Ross, who considered his two years at Arvin among the most "supercharged" periods of his life. In his writings, Ross later claimed that the strike was the largest in the history of the San Joaquin Valley, but it wasn't: a far larger cotton strike occurred in 1933, made up overwhelmingly of Mexican workers. The 1939 strike was instead the last notable conflict of the 1930s, a tumultuous decade that saw more than 127,000 California farmworkers engage in at least 140 strikes.[35] Ross knew this history very well and likely exaggerated the size of the strike to dramatize the experience. But this exaggeration also likely reflected an emotional truth: for someone with a front-row seat, the strike was an exhilarating and unforgettable experience, at once cautionary and inspiring.

Life at the camp settled down after the strike, with Ross's days taken up by more mundane administrative duties. Talk of the camps as laboratories of democracy obscured the less romantic side of communal life: complaints about men gambling over dice, children who made too much noise, a camper who shot at stray dogs with his rifle. After long days spent picking cotton or grapes, workers could return to their tight quarters exhausted and testy, with tempers flaring over perceived slights. Labor struggles were replaced with something less inspiring. "Anyone caught dumping slop-jars, night chambers, or garbage in the wash tubs will be summoned before the camp council for eviction," warned Ross in the camp paper.[36] In another dispatch, he wrote that it "has gotten beyond the joking stage," promising to notify the health department about those who "job" on the floor instead of using the toilet; they would be "booked as a menace to the health of the entire community."[37]

As the weeks turned into months, an authoritarian streak in Ross emerged. He grew increasingly frustrated with campers who, having agreed to complete certain tasks in exchange for waiving of the rent, departed without finishing the work. Like some managers, he kept what he referred to as a "blacklist" of people who had left the camp without working off their debts, who wouldn't be allowed to return. While he emphasized the democratic potential of the camp council, he also sought ways around it. At one point, he expressed a "keen interest" to his supervisor in securing a mechanism to quickly evict campers whom, although not breaking any regulations, he considered to be troublesome.[38] But this dogmatic tendency could also have an egalitarian edge. Against the wishes of the majority of the residents, he marched a Mexican family in who needed shelter, single-handedly desegregating the camp. (The other FSA camps were set aside for whites.)

Though daily life at the camp wasn't glamorous, it had its fair share of joys. Every Saturday night, bands with names like the Crystal Valley Ramblers and Circle K Ranchers fiddled away to dancing crowds. People flocked to the social hall for community "sings" and movie screenings. If there was some fighting and some drinking, the camp was also a good place for teenagers to fall in love—more than one dusty wedding ceremony occurred while Ross was manager—with budding romances noted in the gossip pages of the camp paper. ("We noticed Bill Broadway was having quiet [sic] a time playing Dominoes Tuesday Night. Who was she Bill?")[39]

Ross was also busy managing a steady stream of visitors. The Okies had become front-page news, with three books about farmworkers in the Depression, all destined to be classics, hitting the shelves in 1939. First came *The Grapes of Wrath,* followed in the summer by McWilliams's *Factories in the Field* and finally, that winter, by Dorothea Lange and Paul Taylor's *An American Exodus.* On April 4, 1940, Eleanor Roosevelt arrived without fanfare at the Bakersfield airport. Ross was among the party that greeted her, and she was given a tour of a ditch-bank settlement in East Bakersfield where Ross knew conditions were particularly horrendous. Walking down an alley-way, Roosevelt suddenly stopped in her tracks, outraged to see that a drink-ing-water faucet had been installed alongside a filthy outhouse. She tracked down the manager and chewed him out, surrounded by a crowd of migrants who were amazed at the unannounced guest. At another point, several ine-briated women began to taunt Roosevelt. When someone started over to shush the women, she held them up. "Don't pay them any attention," Ross recalled her saying. "You and I would probably be the same way if we were in their shoes."[40] Ross also told an interviewer in the 1980s that he gave Roosevelt a tour of the Arvin camp, but this doesn't appear to be the case: in her daily column, Roosevelt didn't mention visiting the camp, nor did any other peo-ple in the group who wrote about the visit. They did tour the Visalia camp, however, where manager Robert Hardie and a media scrum were waiting. Asked by a reporter about the conditions she had witnessed, Roosevelt replied, "I never believed that *The Grapes of Wrath* was an exaggeration."[41]

Soon after Roosevelt's departure, two new guests arrived from the East Coast, lugging along an eighty-pound piece of recording equipment. Charles Todd and Robert Sonkin were traveling through migrant camps to capture the ballads of the Dust Bowlers for the Archive of American Folk Song, part of the Library of Congress. Though residents were initially leery—in their field notes, Todd and Sonkin complain that upon their arrival the "best fid-dler in camp was on guard duty and refused to relinquish his post"—people eventually warmed up, volunteering songs and bringing along their harmoni-cas, guitars, and fiddles.[42] Among the recordings, which are archived online, one can hear Ross recite "Cotton Fever," which includes an indictment of rapacious growers:

> You kin live on the lan' till the day you die
> Jus' as long as you leave when the crop's laid by.
> So hunker on along an' grabb'er all around'—
> Payin' the man fer the use of his groun'.

Ross initially told Todd and Sonkin that the poem had been submitted anonymously to the camp paper. Later, Ross admitted that he had in fact written the poem. "Fairly good," the men write, "but Ross is no Okie." (Two years later, the poem would be published in the *Saturday Evening Review*.)

The preserved audio recordings and field notes provide an invaluable snap-shot of camp life, much more intimate and earthy than the official monthly reports filed by FSA staff. One migrant, who praised *The Grapes of Wrath*, tells Todd and Sonkin that he had arrived knowing full well that relief wasn't coming; facing a "root-hog or die" scenario, he got to work picking cotton, which "kicked the dog outa me." Others shared their tales of coming to California, what many called their "migracious" stories. One woman, originally from Arkansas, crossed with her family through half a dozen states looking for work, arriving at the camp with just seven cents to her name. As the tape rolls, Todd and Sonkin take notes on the day's activities. Men are in the fields chopping grapes. In unit 117, a child is laid up with fever. A woman pores over a road map to plan her next move. A fire starts on a nearby ridge. Ross threatens to evict a man for beating up his son. A boy falls off a fence and breaks his arm. There was, clearly, no shortage of drama.

Those men chopping grapes, sweating under the sun for just thirty cents an hour, worked for the DiGiorgio Fruit Company. Under the direction of Joseph DiGiorgio, who had packed lemons on his father's small farm in Sicily, the company had become the largest grape grower in the world, with ten thousand acres in Arvin alone. DiGiorgio was ruthless and brash, a short man with an outsized ego who didn't hesitate to crush workers' attempts to organize. "All this I create myself," he told a reporter from *Fortune*, looking out over his Arvin empire.[43] DiGiorgio, whom the reporter noted was shaped "like one of his own select plums," had all the makings of a cartoon villain: apartment on New York City's Central Park, vast acres filled with impoverished laborers, even a bust in town to honor his good deeds. (None too subtly, Steinbeck named the evil grower "Gregorio" in *The Grapes of Wrath*.) But if Ross harbored any animosity toward the company, he successfully concealed it, even going so far as to have DiGiorgio's chief foreman visit the camp to talk with workers. When Ross left Arvin in 1941, he did so on good terms with the company. In twenty-five years' time, he would return to direct a historic union election at DiGiorgio, and relations wouldn't be so sweet.

Arvin transformed Ross personally as well as professionally. On May 3, 1940, sandwiched between the visits of Roosevelt and then Todd and Sonkin, Yvonne gave birth to a baby boy, whom the couple named Robert—after Ross's brother—and gave the nickname Robin. One of the first congratulatory telegrams came from UCAPAWA organizer Wyman Hicks. "I hope you will be as determined and successful in your future fight for freedom as you were in this recent affair," Hicks wrote, addressing the newborn.[44]

The birth was a joyous occasion, but soon afterward Yvonne entered a deep funk, likely an undiagnosed case of postpartum depression, and never managed to fully climb out of it. She had other reasons to be unhappy, too. Even in the best of times, Arvin was hardly a dream post for Yvonne. Gregarious, charismatic, a city girl who loved theaters and parties, she had followed Ross to a place that could be fairly described as the middle of nowhere. Distant from friends, surrounded by dirt, with a husband who was often attending camp meetings at night, Yvonne must have been both deeply suffocated and profoundly bored. She was employed as a social worker for the State Relief Administration in 1939, but this was not the sort of life she had planned for herself. An especially supportive and attentive partner might have made it work. Ross, however, was neither. Buried in work and fascinated by the campers, he managed, month after month, to overlook the plain fact that his wife was miserable.

Yvonne had been a drinker in her early twenties, and after Robin's birth she took up the bottle again, buying wine at a store on the other side of town to avoid running into someone she might know. But Ross, although later realizing his wife at times seemed to be in a "fairly fuzzy condition," didn't pay much attention. It wasn't until he cleared out the garage, preparing for a move to San Francisco, that he realized the extent of her alcoholism. Bottle upon empty wine bottle was stashed in the dark corners, marking a record of unhappiness that even the most unaware of husbands couldn't miss. "By the time I knew how serious her problem was," he would later write, "the only thing I wanted to do with our marriage was end it."[45]

The family moved to San Francisco in April 1941, where Ross had been bumped up to a supervisory position working out of the FSA's regional headquarters on Van Ness Avenue. The change in setting wasn't enough to rekindle the relationship, and within months Yvonne and Robin had relocated to Southern California, where they stayed with relatives. The family was briefly reunited in the fall in San Francisco, but only to make the separation permanent. "Mummy divorced daddy," Yvonne wrote in her notebook on October 31, 1941.[46]

In San Francisco, Ross was the assistant chief of community services. He held the position for a year and a half, overseeing community activities at twenty-two FSA camps. The promotion out of Arvin, which included a significant raise, might have been based on Ross's solid track record. Or it might have been meant to get him away from daily contact with migrants. Ross was known as a staunch union supporter, and his supervisor, Laurence Hewes, was set on reigning in the leftists. In his autobiography, Hewes wrote that he had "transferred some of the more obstreperous juniors to positions remote from the powder keg of the San Joaquin."[47]

While Ross's new position was more bureaucratic, he did still get to travel the state to visit camps to monitor their community-building activities. During one such trip, likely in the latter half of 1941, he met Frances Gibson at the Marysville camp, located north of Sacramento. Bright and self-assured, the twenty-seven-year-old brunette taught nutrition and cooking classes to migrant women. They fell for each other, quickly and deeply. Frances was a seasoned political activist who hailed from a long line of radical women. Her grandmother so despised the rigid class system of London that she married an Irishman from a lower status and moved to America. Frances's mother took her to watch the sensational trials of Communist farmworker organizers Caroline Decker and Pat Chambers, both eventually found guilty of criminal syndicalism. Like the migrants she helped, Frances, whose father worked for the railroad, had spent much of her life in transit, attending sixteen different schools before graduating from Polytechnic High in San Francisco. She continued on to San Francisco State University, graduating in 1937, and served as the campaign manager for California lieutenant governor Ellis Patterson, who won office the following year. Like Ross, she was an idealist who wasn't afraid to get her hands dirty.

By the time she met Ross, Frances had been divorced twice, both at her initiation—another mark of her independent streak. Her first husband had been an alcoholic, the second old and impotent. Ross was a welcome contrast: a dedicated activist with similar politics, who also happened to be handsome and charming. In January 1942, less than three months after Ross and Yvonne were officially divorced, Ross drove to Marysville to pick up Frances. During her year at the camp, she had become popular with the farmworkers, who raised ten dollars to throw her a farewell party. When Ross arrived, the campers staged a mock wedding for the couple (they would officially marry the following year). Frances, sporting an orange crepe dress and matching hat and veil, carried a "lovely bouquet of celery centered with red radishes" and took the arm of Ross, who wore a tailored brown suit and hat, with a celery leaf in his lapel. After the ceremony they gathered to eat around a table filled

FIGURE 6. Frances Gibson, circa 1935. Ross's second wife was also a dedicated activist. Courtesy of Fred Ross Jr.

with sandwiches, macaroni salad, and Jell-O, with the bride and groom belting out the "latest song hits throughout the luncheon" before heading south to San Francisco.[48]

The San Francisco that Ross and Frances returned to was in turmoil. On December 7, 1941, beginning at 7:48 A.M., waves of Japanese fighter planes had launched a surprise attack on Hawaii's Pearl Harbor. In less than two hours, the assault sunk four naval battleships, killed 2,402 people, and led the United States to enter World War II. It also sparked a wave of anti-Japanese hysteria that would directly affect the direction of Ross's life and work.

For Ross, the attack also had a personal twist. Exactly one week after their divorce, on November 7, Yvonne had boarded a ship bound for Honolulu, carrying eighteen-month-old Robin. After Ross heard the news about the bombing, he was among the thousands of stunned people who gathered at

San Francisco's Ocean Beach, looking to the horizon and wondering if an invasion was imminent. For all he knew, staring into the churning sea, his family was dead on the island, buried beneath the rubble. Both Ross and his brother volunteered to enlist, but Ross was declared 4-F due to a back ailment, likely caused by the heavy weight lifting he did in his youth. (His brother would become a decorated pilot.)

Ross was relieved to learn that his ex-wife and son were not among the sixty-eight civilians killed in the attack. Still, the trip would prove to have dire consequences for Yvonne. If she was searching for a new beginning, Hawaii, with its warm winter weather, sandy beaches, and coconut trees, must have seemed the perfect destination, a peaceful vacation spot to try to relax, rebuild, and clear her head. Instead, she was surrounded by the constant scream of air-raid sirens and beaches strewn with barbed wire. She fell for a sailor in the navy, who was also an alcoholic. On the surface, she put up a good front. An article in the *Honolulu Adviser,* from January 13, 1942, includes a photo of a smiling Yvonne, who is "reading a missive from husband" while holding onto a child leash that is attached to young Robin, who stares into the camera. But she had, at this point, likely begun drinking heavily again, and met someone who would only encourage the habit. During the next few years, Ross would make regular child-support payments, but he would hardly communicate with Yvonne or Robin, as she went on one bender after another. Before the decade was over, she would drink herself to death.

FOUR

Doing Penance

IN THE AFTERMATH OF PEARL HARBOR, not many people kept a cool head when it came to the treatment of Japanese Americans. Rabid columnists proudly proclaimed their hatred for the "enemy race." The *Los Angeles Times* likened them to vipers. California's liberal governor, Culbert Olson, announced that while he could simply look at a German American and discern his loyalty, "it is impossible to do so with the inscrutable Orientals, and particularly the Japanese."[1] Many others on the left end of the political spectrum were no better. Even the radical newspaper *PM* ran a cartoon by Dr. Seuss that portrayed Japanese Americans as bomb-throwing spies.

One of the least cool heads belonged to one of the most powerful people: army general John DeWitt, based in San Francisco's Presidio and leader of the Western Defense Command. Bony, square-jawed, and with a facial range that expressed various degrees of severity, DeWitt repeatedly sounded the alarm about the threat posed by the treacherous Japanese. Everywhere he looked, chaos was brewing. Twenty thousand Japanese Americans in San Francisco were secretly organizing a revolt. Spies were communicating by radio with submarines offshore. Enemy fighter planes were flying over Los Angeles. Fires were being set as signals. Each story, it turned out, was false.[2] The San Francisco uprising was imagined; the radio stations were actually operated by the US Army; the "enemy" planes were American; the brush fires were set by ordinary farmers. In his journal, an official who served under DeWitt wrote, "Common sense is thrown to the winds and any absurdity is believed."[3] Even J. Edgar Hoover called the army's West Coast intelligence operation full of "hysteria and lack of judgment."[4]

But for DeWitt, that each supposed plot unraveled upon inspection was cause for even greater concern. "The very fact that no sabotage has taken place to date is a disturbing and confirming indication that such action will be taken," he wrote to Secretary of War Henry Stimson, in his recommendation for the removal of the ethnic Japanese from the West Coast.[5] Five days later, on February 19, 1942, President Roosevelt approved the request with Executive Order 9066. DeWitt wasn't particularly concerned that nearly two-thirds of the 120,000 evacuees were US-born. "A Jap's a Jap," he said at a congressional hearing. "It makes no difference whether he's an American citizen or not."[6]

But if DeWitt had few civil liberties scruples, he did recognize one logistical challenge posed by the evacuation. Nearly half of working-age Japanese farmed, a vocation in which they had proven themselves especially skilled. Once they were whisked away, their crops would rot. To prevent such a disaster, DeWitt ordered the Farm Security Administration to ensure that any "lands voluntarily vacated"—the language of the evacuation is nothing if not Orwellian—would be continued to be used for agriculture, to meet the food needs of a wartime nation.[7]

In the spring of 1942, Ross was sent from San Francisco to San Diego to help facilitate the process. As an FSA agent, Ross was theoretically responsible for ensuring that the Japanese received a "fair disposition" for their land and farming equipment, but such assurances were a cruel joke. The evacuees were desperate sellers, with little idea of where they were going or when—if ever—they would return. Without any bargaining leverage, they received an average of just fifteen cents on the dollar for their properties.[8] White growers, who had long coveted the valuable Japanese land, pounced at the opportunity for a naked land grab. And it was a land grab they helped into being: groups like the California Farm Bureau had lobbied hard in support of expelling the Japanese. "We're charged with wanting to get rid of the Japs for selfish reasons," a representative from the Grower Shipper Vegetable Association told the *Saturday Evening Post*. "We do. It's a question of whether the white man lives on the Pacific Coast or the brown man."[9] In the final tally, some 6,789 farmers lost nearly a quarter million acres, worth an estimated seventy-three million dollars.[10]

Ross arrived in San Diego supportive of the evacuation. Like many Americans, he was deeply affected by the bombing of Pearl Harbor—a national tragedy that had a personal significance for a man whose son and ex-wife were on the island. Since graduating from college, the only jobs Ross had held were with the government, which he saw as largely a force for good. He trusted DeWitt's claims about the threats posed by the Japanese, and prior to his arrival in San Diego he had had little contact with people of Japanese descent. But now he witnessed a "shocked and sort of benumbed" people line up to have their most important possessions taken from them. Some remained quiet; others grew "semi-hysterical" as they realized what was happening.[11] It was one thing to read diatribes about an exotic and conniving enemy race, quite another to watch heartbroken men with callused hands have their livelihoods stripped away. That big growers were playing a leading role in the affair complicated the picture as well, suggesting forces at work other than simple national-security concerns.

Ross wasn't in San Diego long. Events moved with bewildering speed: Japanese were given just six days' notice to report to the city's train station downtown. They arrived wearing ID tags and taking only what they could carry. Large crowds gathered to watch hundreds of families step into the cars, bound for the Santa Anita racetrack, located 120 miles north in the city of Arcadia. There they disembarked and found themselves surrounded by armed guards, barbed wire, and searchlights; their new homes, converted horse stalls, still reeked of manure.[12] Six months later they would be forcibly moved again, this time to an internment camp in the interior. In San Diego, local press and politicians had been calling for the removal of the Japanese for weeks. Now, as more than a thousand people headed into an uncertain future, a local journalist breezily reported, "Each realized that the U.S. was doing everything in their power to make the pathway as easy as possible for them."[13]

Ross returned to San Francisco to receive his final assignment with the FSA. As he had witnessed in college, the US government had launched a massive deportation project during the Depression, resulting in the repatriation of hundreds of thousands of Mexican immigrants (and, in the messy rush, some US citizens). Now, worried about a wartime labor shortage, the United States wanted them back. Ross was told to inspect private labor camps and report on whether they were suitable to house the first wave of *braceros,* as the Mexican guest workers came to be called. Ross paid a visit to Carey McWilliams, then in his final year with the Olson administration, who handed him a long list of camps. Ross traveled the state, finding that little had changed since his days at Arvin. The camps were in horrendous condition, and few met even the state's minimal standards. Many stood empty and condemned. He wrote up his findings, singling out several prominent growers for condemnation, and was promptly called into the office of a superior.

What followed was a short, frank discussion. The rules, he was told, had changed: with a war on, there was no room to criticize growers—they were the ones who would be feeding the nation and soldiers. Years later, Ross would recall that the supervisor told him that Ross didn't have enough "petty larceny in his blood" to cooperate in this next, more conciliatory phase.[14] He suggested that Ross transfer to the War Relocation Authority (WRA), the civilian agency recently created to run the internment camps, which had plenty of vacant positions to fill. Seeing the writing on the wall, Ross interviewed with the WRA and was hired in the Community Services division, assigned to the Minidoka internment camp in southern Idaho. It was, in one way, a natural fit. As camp manager at Arvin, Ross had years of experience in trying to create a sense of community among people living in distress. But that was where the similarities ended. The FSA camps had been voluntary and progressive, designed to aid poor farmworkers. Now he would be working inside what amounted to a prison, with people who were incarcerated based solely on their ethnicity. For a person fundamentally optimistic about the country in which he had been born, the time Ross spent at Minidoka would serve as a sobering counterpoint, revealing how quickly a democratic country could abandon its principles. But that was to come. In September 1942, as he and Frances set out for Idaho, he thought of Minidoka in relation to Arvin and was eager to "help the people set up their own self-government."[15]

When the idea first surfaced of relocating Japanese Americans eastward, Idaho governor Chase Clark made sure no one could misinterpret his feelings. "The Japs live like rats, breed like rats, and act like rats," he said. "I don't want them coming into Idaho."[16] His preferred solution to the "Jap problem" was to ship them home and "sink the island."[17] If all else failed and they were brought to Idaho, he told a congressional committee, they should be held "in concentration camps under military guard."[18]

Which is precisely what Ross found at Minidoka. Located in remote desert scrub, just north of a small town with the ironic name of Eden, the camp was surrounded by five miles of barbed-wire fencing and eight towers manned by armed guards. (The government claimed the guards were in place to protect the inmates; that the gun slots opened toward the camp suggested otherwise.) Minidoka's population would peak at ninety-five hundred—becoming, briefly, the seventh-largest city in Idaho—and was made up of first-generation Japanese immigrants, the Issei, and their American-born children, the Nisei. Internees, whom the WRA workers preferred to call "colonists"—as if they were simply settlers of vacant land—were housed in primitive tar-paper barracks, furnished with canvas cots, a stove, and a bare lightbulb hanging from the ceiling.[19] Space was tight, forcing many families to share a single room with strangers. The hastily built camp did not have a sewage system when it opened, so internees used overflowing latrines outside, leading to epidemics of typhoid and dysentery. To stay warm during the winter, when temperatures could drop to twenty-five degrees below zero, the Japanese went outside to chop sagebrush to heat their rooms. They received coal only after rumors of a riot began to spread. (One unfortunate man, lost while looking for wood, was found dead two days later.)[20]

For many people, the defining feature of Minidoka was the dust. Severe winds could whip the sky into a black menace of pelting sand, creating dust storms so powerful that they stopped construction of the camp several times. Here's how one Japanese-American girl described her arrival: "We felt as if we were standing in a gigantic sand-mixing machine as the sixty-mile gale lifted the loose earth up into the sky, obliterating everything. Sand filled our mouths and nostrils and stung our faces and hands like a thousand darting needles.... At last we staggered into our room, gasping and blinded.... The window panes rattled madly, and the dust poured through the cracks like smoke."[21]

Despite the many hardships, internees did their best to create something resembling normal life inside the camp. Schools were established, gardens were planted, drama clubs were formed, Boy and Girl Scouts troops were organized. Ross quickly found that they had little need for his services. As he testified before a government committee in 1981, the Japanese Americans "were infinitely more capable of taking care of their problems ... than I, or the rest of the *Hakujins* [white people] were."[22] There were modest tasks to perform that felt useful: Frances obtained fabric for internees, which was used to create partitions, offering residents a modicum of privacy. But given the scope of the situation, Ross felt superfluous.

His official duties seemed designed to go nowhere. He listened to internees who had grievances against the WRA, but all he could do was scribble notes and nod sympathetically, knowing that few higher-ups would act on the complaints. He tried his hand at organizing a council but found that his autocratic supervisor wasn't supportive. "He felt that if you gave the people any real power or self-government, it would just cause problems," he recalled.[23] None of this, of course, is surprising; that Ross was surprised is a reflection of the naïveté he carried to Minidoka. It was absurd to speak about power or self-government in an internment camp where movements were monitored

FIGURE 7. Minidoka Relocation Center, August 18, 1942. One of ten internment camps built by the federal government, Minidoka was in the high desert of Idaho. At its peak, it housed nearly ten thousand ethnic Japanese—the vast majority US citizens. Courtesy of Bancroft Library, University of California, Berkeley.

and mail censored. Internees at Minidoka recognized as much. At meetings they expressed skepticism about forming a community government. How could they have a voice in policies, one man asked, if the director could veto anything? How was it a democracy if WRA policy prevented the Issei, or first-generation elders, from participating in the council? After much debate, Ross's supervisor at Minidoka, George Townsend, bluntly acknowledged the critiques. "There is no real democratic power in the council if the project director has the final say in all its reservations," he said.[24] The issue was dropped.

As the fall turned to winter, the hollowness of the assignment wore on Ross, who felt he "had nothing to do that amounted to a damn thing."[25] Even more important was his conviction—which he came to not long after arriving in Minidoka—that the internment was unnecessary and immoral. He had initially bought the DeWitt line that Japanese Americans were plotting fifth-column activities. If they didn't represent a threat, after all, why would Roosevelt—whom Ross so admired—order them out of the West Coast? But the claims of widespread treachery unraveled at Minidoka. For families stuck in the camp, Ross saw that "life was filled with so much humiliation and indignity." Yet these people, who had every reason to be disloyal, weren't.[26] When it was announced that Japanese Americans could register for the draft, the men of Minidoka signed up in droves. A 1943 report pointed to the "model" that Minidoka had become. Among the internees, announced the camp director, there were no major crimes, no disloyal activities, no unreasonable complaints, no breaches of trust.[27]

As Christmas approached, Ross busied himself with soliciting donations from outside groups like the Quakers to pay for gifts for the children. But already he was planning his exit. He felt like a pointless cog in a machine that wasn't headed in the right direction. And there was an out. Under the new leadership of Dillon Myer, the WRA was making a serious push to empty the camps. If internees could show that a job and housing awaited them back east—and they cleared a background check—they were free to relocate. To assist in the process, the WRA would soon open dozens of relocation offices, and the agency needed staffers to convince employers and landlords to hire and rent to the Japanese. That winter, as Ross chaired weekly meetings of Minidoka's Christmas committee, he was greatly relieved to learn he had been selected to open the newest relocation office, in Cleveland.

Christmas at Minidoka proved to be a mixed affair. The committee raised $1,241 and received seven thousand donated presents, and the barracks were decorated with trees and stockings.[28] But the "success" of the project only highlighted its limits: the Japanese were still behind barbed wire, celebrating the holiday hundreds of miles away from their hometowns. This was not what Ross wanted to be doing. In January, five months after they had arrived, he and Frances loaded up their 1941 Plymouth and left Idaho behind. They had a long and tedious drive ahead, crossing the unbroken snowy plains of Highway 80, but Ross's spirits were high. "I was so anxious to get out of the camp and get someplace where I could do something that I considered productive," he recalled.[29] By refusing to protest—indeed, by initially supporting the evacuation and internment—he now felt he had failed a major test. He arrived in Cleveland with a guilty conscience, eager to, as he put it, "do penance."[30]

After enduring the lonely high desert of Idaho, the hustle and bustle of Cleveland must have been a relief for Ross and Frances. With nearly 900,000 residents, it was the sixth-largest city in the nation, with more people arriving every day to fill jobs in war-related plants.[31] The couple settled into a tiny one-bedroom house on Cleveland's west side, and Frances found work at one such plant, operating a drill press for an airplane parts manufacturer. While her husband would spend the next two years helping the Japanese, she would engage in shop-floor activism, leading a successful drive to integrate the plant with African Americans and, afterward, joining the staff of the Fair Employment Practices Commission, set up by President Roosevelt to prohibit race-based job discrimination.

Ross opened the Cleveland WRA office on January 16, 1943. He approached his mission with characteristic zeal; one coworker described him as a "crusader" who put in impossibly long hours.[32] The job demanded that sort of energy. Cleveland was virtually unknown to internees—the 1940 census listed just eighteen residents of Japanese descent—and Ross's unenviable task was to explain to landlords and employers why they ought to do business with a group that, less than a year ago, had been considered so dangerous that they were locked away in remote camps. He was given a list of job openings each week, but he found that many employers, though desperate for workers, would hang up upon hearing the word "Japanese." Ross shifted tactics, identifying himself instead as representing the War Manpower Commission, excited to share news about a new pool of hard workers—the "very cream of the crop," he gushed—that had recently been discovered.[33] Any smart manager would snatch them up in a second; might he stop by for a few minutes to discuss this marvelous business opportunity? Ross deflected any specific questions about the workers and rushed over to make the case "eyeball to eyeball."[34]

This approach worked better, but the next group to win over was the white employees. Early on, when Ross omitted this step, workers at one plant staged a spontaneous walkout upon learning they would be laboring alongside "dirty Japs." From then on he made sure to speak beforehand to workers and union officials. He visited 125 plants the first year, explaining the relocation project and stressing the patriotism of the Japanese. After hearing Ross, most voiced no opposition. When someone raised a fuss, Ross told the dissenter that, by refusing to accept additional hands, he was actively impeding the war effort. If that didn't work, Ross reminded his audience about the Depression and how terrible it felt to be without an income and forced to rely on meager relief checks. How could a worker in good conscience keep a fellow worker from a job? Being a relocation officer, Ross was learning, required "great finesse in some instances" and at other times "something approaching intimidation."[35] He could bend, but he could also bend others, and after applying pressure in the right spots he found that "the workers were usually very good about accepting."[36]

The other critical people to be won over were the Japanese. Although leaving the camp was a step toward greater freedom, many internees had little money to relocate and no idea how they might be received outside the barbed-wire fences. This was the same country, after all, whose citizens had cheered their incarceration. It also didn't help that most of the initial positions available in Cleveland were either in domestic work or agriculture, neither of which paid well. When Ross visited internment camps, he found that many were less than excited by what he had to offer. "Here are these people—electrical engineers, aeronautical engineers, doctors, lawyer—and we wanted them to come out and do farm work or be gardeners or maids," he remembered. "They said, 'No, get us some good jobs.' So we had to get the jobs. They just forced us to do it, because it was an insult."[37]

Many of the good jobs were in war-related plants, which presented a special challenge. These positions needed clearance from the US Army's provost marshal general, who repeatedly rejected individuals without a shred of evidence that they were disloyal. The process, Ross reported, was "slow and complicated" and could lead to people he had already placed in plants being yanked out.[38] So he created a work-around. Ross had a friendly contact at the Military Intelligence Service, which was running a confidential map translation project in Cleveland with the help of Japanese Americans. Instead of dealing with the army provost, each month Ross sent over a new batch of names to his contact, and each month they were cleared for defense-plant work. The solution highlighted a Ross trait that would show up in his future organizing: he preferred to work within the rules of a system, but he didn't mind going around them if need be.

Soon he was placing workers in dozens of plants, but a new problem emerged: the Nisei worked too hard. At the Cleveland Steel Products Company, for example, Ross had found work for eighteen Japanese. One day the boss called him, upset. The new workers, "full of vigor and patriotism," failed to take breaks and maintained such a rapid pace that it made the old-timers look bad, and they had begun to grumble.[39] Ross sat down with the Japanese workers and explained the problem, instructing them to watch their coworkers. When the whites took a break, they were to take a break. If the whites slowed down, they were to slow down, too. As Ross spoke, the Japanese looked at him with growing incredulousness. "Once they understood, it seemed kind of crazy to them," he said. "We're in the middle of the war, and they're slowing down when they should be really working for all their worth."[40]

More than three thousand Japanese Americans would settle in Cleveland during the war years. For the newcomers it could be a strange, cold city. They were told by the WRA to stay quiet and avoid congregating in groups, but following these instructions—which seemed to blame them for the situation the government had created—didn't guarantee a friendly reception. Retail stores refused to hire them; certain landlords wouldn't rent to them; their children were teased and beaten up at school. The local university, Western Reserve (now Case Western Reserve), prohibited Japanese American students from enrolling, relenting only after a local paper—alerted by Ross and others—exposed the policy.

Ross came to appreciate the guts it took to leave a camp and venture into an unknown city. One of the earliest arrivals in Cleveland was Kay Uweda, a nineteen-year-old whose parents stayed behind at Utah's Topaz relocation camp. As the train roared toward Chicago, Uweda, who was riding with three other young women, looked over the list of commands she had been given, essentially orders to remain as invisible as possible: *Don't talk to strangers. Don't get into arguments.* At Chicago the three other women disembarked; Uweda was making the rest of the journey alone. "If anybody bothers you, run into the bathroom and stay there until you get to Cleveland," one woman advised.[41]

It was nearly midnight when the train pulled into Cleveland. Uweda had been told that she would be meeting a short, redheaded man, so she grew concerned when a towering dark-haired figure called her name and instructed her to grab her bags. Alone in a strange city, with the person she had expected nowhere in sight, her heart began to beat faster. She retrieved her luggage and followed the man to his waiting car. She knew that a Quaker family had volunteered to house her, but the man said that it was too late to disturb them. Instead, she'd stay the night at the YWCA. *Likely story,* she thought. They drove down one dark street after the next. Uweda realized she had fallen into the very trap she'd been warned about in the camp: never follow a stranger who offers to help. She would be robbed, probably killed, her body dumped in the bushes. *Well, this is it,* she thought, just before the sign of the YWCA came into view.

"And that," she said, laughing during an interview many decades later, "is how I got to know Fred Ross."[42]

Uweda would go on to work alongside Ross for nearly five years—first as a receptionist at the WRA office in Cleveland and then, once the West Coast reopened, back in San Francisco, helping anxious Japanese Americans feel a bit more at home. Part of her time was spent responding to job applications and sitting for interviews; when she was rejected, Ross would follow up with the employers and lean on them to accept Japanese workers. Uweda also spearheaded a large community dance—unusual for the time because she explicitly invited whites, blacks, and Japanese—which went off without a hitch, despite warnings from some that it would lead to trouble. Ross found Uweda to be an invaluable worker; Uweda thought Ross was an inspiring person with an uncanny ability to convince people of all walks to work with him.

Organizers must have their feet planted firmly on the ground, but sometimes their heads need to be in the clouds. In Cleveland, Ross envisioned an ambitious social experiment—which hints at his desire, after nearly a decade of government work, to move beyond his ordinary responsibilities and set something grander in motion. The plan, which Ross called the Lakewood Experiment, aimed to build community ties between Japanese Americans and their neighbors. Starting in the Lakewood neighborhood, Ross helped organize a group of Nisei who joined whatever local groups existed—school PTAs, block associations—in order to more fully integrate the area. The experiment apparently worked well enough that Ross drew up plans to create a Nisei council in every neighborhood, which would serve as a "focal point" in integrating any new arrivals. Once each neighborhood had a committee, Ross imagined, the next step would be to form a citywide group. The city group, in turn, would link up with similar councils, building a committee across the nation that would . . .

The point isn't that any such thing was achieved. While Ross wrote up the experiment in his final WRA report about his work in Cleveland, it doesn't appear that the project got much beyond the original Lakewood group. But his imaginings hint at the organizer to be. By 1944, Ross had spent the better part of a decade assisting and advocating for the marginalized: the out of work, the Dust Bowl migrants, the interned. He had handed out relief checks and food, counseled people behind barbed wire, sat across the desk from racist employers and convinced them to hire Japanese Americans. But the problems to be confronted were immense, and thus far he had largely acted alone. The Lakewood Experiment showed that Ross was beginning to sense the limitations of such an approach. He was growing impatient, ready to bite off a new challenge, taken with the idea of creating a snowball of people who could transform their community. Ross the social worker was receding, soon to disappear. The outlines of Ross the campaigner, Ross the organizer, were beginning to take shape.

As relocations proceeded more or less smoothly in Cleveland, the US government faced mounting pressure to figure out what to do with Japanese Americans. By 1944, several lawsuits had been filed that challenged the legality of the evacuation, and the status quo was so filled with contradictions that it threatened to implode. It was impossible to determine if Japanese Americans were loyal—or so claimed General DeWitt—and yet tens of thousands of them were being declared just that and allowed to leave the camps. Others were fighting for their country in the Pacific theater. By what logic could someone who was determined by the government to be a "loyal American" be prevented from settling down wherever they chose? How could such a person be a military threat? In December 1944, as these questions swirled, the army finally announced the end date of the evacuation. As of January 2, 1945, the West Coast would be reopened.

Ross filed for a transfer to San Francisco and in early January drove to California to open a new WRA office, accompanied by two Japanese Americans. He arrived in the city on January 10, 1945, and five days later opened the office, located at the De Young Building on bustling Market Street. Ross was in charge of the San Francisco district—whose territory included the city and San Mateo County to the south—and he would spend the next year and a half trying to smooth the way for the Japanese trickling out of the camps. But first he had a birth to attend to. He rushed back to Cleveland by train, in time for the arrival of his daughter, Julia, on January 22, 1945. Once Julia was a month old, the family packed up and moved west, leaving by train during a ferocious snowstorm.

The work in San Francisco was similar to what Ross had done in Cleveland, only more intense. Housing was the biggest challenge. "This topic could be covered by a single word, 'none,'" Ross reported.[43] Before the war, the Japanese had primarily lived in the neighborhood of Western Addition.

When they were forced to evacuate, a new wave of people—African Americans streaming north and west for war-related work—took refuge in the empty units. Now, with vacancy rates approaching zero, the returning Japanese Americans had few options other than to cram into impossibly tight quarters. At one point, the WRA estimated that eighteen hundred resettlers were living in housing meant for just six hundred; many took low-paying live-in domestic work simply to have a roof over their heads. Some relief finally arrived when eight hundred public housing units in Hunter's Point were made available, but it was hardly an ideal solution. Large families were crowded into wartime dormitories meant for single people, a living arrangement that, Ross noted, "resembled [internment] camp quarters."[44]

Fearing anti-Japanese hostility, the WRA had offered to provide financial assistance to anyone who decided to remain east of the Rockies. Most chose to return west, however, and the predicted wave of violence in California did indeed result. During the first six months of 1945, Japanese were targeted in twenty-two shootings, along with twenty cases of arson. Most of the vigilantism occurred in rural inland areas, in what the WRA characterized as a "widespread campaign of terrorism."[45] Japanese Americans had their sheds burned to the ground, their homes fired on with shotguns, their windows shattered by rocks. The fiercest violence was directed at the earliest arrivals, in the hope of discouraging others. But the Japanese showed remarkable determination. "They will have to blast me out," said one Japanese American farmer, refusing to leave after his home was the target of repeated nights of drive-by gunfire.[46]

San Francisco was friendlier territory, but there was still plenty of prejudice, evidenced by the smashing of windows of a hostel that housed the Japanese. As in Cleveland, Ross spent much of his time trying to win over union leaders, finding allies in people like Harry Bridges of the International Longshore and Warehouse Union. On one occasion, Ross accompanied Bridges—who would later marry a Nisei—to a warehouse in Petaluma, where workers had threatened to strike if they were forced to work alongside Japanese Americans. Bridges entered the building and, without hesitating, told the men that he would revoke their union charter if they didn't get with the program. (They did.)[47]

The most dramatic expression of anti-Japanese sentiment came in the summer of 1945, when machinist Takeo Miyama attempted to show up for his new job at the Municipal Railway bus repair shop. One hundred members of the Machinists Union rebelled, threatening to strike. When Mayor Roger Lapham arrived, telling the workers that Miyama had the legal right to work, he was greeted with shouts of "Remember Pearl Harbor!" and "We don't want him!" If Miyama returned, they promised to "escort him out."[48]

Such threats caused the thirty-seven-year-old to have second thoughts. It was one thing to want a job, quite another to have to face down a mob of angry whites to get it. But a lengthy meeting with Ross and a representative from the Japanese American Citizens League shored up his strength. Ross stressed the historic importance of the moment. To back off now, when the entire city was watching, would send precisely the wrong message at precisely the wrong time. Ross also penned Miyama into a corner, telling a newspaper that Miyama "must face his duty to his people and not stay away like a coward."[49] The next morning, Miyama returned for his morning shift. Word of his return spread quickly, but when sixty angry men threatened to strike, a white worker—and war hero—spoke up in opposition. "I didn't go out to fight in the Pacific so people with differently colored skin would be discriminated against when I got home," Harold Stone told the crowd.[50] Later that day, workers voted to accept Miyama.

By early 1946, Ross knew his days at the WRA were coming to an end. The internment camps had been emptied and the San Francisco office would soon be shut down. Ross had misgivings about the decision—he felt that the WRA "pulled out too soon" and abandoned many struggling Japanese—but he began to reach out to acquaintances in a search for other work.[51]

Laurence Hewes, his old supervisor at the Farm Security Administration, had left the government to work out of the San Francisco office of the American Council on Race Relations (ACRR). Like many nonprofits, the ACRR was an underfunded group with an oversized mission, seeking to "bring about full democracy in race relations." Based in Chicago, it had been established in the wake of race riots that swept the country in the long, hot summer of 1943. Mostly forgotten amid the overseas drama of World War II, hundreds of whites armed with lead pipes had attacked their black coworkers in Mobile, Alabama. Nearly ten thousand vigilantes had laid siege to a black neighborhood in Beaumont, Texas. Street fighting in Detroit and Harlem had left forty people dead and another thousand injured. And in what became known as the Zoot Suit Riots, rampaging servicemen had taken to the streets of Los Angeles, beating Mexican American and black youth who dared wear the offending outfit. "National Race War Feared," had warned a headline in the *Amsterdam News*.[52]

ACRR

One response to the violence was the creation of "councils for civic unity"—essentially multiethnic groups—that would work to resolve conflicts, resist segregation, and generally act as an organized antiracist force in the community. On April 8, 1946, Ross officially joined the ACRR as a "field representative," responsible for investigating conditions in Southern California and organizing councils to improve them. He and Frances gathered their belongings yet again—this was the couple's fourth move in as many years—and headed south, where Ross had found a vacancy in a public housing development in Long Beach. At thirty-five, he was now on the path he would travel for the rest of his life.

FIVE

The Mexican Problem

IN THE FALL OF 1945, while Ross struggled to find housing for the returning Japanese Americans, a man named O'Day Short purchased a house in the
city of Fontana, about an hour's drive east of Los Angeles. Short, who had
developed a reputation in Los Angeles for his civil rights activism, was the
first African American to move into the southern section of the San
Bernardino County community. It wasn't long before he received a hostile
visit from a group of men, likely members of the resurging Ku Klux Klan
(KKK). If he stuck around, they warned, bad things could happen. Better for
everyone if he moved along.

Short proved a hard man to intimidate. He sent the group on its way,
dashed off a letter about the threat to a black-owned newspaper, and lodged
complaints with the FBI and sheriff. The FBI ignored the complaint; the
sheriff advised him to move out in order to prevent any "disagreeableness."
The Chamber of Commerce offered to purchase his property in order to get
him out of town. Short declined. One night in December, his house was
rocked with a loud explosion. Neighbors watched as his family, engulfed in
flames, staggered outside. His wife and two young children died immediately;
Short survived an additional two weeks. After a cursory investigation, local
officials ruled the fire an accident, a conclusion contradicted by evidence discovered at the scene by an arson expert hired by the NAACP. The murders set
off a series of protests, but local law enforcement refused to reopen the case.[1]

In his first assignment after settling in at Long Beach, Ross drove out to
San Bernardino to investigate. After several wrong turns, he found himself
traveling along dirt roads lined with "hovels two and three deep."[2] Ross
had inadvertently landed in the middle of a Mexican American barrio, and
the discovery of a hidden village within the city stirred his imagination.

63

He stopped at a local diner, partly to lunch but mostly to linger, and heard angry shouts in Spanish coming from a nearby booth. Before leaving, Ross asked the waitress about the commotion. She explained that the teenagers had been barred from entering a skating rink in nearby Redlands the previous evening: normally, Wednesdays were "Mexican Night" at the rink—the only day they were allowed to enter—but the youth had been turned away due to a local tournament.

During the trip, Ross attended a meeting of San Bernardino's Council for Human Rights, which was launching a campaign against the KKK. Listening to representatives of the NAACP document their ongoing investigation, Ross grew convinced that he had little to offer in the way of organizational assistance in the Short case. Still, thinking about his earlier wanderings in the barrio, he noticed that not a single Mexican American was present. After a rabbi warned that the KKK could soon be targeting Jews and Catholics, Ross stood up and mentioned the Redlands skating rink. Was the council doing anything about such blatant segregation? And why weren't any Mexican Americans at the meeting? If they wanted to stamp out the KKK, Ross argued, they ought to make common cause with Spanish speakers.

 Seated behind Ross was a professor from the University of Redlands named Ruth Tuck. Years later, Ross would remember his encounter with Tuck as one of the key pivots upon which his life turned. Tuck had lived in San Bernardino's barrio while working on a recently published book, *Not with the Fist: Mexican Americans in a Southwest City,* part of which described the lack of stable organizations in the region. After the meeting, Tuck invited Ross to her house, where they talked into the early morning on a porch overlooking the citrus groves of Redlands. She told Ross what she knew. Yes, the conditions in the barrio were shocking, but he could drive through any number of towns and find similar circumstances. With neighborhoods of unpaved streets and segregated schools, Mexican Americans lived in what felt like a parallel universe. There was plenty of potential. As a voting block, they could swing local elections. Organized, they could form their own version of the NAACP. But most Mexican Americans weren't registered to vote, and most of the organizations in the barrio didn't challenge the dominant—white—society.

Tuck thus planted the seed of a grand idea. But it was just an idea; Ross also needed an example. Which was where Tuck's friend Ignacio Lopez came in.

Ross had every reason to be impressed by Lopez, whom he would call a "tireless crusader for his people" and an "organizer of surpassing ability."[3]

Born in Guadalajara, Lopez had moved to the United States as a child and graduated from college, a rare achievement for a Mexican immigrant of the period. After college he launched *El Espectador*—the Witness—a Spanish-language paper that specialized in documenting abuses committed against Mexicans. Soon, Lopez was not just documenting but fighting, using the publication as an organizing tool that resulted in a string of victories: the release of a wrongfully arrested man; the desegregation of a movie theater; even the election of a Mexican American to the city council in Chino. Lopez took his struggle to the courts as well, successfully suing San Bernardino after he was prevented from using its swimming pool.[4] But his could be a lonely fight, and at times he grew frustrated with what he saw as complacency within the Mexican American community. "People must be awakened from lethargy," he commanded his readers.[5]

There were plenty of reasons for Lopez and Ross to become quick allies. But there were also factors that could have pushed them apart. Ross was white, didn't speak Spanish, and had never worked in Mexican American communities. As Tuck wrote to Ross, "Ignacio seldom admires anyone, particularly Anglos who are fishing in *colonia* waters."[6] But at one of their first meetings, Ross surprised Lopez by asking for advice about how to proceed. It was, Lopez later remarked, the first time an Anglo had ever posed the question to him; the whites he had come across were often condescending, eager to lecture about what needed to be done. That Ross started with questions—admitting he didn't know what he was doing—was refreshing, and Lopez took him under his wing during what Ross called his organizing "toddling" period.

Ross was certainly drawn to Lopez, but he was also searching for new models, frustrated by the existing unity councils. Ross found that despite their good intentions, most were inherently conservative. They wanted change, but they didn't want to risk alienating their peers in the process. "The average member thinks he is dependent upon community good will for his livelihood," Ross wrote. Compromised in such a manner, Ross complained, they were destined to "meet, seat, eat, and repeat (or retreat)."[7] Tuck had reached a similar conclusion, lamenting that many groups of Anglo do-gooders were "floundering along in a morass of minutes, letter-heads, and empty objectives."[8]

Lopez advocated a different path: go directly into the barrios and organize. If Ross was to help "bring about full democracy in race relations," it made little sense to spend his time assisting those who were already active citizens. For Lopez, the vote was critical, and his success in Chino provided Ross with concrete proof that progress was possible. With Lopez's support, Ross set his sights on the Mexican American communities of the Citrus Belt, an area that stretched east from Los Angeles to the foothills of the San Gabriel Mountains. This became the backdrop for Ross's first organizing attempts, a region aptly described by Carey McWilliams as "neither town nor country, neither rural nor urban," but instead "a world of its own."[9] Ross would spend most of the coming year in this world, living out of motels for weeks at a time while Frances and Julia were in Long Beach.

The world of the Citrus Belt was a mess of contrasts and contradictions. The symmetry of the orange grove is a beautiful thing to behold, and the orange itself had become a symbol of health and optimism (and California itself, where health and optimism were supposedly in abundance). The wealth generated by the crop was also fantastic: in 1930, Southern California citrus growers grossed nearly $150 million, rivaling the manufacturing wages earned in the movies, oil, and aircraft industries combined.[10] But if the "orange curtain" was raised, a different picture emerged, that of an exploited Mexican workforce and patterns of discrimination—sometimes enforced by laws, sometimes by custom—designed to ensure that Mexicans knew their proper, subservient place.[11] Businesses posted WHITE TRADE ONLY signs in their windows. Movie theaters forced Mexican Americans to sit in the balconies or in the first few rows, noses pressed to the screen. Restrictive housing covenants kept them locked into the barrio. At least one cemetery in San Bernardino refused to bury Mexicans.

All of these measures were attempts to deal with what was called the "Mexican Problem." The "problem" was straightforward. Without Mexicans, entire industries, such as citrus, would collapse. But—and herein lay the problem—Mexicans were thought to be dirty and dim-witted. Any workable solution would have to keep "Mexicans" around (which included Mexican Americans, not that many people made the distinction) without allowing them to drag whites down to their level. While cities might come up with customized solutions, the "problem" they faced was the same. San Bernardino, for example, had barred anyone of Mexican descent from swimming in its pool—that is, until Lopez sued. The City of Orange, instead, permitted them to use the pool on Mondays. To protect white children from contamination, the pool was drained each Monday night, cleaned and refilled on Tuesday, and reopened on Wednesday.

If sharing pool water posed a threat, segregated schools were a bulwark in the fight to preserve the integrity of white children. Indeed, segregation was widespread: at the time, according to one scholar, 85 percent of California school districts segregated students prior to high school.[12] One influential study published in the late 1920s sought to understand the reasons for the "over-agedness" and "retardation" of Mexican American children. It found that children of Mexican descent demonstrated only 58.1 percent of the academic ability of whites, while exhibiting 90 percent of their ability to perform manual work. The study's author recommended that boys learn how to "make use of discarded tin cans in the development of useful kitchen utensils" in order to become "skilled workers with their hands."[13] With retarded minds and skilled hands, Mexican American students would be perfectly positioned for a life in the fields—an arrangement that was also convenient for powerful growers. That high schools remained desegregated meant little for Mexican American students, as few would reach them and even fewer graduate.

Such segregation was on full display when Lopez took Ross, in May 1946, to a community of black and Mexican American residents in an unincorporated section of Riverside. The area, known as Bell Town, was little more than a collection of shacks huddled around a church, store, and tottering wood schoolhouse, which was perched on the edge of a gaping chasm left by a cement company. Inside the school, more than one hundred children were jammed into three dimly lit rooms, while white students who lived nearby were bused to a newly constructed school complete with everything Bell Town lacked: playground, indoor plumbing, even a cafeteria.

Bell Town residents were now being asked to support a bond measure to make improvements to the *new* school. This proved too much for women like Blossie Adams and Claudia Maldonado. By the time they met Ross, the pair had delivered a petition protesting the bond to the school board. Like all concerns coming from residents of Bell Town, their petition had been ignored. Ross suggested the women call a meeting, and nearly one hundred locals turned out, evidence that people were frustrated and ready for action. Though Adams and Maldonado had originally wanted to stop the bond, Ross convinced the group to support it—provided that the district became integrated, which would allow the children of Bell Town to enjoy the improvements.

Ross registered his only concern. The close friendship of Adams and Maldonado was unusual, as blacks and Mexican Americans in Bell Town typically kept to themselves. Looking out at the self-segregated audience, he told them that they would have to work together if they hoped to win. When Ross finished, Maldonado stood up and delivered the lines they had practiced earlier: "I want to motion that we form an organization of *all* the people of Bell Town."[14] The group enthusiastically backed the motion and the Bell Town Improvement League was born. Ross had helped organize his first group.

Events moved quickly. A parent agreed to file a discrimination charge against the district and a voter registration committee was formed. After the county clerk refused to deputize Maldonado so that she could register voters, Adams alerted the NAACP, and Maldonado was quickly sworn in. Maldonado and her husband were so impressed that they joined NAACP's Riverside chapter. An annual party held by Mexican Americans was turned into a fund-raiser for the Bell Town Improvement League, and for the first time blacks were invited. People weren't suddenly the best of friends, but "gradually this sort of give and take took hold," Ross wrote.[15]

Still, when a large group of parents attended the next board meeting to demand that the schools be integrated, they were rebuffed. None of the school board officials had even heard of the Bell Town group. The frustrated parents left, but not before Adams promised the school board that they would soon hear from them again.

When Lopez had decided to sue San Bernardino over its segregated swimming pool, the lawyer he turned to was David Marcus. Now Ross and leaders from Bell Town traveled to the attorney's Los Angeles office to seek advice.

Marcus seemed an unlikely candidate for civil rights litigation. After graduating from the University of Southern California's law school, he had developed a lucrative private practice and lived in a Pasadena mansion, complete with a tennis court, swimming pool, and live-in servants. But for all his success, Marcus had sharp memories of a painful past. Raised in the Midwest, he had taken violin lessons as a young child and performed recitals on stage. But he played from behind a curtain, lest the audience be forced to view a Jew. The lingering sting, along with the anti-Semitism he faced at USC, left him with a passion for representing the underdog. So while he maintained his private practice, he had also taken on a string of unconventional civil rights cases. A year earlier, in what would become the first successful federal school desegregation case in US history, he had sued four school districts in Orange County for segregating Mexican American students.[16]

The case was known as *Mendez v. Westminster,* and it became a precursor to the more famous *Brown v. Board of Education,* which was still eight years in the future. But there was a key difference. According to law, "Mexicans" were legally "white," which prevented Marcus from arguing that the segregation was unconstitutional based on race. Instead, he focused on ancestry, hoping to convince Judge Paul McCormick that "segregation within the white race, as opposed to segregation of different races, was unconstitutional."[17] In their defense, the school districts justified the segregation primarily by citing "language deficiencies": students who didn't speak English needed more attention. This defense collapsed when it became clear, during the course of the trial, that schools didn't actually test students for language proficiency (the three Mendez children named in the suit, for example, spoke English fluently).

The five-day trial began on July 6, 1945. Its most memorable witness was James Kent, a superintendent of one of the districts being sued. Kent's master's thesis had been called "Segregation of Mexican School Children in Southern California," and his breathless findings more than made up for the bland title. He wrote that Mexican children grew up in homes that were "veritable junk heaps" and were malnourished due to a diet of "tortillas, a greasy mixture, or enchiladas and beans." As a consequence, Mexicans were made up of a "less sturdy stock than the white race,"[18] and in court he argued that such students possessed more "physical prowess" than "mental ability."[19]

The case flew beneath the media's radar until seven months later, when Judge McCormick decided against the school districts. "Ruling Gives Mexican Children Equal Rights," announced the *Los Angeles Times.* Marcus had the wind at his back. After listening to the people from Bell Town, he drew up a preliminary lawsuit against the West Riverside school district for violating the Fourteenth Amendment guaranteeing equal protection.

By now the school board knew something was afoot in Bell Town. Ross and Maldonado were registering voters—with the implicit threat that they could throw their weight against the bond measure—and plans were made to file the lawsuit. With no movement from the board, the Bell Town organization invited school representatives to a community forum with Marcus. Now that the community was organized and in a fighting mood, the old schoolhouse was packed to capacity. Marcus, who loved a good row, outlined the *Mendez* case and the judge's decision. Before an audience that included the school superintendent and board members, he assailed those who believed Mexican Americans were an inferior race. The board members huddled tightly together, a small island of white in a sea of brown and black.

The large meeting was followed, as promised, by legal action. "Segregation Suit Hits School Here," announced the *Riverside Daily Press* on August 10, 1946. As the paper reported, "five Mexican and Negro parents" charged in federal court that their children were forced to attend a "vermin infested school without recreational facilities." On behalf of fifteen hundred other "Latin or Negro" parents, they demanded their schools be desegregated. The school board acted immediately, sending a letter to residents of Bell Town announcing that the West Riverside school district would be desegregated in September. A month later, an adjacent town—citing the Bell Town controversy—announced it would follow suit.*

Ross took two important lessons from Bell Town. The first was to remember that the issue that gets people upset might not be the issue to tackle. In Bell Town, the catalyst hadn't been school segregation but the proposed bond measure. Part of the organizing process was to encourage others to think through a problem, to turn it around in their heads and talk through the merits of various solutions. An organizer always starts out where the people are, but that doesn't mean that he or she can't help them get to a different place.

The other important lesson was this: look for the women. At Bell Town the ringleaders were women; they did most of the organizing and were unafraid of public confrontation. Adams stared down the school board chairman. Maldonado spearheaded the voter registration drive. For a man of his time, Ross would prove remarkably egalitarian when it came to gender. His primary bias was toward those with a willingness to work: find and invest in people who will, quickly leave behind those who won't. Summing up his

* The case, had it proceeded in court, would have been intriguing, as the parents included both "white" Mexican Americans and "nonwhite" African Americans. The extent to which Marcus reflected on these broader implications is not clear. The NAACP was certainly aware of the *Mendez* case and filed an amicus brief during the appeal process, signed by Thurgood Marshall.

activities, he wrote, "In some instances women are assuming more than their proportionate share of Colonia improvement responsibilities. Frequently they make diligent, hard-driving members. Lastly, of course, as representative of more than half of the Colonia population, they will command a good deal of the worker's consideration."[20]

His tone is matter-of-fact. He is reporting what he discovered, and he would never find reason to reverse course. As an organizer he would encounter many "diligent, hard-driving" women—words that describe Dolores Huerta, whom Ross would meet and mentor in a decade's time. But his readiness to see women as powerful actors, which he considered nothing more than a common-sense observation, was a step that many male organizers would not take at that time. Beyond whatever blows Ross struck for gender equality, his outlook made him a much better organizer.

While still organizing in Bell Town, Ross had begun to turn his attention to Casa Blanca, another racially mixed colonia a few miles from downtown Riverside. On August 19, 1946—just over a week after the Bell Town lawsuit was filed—the *Riverside Daily Press* announced that a "civic unity council" had been formed in Casa Blanca. Ross had been called in by a local priest and quickly learned that residents had a problem named Jesse Rathgeber.

Rathgeber was an orange grower and city councilman whose district included the three thousand residents of Casa Blanca. Ross had already crossed paths with Rathgeber. When the NAACP proposed an ordinance to ban businesses from displaying WHITE TRADE ONLY signs, Rathgeber had led the opposition against it. After the council voted down the bill in early August, Ross asked members to justify their action. An outraged Rathgeber demanded to know more about Ross. (A whisper campaign had suggested that the Communist Party was behind the proposed legislation.) Ross identified himself, but the councilmen still moved to other business without explaining their objections to the proposal. According to the *Riverside Daily Press*, "members of the NAACP sat as if stunned" before silently filing out of the chambers.[21] (The following day, underscoring the city's hostility to blacks, the paper reported that a woman had received a note from the KKK stating that Klansmen would "get after her" if she didn't move out of the neighborhood.)[22]

But it wasn't just blacks who felt slighted by Rathgeber. In May 1946, a proposal had been floated at a city council meeting to build new playgrounds, including one slotted for Casa Blanca. Parents were thrilled; Rathgeber voted against the measure. If it was unusual for a politician to vote against a benefit for his constituents, there was history to consider. Several years prior, seeking higher wages, workers in Casa Blanca had struck a number of orange groves, including those owned by Rathgeber. So the kids of Casa Blanca would get no playground.

The first meeting of the Casa Blanca Unity League was held in early August. People listed their complaints against Rathgeber. Ross asked how many people were registered to vote. Only two hands went up. Two weeks later, the small group had grown to seventy-five. A team of officers was voted in—three blacks and four Mexican Americans—with Belen Reyes, who owned Casa Blanca's grocery store, elected as president. A veteran named Frank Martinez was especially eager to dispose of Rathgeber, and he volunteered to become a deputy registrar. With only eight days before the registration deadline, Martinez, who worked the graveyard shift, spent his days going door-to-door with Ross. When they were done the pair had registered 245 new voters.

It was during this period that Ross stumbled upon a tactic that would become the building block for his method of organizing. After holding a small meeting, Ross asked if people knew anyone else who might be interested in getting involved. One man who worked in the orange groves told Ross to come over to his house; he would invite the entire crew. At that meeting, Ross asked the same question, and another worker volunteered, saying he had a friend in a different crew, who could invite *his* crew to another meeting. "I began to get the idea," Ross later said, "that this was a really good way to organize, because each meeting was linked with the last one."[23] The house meeting method was born.

The house meeting, which would become synonymous with Ross, was effective because it recognized that people existed within a social network of close friends and relatives. By using house meetings—a simple gathering in a living room—an organizer could tap into and activate that network. In this relatively intimate setting, Ross would describe the organizing work and, at the end, ask each person to hold their own meeting. Even the person who said he "knew nobody" likely had a few family members he could invite. As Ross continued to experiment, he found that the approach had other advantages as well. The meetings were small enough to allow quieter voices to be heard but large enough that they felt productive and built momentum. They didn't require people to do something out of the ordinary, such as attend a rally or speak in public. He noticed, early on, that the meetings were a forum in which skeptical people could be won over—not by arguments from an outside organizer but by their close companions. Ross would eventually turn house meetings into something of a science and train thousands of people in this method, which he refined over the years in great detail. (One portion of trainings he gave in the 1980s, for example, covered how to make effective small talk, which Ross called "the meeting before the meeting.") It was in house meetings that Ross would meet Cesar Chavez and Dolores Huerta, and it was through house meetings that Chavez built what became the United Farm Workers. But that history began with some orange pickers in Casa Blanca.

Election day was Tuesday, September 17, 1946. Several weeks earlier, the Casa Blanca Unity League invited both council candidates to a forum. Rathgeber didn't show, leaving his opponent alone on the stage. Zollie Hair was a former deputy sheriff who didn't need to be the most astute politician to realize the opportunity presented by the overflow crowd. Hair promised to fight for a playground for Casa Blanca, and his subsequent political advertisements promoted "adequate recreation for ALL" as the central plank of his campaign.[24] At a follow-up meeting, in a move encouraged by Ross, league members decided to vote en masse for Hair. (None of this overtly political activity was what Ross's superiors in Chicago had in mind when they had hired him as a consultant for the American Council on Race Relations.)

Ross would become known for his preparation and attention to detail. He never tired of sharing a favorite line about the craft of organizing: "The incidentals make up the fundamentals." And nowhere were the incidentals more important than on election day. It was one thing to register people to vote, quite another to make sure they voted. In two decades' time, Chavez would call on Ross to direct a union election that would make or break the fledgling farmworker union; as the director, Ross insisted that organizers meet three to four times a day, cementing his reputation as a hard-driving disciplinarian. But looking at his first get-out-the-vote operation in Casa Blanca, it's clear that even as a rookie organizer he already knew the importance of leaving as little to chance as possible.*

* In 1950, Ross was asked by Congresswoman Helen Gahagan Douglas of Los Angeles to direct the get-out-the-vote operation for her senatorial campaign, which was proving to be an especially tough fight. Ross declined, citing his busy schedule. In that election, Douglas would lose to a thirty-seven-year-old upstart named Richard Nixon.

A week before the election, Ross called everyone together to explain how to mark a ballot. On the morning of the election, Reyes was stationed in her store next to an oversized map of every home in Casa Blanca. Vehicles were dispatched to pick up voters, babysitters were made available, street captains went door-to-door to make sure the stragglers turned out. When a captain actually witnessed someone enter the voting booth, Reyes crossed the person off the map; when captains returned from a house without any luck, Ross dispatched the local priest to make a personal visit. Meanwhile, the veteran Martinez put a loudspeaker on his truck, which was festooned with signs reading "Justice for Casa Blanca," and drove through the streets imploring people to vote.

Even in light of these efforts, there was little indication that Rathgeber felt the least bit threatened. In the run-up to the election, the two-time incumbent had vacationed in Mexico, and he had failed to take out a single newspaper ad. While little Casa Blanca buzzed with activity, Rathgeber spent election day in the council's chambers, again voting against the most recent version of the NAACP's antidiscrimination bill, which went down to defeat for a third time.

It would prove to be one of his final acts as councilman. That night in Casa Blanca, leaders huddled around the phone in the store-cum-campaign headquarters, impatiently waiting the results. Early news wasn't positive: a city clerk reported that Rathgeber had won six of nine precincts and was maintaining a 555 to 472 advantage. There was some grumbling in the room—no one wanted to imagine living with Rathgeber for another four years—until they learned that the numbers didn't include Casa Blanca. An hour later, after all the votes were tallied, Rathgeber had been tossed out. Casa Blanca had the highest turnout of any precinct, with 193 of the 240 votes going to Hair. Rathgeber had lost by 63 votes.[25] Several days later, when the paper published a breakdown of votes by precinct, Rathgeber cried foul, promising to launch an investigation into whatever strange goings-on had occurred in the usually quiet Casa Blanca. There is no record of that investigation ever taking place; either way, by then Ross had already moved on to a new town, where his organizing record would finally catch up with him.

SIX

Red Ross

BY THE FALL OF 1946, Ross was a marked man. You didn't just waltz into a conservative city like Riverside, help desegregate a school district and toss out a councilman, and expect to go unnoticed. Certainly not when the losing council member was a citrus grower, when your name repeatedly appeared in the paper, and when a group like the Associated Farmers started getting wind of your activities.

Formed in the wake of the great cotton strike of 1933, the group of wealthy agriculturalists was faced with a choice: they could grant modest raises to tamp down labor unrest, or they could crush any organizing attempts with overwhelming force. As Ross discovered while at Arvin, they chose the violent option, beginning with Salinas in 1936. After lettuce workers went on strike, local law-enforcement authorities stepped aside to allow the Associated Farmers to virtually run the city. The new governing body—operating without a shred of legality—quickly installed an army reserve officer named Colonel Sanborn to direct the police in a campaign of mass arrests and violence, including widespread use of tear gas. When that didn't prove sufficient, every man in Salinas between the ages of eighteen and forty-five was ordered to form a "citizens' army." Anyone who refused could be arrested. More than two thousand armed men turned the town into a war zone, bombing a union office with tear gas and threatening to lynch a photographer from the *San Francisco Chronicle* for documenting the scene. It was costly, but it worked. Within a month the union was crushed and the lettuce harvested.

When Carey McWilliams described the Associated Farmers as "fascist" he wasn't speaking in hyperbole—he was thinking about Salinas. Along with its reliance on brute force, the Associated Farmers also kept detailed records of "dangerous radicals," which McWilliams somehow obtained in 1935.[1] The group would share this information among its wide network of members and law-enforcement agencies, and by the time Ross left Riverside, there was likely a folder somewhere with his name on it.

Free to chart his course—Ross seemed to have only minimal supervision from Laurence Hewes and the American Council on Race Relations during this period—in August 1946 he decided to focus his work in Orange County. Orange County was home to the four school districts named in the federal *Mendez v. Westminster* case, including one in the small town of El Modena. In El Modena there was nothing subtle about the segregation. The two elementary schools, Roosevelt and Lincoln, were right next to each other, separated only by a playground. Roosevelt, set aside for whites and a handful of prosperous light-skinned Mexican Americans, was lined with palm trees and pillars. Lincoln was the "Mexican" school, for the children of farmworkers. It was a dark and drab brick building, where students were searched for fleas and classes were cut short so the children could harvest walnuts.

El Modena was proving to be a hard case to crack. Even after Judge McCormick ruled against the districts, the school board refused to obey his injunction, citing the appeal still waiting to be heard. Several small Mexican American groups in Orange County had pushed for integration, including a newly formed chapter of the League of United Latin American Citizens (LULAC), which had been founded in Texas during the Depression. Ross attended a LULAC meeting but wasn't particularly impressed: the discussion focused on the importance of flying a California flag during sessions, and the chapter's president, Manuel Viega, struck Ross as cold and not particularly ambitious. (As Ross put it, Viega was an undertaker who "looked like one.")[2] But Ross was immediately drawn to the group's secretary, Hector Tarango, who expressed enthusiasm after hearing about Ross's work in Casa Blanca and Bell Town.

In September, when the El Modena schools opened, ten Mexican American parents asked that their children be transferred to Roosevelt, but only two were accepted. Ross and Tarango held a meeting with the parents, who organized the El Modena Unity League. One father filed a petition asking Judge McCormick to hold the school board in contempt. In nearby Santa Ana, also named in the lawsuit, the school board was dragging its feet as well. Ross and Tarango met with the superintendent, who later reported at a board meeting that Ross, whom he described as "antagonistic and belligerent," told him that "he had instructed the Mexican children to go to the school of their choice on the opening day of school, and if they were not admitted, the Board of Education would be cited for contempt."[3]

It soon became clear, however, that the school boards were unwilling to budge until the appeal ran its course. (In April of the following year, Judge McCormick's ruling would be upheld and the schools desegregated.) The district superintendent of El Modena dismissed protests, arguing that the children were happy to be segregated and that it was "only the parents who don't know what is best for them."[4] So Ross and Tarango shifted the fight to the streets. Ross received a list of registered voters from the county clerk and sent off hundreds of postcards to people with Spanish surnames, inviting them to a meeting. After initial objections—objections that Ross would face many times in the coming decade—the county clerk finally agreed to deputize five Mexican Americans as voter registrars, who went door-to-door to sign up new voters, with the aim of voting out a particularly racist school board member. The El Modena Unity League also floated an antisegregation petition and supported the California Fair Employment Practice Act, a statewide bill that would prevent discrimination in hiring.

LULAC president Viega was on vacation during much of this activity. On his return, Ross expected words of appreciation. Viega instead launched into a litany of complaints. The new members of the Unity League were mostly common farmworkers, instead of the business owners LULAC had organized. They would soon lose interest and drift away. The antidiscrimination proposal, Viega told Ross, was "nothing but a bill to help the Negroes," and if passed he could be forced to hire one at his mortuary.[5] Ross had thought the long hours of door-to-door work would win over the president. Instead, Ross had organized a threat to Viega's power.

Ross and Tarango nevertheless put aside Viega's objections and continued registering voters up to the election. At the last minute, the El Modena school board, concerned about the possibility of an upset, announced that voting hours would be cut short, ending at 2:00 P.M. instead of the customary 7:00 P.M. The hope was that farmworkers wouldn't be able to get the time off. Instead, outraged parents skipped work entirely and overwhelmingly replaced the white board member with a Mexican American barber.

The Associated Farmers had seen enough. By now the group was closely monitoring Ross as he moved throughout Southern California. It also likely tipped off the FBI, which opened an investigation into Ross that summer. The agency, which listed Fred Rose (misspelled) as an organizer for the misnamed "American Council of Racial Relations," noted that he was "contacting Mexican and Colored groups ... for organizational purposes" and quoted him as boasting that "[I have a] million dollars behind me for organizational work among minority groups." (Such a statement seems very unlikely to have ever come out of his mouth.) But the agency, which also managed to get Ross's age, weight, and height wrong, was unable to find any dirt on this suspicious man who was "representing himself as an organizer."[6]

That didn't stop the Associated Farmers. Its campaign against "Red Ross" began with a letter to the leaders of LULAC, advising them to cut all ties with the American Council on Race Relations, which the growers claimed was "so infiltrated with communists and fellow travelers" that, while purporting to work to improve race relations, it was in fact "subservient to the aims and purposes of the Communist Party."[7] Next, they contacted religious leaders—including Viega's parish priest—spreading rumors about Ross's subversive motivations. Still not satisfied, the Associated Farmers leaned on the district attorney to call a meeting with LULAC leaders, where the growers passed out documents purporting to show that Ross was a Communist. At the meeting, only Tarango pushed back. "So far, all we've done is recruit voters," he replied. "Is that illegal? Is that anti-American? Is that Communist?"[8]

Despite Tarango's protestations, the Red-baiting campaign worked beautifully. Growers, God, and the law were on one side; Ross, the other. "Everybody got scared," Tarango remembered, one of the few who stuck by Ross.[9] LULAC cut its ties with Ross and severed its affiliation with the ACRR. Upset over LULAC's timidity, Tarango resigned.

But the growers still weren't done. When Ross moved on to San Diego, still working for the ACRR, he found that a campaign against him had already been launched, led by the owner of a large department store. "Yes, there is no longer any doubt about it—the machinery of our old friends, the Farm Bureau boys, has been clicking along with its usual well-oiled precision," Ross reported to Laurence Hewes.[10] Ross stuck around regardless, spending three months in the city, where he organized a unity league of blacks, Latinos, and Japanese Americans, who registered 1,375 new voters during a forty-five-day drive. Despite being frustrated by the constant Red-baiting, Ross came away from San Diego satisfied that his organizing methods were proving versatile. As he noted in a memo, San Diego represented his "first attempt at large-scale, urban organization," which "dwarfed anything I'd dealt with in my rural work." Though he'd begun cautiously, not wanting to step on any territorial toes, he found that the dogged approach he'd taken in "cow-county" worked just as well in the city.[11]

Being pursued across California by private spies was a new, and formative, experience for Ross. He wasn't an easy person to intimidate, and he likely considered the pursuit something of an honor, evidence that he was on the right track. But there was no denying that Red-baiting opponents could quickly derail his work, destroying in a matter of days what he had spent months putting together. And it was only going to get worse: as the Associated Farmers hounded Ross in 1947, a paranoid mood was building across the country. In the nation's capital, President Harry Truman signed Executive Order 9835, launching investigations into two million federal employees in search of any ties to Communism. The House Un-American Activities Committee would soon hold hearings into alleged Communist influence in Hollywood. And in Wisconsin, a young and ambitious Marine Corps veteran named Joseph McCarthy had just been elected senator. Ross was launching his organizing career just as the country's post–World War II Red Scare was gaining steam, and as he had learned, it would require diligence if he hoped to avoid, as he put it, "being labeled."[12]

Word about the anti-Ross campaign began to reach the ears of his ACRR superiors, and Ross took care to portray the controversies as the desperate work of reactionaries willing to fling any labels to preserve the status quo. "I think you know me well enough to realize that I don't go in for 'rabble rousing,'" he wrote to Hewes, after returning from a trip to San Diego. "I'm glad you called me on the matter immediately and hope it's settled. However, I'm sure you have sufficient confidence in my work to give me full backing again, should it or similar matters crop up in the future."[13]

Hewes stood by Ross and remained confident in his work. But the same couldn't be said for Louis Wirth, a University of Chicago sociology professor and the president of the ACRR. In March 1947, Wirth sent a sixteen-page memo to the ACRR board, dense with academic jargon, which essentially repudiated everything Ross was doing. The ACRR would be shifting away from "programs of action," Wirth instructed, to become a "neutral agent to build bridges to enable other organizations to come together."[14] New priorities would include compiling data, disseminating information, analyzing programs—in short, doing anything but directly challenging discrimination. Ross was informed that his position would end that summer.

But as Wirth closed one door, he inadvertently kicked open another. Among Wirth's card-playing buddies in Chicago was Saul Alinsky, the irreverent community organizer whose book, *Reveille for Radicals,* had recently become an improbable best seller. One night over pinochle, Wirth complained about the trouble Ross was stirring up out west, where he always seemed to rile up the communities he was supposed to be studying. Alinsky, a professional troublemaker, dashed off a letter to Ross; in June, he came west to visit. They met at the Biltmore Hotel in downtown Los Angeles. Ross had read Alinsky's book and was a bit anxious about meeting the man who had cut his organizing teeth among slaughterhouse workers in the Back of the Yards, the Chicago neighborhood made famous by Upton Sinclair's *Jungle.* But the pair quickly hit it off, with Ross updating Alinsky on his work and giving him a tour of the areas he'd organized. In some ways, the men were stark opposites. Alinsky grew bored easily, having little patience for the sort of grinding organizing work that would become Ross's life. He was quick with the quip and filled, as one of his student's later put it, with "terrific bluster,"[15] once threatening to hold a fart-in at a Rochester symphony. (Prior to the event—which never actually occurred—protesters would eat baked beans.) But for all their differences in style and temperament, Alinsky and Ross shared a very similar organizing philosophy, based in large measure around contempt for what they considered social-work do-gooders who believed progress could somehow come about without conflict.

Ross raised one area of concern. In Chicago, Alinsky had made his name by building a coalition—the Back of the Yards Neighborhood Council—that included representatives from neighborhood groups, various parishes, and the packinghouse union. This successful experiment of an "organization of organizations" was the model for social change that Alinsky championed in *Reveille for Radicals.* But Ross's experiences thus far had soured him on the idea of building an organization by pulling together already formed groups. What groups that did exist in the barrios and colonias, he told Alinsky, usually lacked political power. Others buckled easily under pressure. Bringing weak or apolitical groups together would only result in a weak and apolitical coalition. It was better to build something new.

Alinsky trusted Ross on this account, though at the moment he didn't care too much about the lay of the land in California: he wanted to hire Ross to organize in Butte, Montana, for a project targeting Anaconda Copper.

The prospect held little interest for Ross, who was dead set on staying in California to organize Mexican Americans and had begun hanging out in East Los Angeles to survey the scene. Alinsky gave in. Campaigns would come and go; good organizers were rare. When he returned to Chicago he wrote to a friend, "I have hired a guy who I think is a natural for our work. It will really be the first time that I have had a capable associate who understands exactly what we are after."[16]

Ross spent his last month at the ACRR writing up a report of his activities. The result, "Community Organization in Mexican American Colonies: A Progress Report," was nearly a hundred pages long, and it was divided into seventeen subsections, with titles like "Attitude of the Church" and "Determination of Organizational Structure." Throughout, one feels the intellectual excitement that Ross was discovering in the work. Organizing was fundamentally a people-based endeavor, but it was also something of a societal chess match, and Ross spent the first third of the report discussing the different organizations operating in the colonias. Here are the groups— social-service agencies, private welfare federations—that Wirth, in his memo, thought so critical to eliminating discrimination. Ross dispatches them swiftly, arguing that most are too compromised to take meaningful stands: social-service agencies because they must answer to the same political powers that benefit from the status quo, private groups because they avoid controversial issues that might "offend the financial interests which control its board." As Ross argued:

> But the most urgent problems of the Colonia are all intensely controversial. The private agencies have, from time to time, come into the Colonia and set up clinics, classes in hygiene, homemaking, etc, giving instructions in budget making, and organized the children around various craft and recreational interests; and this has all been to the good. But what the Colonia needs most is opportunity to get decent jobs, decent food and housing so they won't have to use those clinics so often, so they'll have a reasonable budget to keep within, so they can have something to take pride in.[17]

Ross didn't trust outside agencies. But he was also suspicious of colonia groups that came from the "razor-thin upper level," like LULAC, which he felt were vulnerable to co-optation. While some professionals, like Hector Tarango and Ignacio Lopez, were hard-charging activists, Ross was convinced that most would retreat when push came to shove, as they were financially dependent on "both sides of the tracks." They could talk a good game, but many advocated "gradualism, patience, endless conciliation and discussion; in short, anything but direct, purposeful action."[18]

If his year with the ACRR left Ross disillusioned with what he considered mushy professional types, it deepened his faith in the abilities of so-called average folks—field hands, blue-collar workers, housewives—to upend the status quo. Having suffered the sting of injustice most acutely, they were more likely to put in the hard work to end it. Alienated from the dominant white culture, they more easily saw through the lies and empty rhetoric of the opposition. Without as much to lose, they refused to back down. They might have dropped out of school early. They might find it difficult to read and write. They might not be able to deliver an eloquent speech. But what these ordinary people lacked in "more conspicuous statesmanlike abilities" they more than made up for with intestinal fortitude, and they were far more likely to exhibit the type of urgency that got things done.[19] These were the people Ross would be on the lookout for.

PART TWO

Organizing a Movement (1947–1963)

SEVEN

Viva Roybal

WHILE THE FBI TRACKED ROSS'S movements throughout Southern California, a group of Mexican American activists was dreaming big in East Los Angeles. Since anyone could remember, not a single person of Mexican descent had won election to the Los Angeles city council. A potential opening had presented itself in 1946, when aging council member Parley Christensen, who represented downtown and the east-side neighborhood of Boyle Heights, announced his retirement. Christensen was a solid prolabor liberal, and his decision created a vacuum that a number of candidates rushed to fill. One of those candidates was Edward Roybal, a thirty-year-old army veteran who worked as an educator for the county's tuberculosis program. His supporters, initially little more than extended family members, gathered to strategize about how to launch the Spanish-speaking social worker into the city's halls of power.

The campaign was a long shot. At the launch meeting, they collected just thirteen dollars. Roybal's only editorial endorsement would come from a small community publication, *El Pueblo*. "We carried on a campaign of not very great intelligence," admitted Roybal's campaign manager, Roger Johnson.[1] The odds got longer when Christensen reversed course and announced that he would run for another two-year term. Though Christensen was approaching eighty, organized labor stuck with him. Christensen had a solid history on the left; back in 1920, he had even run for president on the Farmer-Labor Party ticket. Labor support and the endorsement of the liberal *Los Angeles Daily News* catapulted Christensen to an easy win, with more than twice the votes of Roybal, who finished third in a field of five. A key reason for his poor showing was the low voter registration rates among Roybal's natural base, the sizable Mexican American community.

But there was a forward-looking energy in the Roybal campaign, whose slogan, "Give a Young Man a Chance," was a none too subtle jibe at Christensen. Several important Mexican American union activists signed on, and Roybal spent his time building a following. He rode streetcars and handed out palm cards that stressed his credentials, emblazoned with the words "veteran" and "progressive." He focused on bread-and-butter issues: cracking down on police abuse, cleaning up the neighborhood, installing better street lighting. The handsome young man with sad eyes lost the election, but anyone could tell he had a future in politics. After the defeat, Saul Alinsky, who had earlier met Roybal at a social-work conference in Texas, sent a seven-word telegram: "What are you going to do next?"[2]

Roybal and his volunteers weren't quite sure what came next. But having tasted the excitement of a political campaign, they weren't ready to disband. In the wake of the defeat they continued to meet, sometimes over beers at local restaurants, sometimes at the East Side YMCA, tackling whatever issues community members brought forward, from evictions to police brutality. It was during this lull, in the summer of 1947, that Ross, after spending a few weeks searching fruitlessly for contacts, finally crossed paths with Roybal, who invited him to a meeting of what they were calling the Community Political Organization (CPO). Having been burned by LULAC, Ross was leery about latching on to an already existing organization, but one meeting with the CPO was enough to make him reconsider. "After the bunch of phonies I had been chasing around after, this group was a real eye opener," he wrote.[3] No loud-mouth wannabes or business owners simply looking to drum up more customers: here were garment and steel workers, dishwashers and short-order cooks. In short, the "plain, ordinary" folks that Ross was after.

On August 1, 1947, Ross become the West Coast representative of the Industrial Areas Foundation (IAF), the organization Alinsky had formed to raise funds and sponsor organizing projects. For two months Ross watched and listened, occasionally crossing the street after CPO meetings to down a beer with members at the Red Rooster, a local hangout. Many of the leaders were active in the labor movement, and Ross had good reason to be impressed. Tony Rios, who would later become president of the group, was a member of the steelworkers union and relished a good fight. Maria Duran, born in Mexico, was a tireless activist with the International Ladies' Garment Workers' Union; she would become the group's first treasurer. Once he felt that he was on good terms with the core leadership, Ross suggested to Roybal that he could serve as an organizer for the group.

For Roybal, the proposal held obvious appeal. Ross had shared his tales of voting out Rathgeber in Casa Blanca and voting in the barber in El Modena, and Roybal's political aspirations were still alive and well. But Roybal registered two concerns. How would Ross prove he wasn't a Communist? And how would he get the other members to go along with a plan that involved bringing in an Anglo outsider? Ross explained that he had already begun to line up religious support for his work, starting with Los Angeles bishop Joseph McGucken, to counter any Red-baiting. On the second matter, Ross suggested bringing the topic up at a meeting and putting it to a vote. But Ross also mentioned the need, if he was accepted, to change the name. The Industrial Areas Foundation was nonpartisan, and so the Community *Political* Organization would become the Community *Service* Organization, or CSO. (Another possible explanation is that the CPO abbreviation was too similar to that of the Communist Party. A third explanation—more colorful, if less accurate—is that CPO, when pronounced in Spanish, sounds a lot like the word for "fart.")

Before the meeting, Ross met individually with Rios, Duran, and others, talking over the plan and gaining their support. "The idea was broached at a very opportune time: the attendance of meetings had dropped from about twenty-five to thirty to around seventeen," Ross wrote to Alinsky. They "realized that since an org either progresses or falls apart, something had to be done."[4] Ross made his pitch at a September meeting, summarizing his work in the Citrus Belt and outlining a plan to comb through Boyle Heights, precinct by precinct, in search of leaders who would build an organization so powerful it couldn't be ignored. In a letter to Alinsky, Ross described how he concluded his talk: "If you accept the plan I'll begin work with the CSO immediately. In making this decision I realize some of you will be full of doubts and suspicions. I've got two strikes against me and I know it: first, I'm an outsider, and second I'm an Anglo-American. But I hope you keep those doubts because having them is healthy. I hope you'll hold on to them until I've had time to prove you're mistaken."[5]

When Ross sat down, CSO members voted unanimously to accept him as organizer. During his talk, he had informed the group that they would be put to work—"this is *your* organization, not mine"—and he immediately made good on the promise. He formed a membership committee of five volunteers, each of whom agreed to go out with Ross one night a week to visit neighbors and talk up the CSO. From Monday to Friday, Ross and a member made the rounds, beginning at 6:00 P.M. and ending near midnight. The legwork paid off. By the next meeting, the original group of 17 had increased to 55. Soon the 55 became 70, then 85, then 175. The meetings grew so large they had to relocate to the YMCA's gymnasium.

"To put it cautiously," Ross wrote to Alinsky, "I'm getting less discouraged about the work here all the time. Let's hope the trend continues."[6]

That fall, Ross and his family moved to a three-bedroom house on the eastern outskirts of Boyle Heights. The move was only twenty miles, but it represented a dramatic shift: from a quiet public housing complex in suburban Long Beach to a working-class neighborhood steeped in radical politics and churning with the energy of new immigrants. Long the center of Jewish life in the city—Boyle Heights was called the Lower East Side of Los Angeles—its main street, Brooklyn Avenue, was lined with shops where one could find customers debating the finer points of socialism in Yiddish. Many of the émigrés from eastern Europe were staunch unionists and sturdy idealists, the sort who, instead of fleeing from the growing Latino population—which would eventually come to dominate the neighborhood—jumped at the chance to build a multicultural community. Alongside the Jews and Mexicans were smaller communities of blacks, Japanese, Italians, and Armenians. Though within view of downtown, Boyle Heights was a world apart from the "lily white" neighborhoods where Ross had been raised—and proud of this fact.

Its embrace of diversity and left-wing politics earned Boyle Heights suspicion in many quarters. The Federal Housing Authority, in giving the neighborhood its lowest rating—and thereby refusing to back mortgages for its residents—noted that it was "hopelessly heterogeneous" and "literally honeycombed with diverse and subversive racial elements."[7] The year after Ross arrived, state senator Jack Tenney, chair of California's Un-American Activities Committee, would characterize Boyle Heights as swarming with Communist-front groups. (The threat of McCarthyism was strong enough to convince Ross and Frances to hide their record albums of Paul Robeson—an unabashed Communist—when they moved to Boyle Heights.) In such a charged environment, Ross knew that an active organization of Mexican Americans, talking politics, wouldn't escape notice. From the outset, he proceeded carefully, anxious to avoid the problems he had experienced in Orange County. He wrote to Alinsky that while he held deep respect for Carey McWilliams, after conversations with a number of people, he had decided not to select him for a CSO advisory committee, as "the MA [Mexican American] situation here is just so damned touchy and tender.... McWilliams is definitely 'labelled,' and even a vague label is more than enough to send the M.A.'s scurrying for cover and send the quasi-liberals and conservative Anglo-Americans in the field out on a crusade to discredit the Committee."[8]

Two months later, the "Red issue" came up during a CSO meeting, when a member of Americans for Democratic Action suggested the group adopt a clause barring Communists from joining. For Ross, avoiding such a clause in the CSO was preferable from both a strategic and principled perspective. On the strategic side, as he explained to Alinsky, the CSO was already labeled by those who opposed it. To adopt an anti-Red clause wouldn't slow down the opposition but would only generate new attacks from the left, especially among the more radical Jews in Boyle Heights. "This was the practical argument," Ross wrote:

> The theoretical one dealt with civil rights, and equal treatment of all who will work for the organization. In other words, no red-baiting. This was agreed upon by the Committee members; and *all* of them were present. The current policy, then, is a positive one—for maximum operation of the democratic processes and participation in CSO [of] all segments of the community; and the only "anti" is anti-discrimination. And all this at the height (what a misnomer!) of the Un-American Activities Hearings in D.C. Nevertheless, I fervently hope and pray that the "boys on the Left" will keep their hot little hands out of the CSO for the time being, at least until a strong, liberal foundation is built. (By the way you never got around to outlining for me the Industrial Areas Foundation line on this. Please let me have it.)[9]

He heard little from Alinsky at this point—about his "line" on Communists or anything else—due to a family tragedy Alinsky suffered back in Chicago, so Ross was alone in navigating the complicated political waters of East Los Angeles.

There is little evidence that Ross was ideologically anti-Communist. Many of his major influences and inspirations, like Eugene Wolman at the University of Southern California and Luke Hinman at Arvin, were members of the party. But that didn't mean he welcomed Communists into the CSO. Ross was leery of dual loyalties: he didn't want people who were taking orders from elsewhere or who viewed the CSO as a pawn to be used for a larger, and unstated, purpose. One of his critiques of Alinsky's strategy of building an "organization of organizations" was that people remained loyal to their original group; this concern spilled over to "the boys on the Left," who he worried would angle to take over the CSO. This related to his second concern: given the political constraints of the day, it would be nearly impossible to build a mass organization that was identified as Communist controlled.

The CSO would have to deal with such considerations throughout most of its existence, and Ross helped it chart a particular course. Unlike groups such as the NAACP, which would purge Communists from its membership in 1950, the CSO theoretically remained open to all—though it proceeded carefully when deciding how to interact with others and took measures to isolate known Communists within its membership. Henry Nava, who would succeed Roybal as CSO president, remembered that Ross "cautioned us" about the possibility that Communists could attempt to take over, and so CSO members tried to minimize their influence.[10] When a representative of the Labor Youth League, an arm of the Communist Party, asked to have the floor at a meeting to speak about a recent trip to China and the Soviet Union, the CSO membership decided that "the speaker not be considered for the next meeting because we already have two candidates."[11] The group was also careful about the alliances it formed. After the Asociación Naciónal Mexico-Americano (ANMA), a radical working-class organization with Communist ties, invited the CSO to formally cosponsor its convention in Los Angeles, the CSO declined but sent Nava as a representative. Ross knew the CSO was being watched—indeed, both the FBI and the California Un-American Activities Committee were monitoring the group—and this awareness affected the group's tactics. At one point, members decided to refrain from picketing a segregated housing complex as it "might lead to the CSO being labeled 'Red.'"[12]

But aside from such behind the scenes maneuvering, along with attempts to marginalize certain individuals through parliamentary procedures, Ross believed that the key to avoiding being taken over by Communists—or any other group—was to keep moving on issues of concrete concern to the community. A decade later, a CSO leader would contact Ross about what he considered a "communist-nationalist" group, led by Bert Corona, that he claimed was attempting to take over the Oakland chapter. Corona is a critical figure in Latino history: a dedicated and talented labor organizer with the Congress of Industrial Organizations, he was also active with ANMA and helped establish the Mexican American Political Association. Corona generally considered the CSO to be a positive force, though he was critical of how it positioned its work as a bulwark against Communism, and he later portrayed Ross as a Red-baiter. In this instance, however, Ross told the worried CSO member to relax. There was little reason for concern; and besides, if the leader was worried, the best course of action was to reenergize the chapter, because "where a CSO has no fighting program it is a sitting duck" for other groups to move in.[13]

The fighting program in Boyle Heights was voter registration. After several months of organizing, the CSO had recruited fifty people to serve as deputy registrars, who could go door-to-door registering people to vote. But an election official told Ross that when it came to voting, Mexican Americans "don't want to be bothered."[14] Ross persisted, turning in dozens of applications and asking that the three-hour class for registrars be given at night in Boyle Heights so that working people could attend. The election official, a balding middle-aged man named Marcus Woodward, refused. Only when Ross took his complaints to the Central Labor Council—which made a quick call to Woodward's boss—did he eventually back down, trekking out to the east side to swear in forty-nine volunteers, who were photographed in the *Daily News* with their hands over their hearts. With this small army of registrars, the CSO set out to transform the political landscape in Los Angeles. Over the next four months, the team registered more than eleven thousand voters, doubling the number of Latino voters in the city.[15]

As the CSO moved forward, Ross heard little from Alinsky. After traveling to Los Angeles to hire Ross, he had returned to Chicago and driven his wife, Helen, and their two children to a vacation spot on Lake Michigan, where they were to stay the summer. In September, just before Alinsky was scheduled to pick them up, he learned that Helen had drowned in a tragic swimming accident. Alinsky was devastated, telling his stepsister that he was ready to end his life. "[He] was absolutely helpless in terms of knowing what to do, how to provide, how to manage alone," one friend told Alinsky's biographer.[16] It would be months before Alinsky had recovered enough to think about the CSO.

Ross was dealing with a family crisis of his own. In June 1947, soon after Alinsky departed, Frances visited her doctor, complaining of back pain. She was told she had "muscle spasms" and given pain-killers.[17] Tests would soon reveal she had contracted polio, which was crippling thirty-five thousand people a year and sending the nation into a panic. She was also pregnant.

FIGURE 8. Marcus Woodward swears in CSO members as deputy registrars at St. Mary's Catholic Church, January 9, 1948. *Los Angeles Daily News*, courtesy of Charles E. Young Research Library, UCLA.

Frances spent nearly three months at the Rancho Los Amigos hospital in Los Angeles and by October had returned home, where she remained in bed and sat up only to eat meals. She would have two painful surgeries to stabilize her pelvis and back in the next three years and would spend many more years in physical therapy before she regained the ability to walk with confidence. Despite it all, she gave birth to a healthy baby boy on October 14, 1947, whom the couple named Fred but would call Gib, short for his middle name, Gibson.

That Ross was able to organize the CSO successfully, in the midst of such an emergency, spoke to his priorities. Although he loved Frances, and would shuttle her back and forth to physical therapy appointments, organizing almost always came first. This must have been obvious to Frances even before the CSO, when her husband was organizing in Santa Ana. Though their Long Beach housing complex was just thirty miles away—a drive of less than an hour—Ross was so consumed by the work that at one point he failed to return home to see his wife and daughter for a six-week stretch. As a toddler, Julia began referring to Ross as "Daddy Dino"—a reference to the fact that her father always seemed to be away in San Bernardino.[18] "My mother told me that I went to the neighbor next door and asked him if he would be my father," recalled Julia. "And he agreed. So every day I would bring him the paper and his slippers. Apparently I abandoned him like a shot when my father would come home."[19]

While in Long Beach, Frances wrote dozens of letters to her mother in San Francisco, a volume that testifies to her loneliness. She tried to remain cheery on paper, but at times she couldn't help but blurt out the truth: she felt overwhelmed and isolated. Judging from the letters, Julia was sick almost as often as well, and she slept terribly, while Frances was stuck in a city where she had few close friends she could rely on for support. "Thurs, Fri, and Sat night she screamed from 1:30 to 4:40," Frances wrote. "I'm a quivering wreck."[20] In one letter, she told her mother that what she needed was a "normal life" but admitted that such a possibility was "not in sight."[21] It didn't help that when her husband was home, he was often a wreck himself. During his first five years' organizing, Ross's ailments—which doctors attributed partly to his heavy workload—would include indigestion, constipation, back pain, a weakened coronary artery, and neuralgia, a painful condition caused by damaged nerves along the neck and face.

Decades later, while training young activists in Syracuse, Ross repeated a story about the period to illustrate the proper priorities of an organizer. In his telling, Frances is finally leaving the hospital by ambulance, to be dropped off at their new house in Boyle Heights. Ross is supposed to be home to receive Frances, who is unable to walk. But when the ambulance arrives, the house is dark: Ross is away at an organizing meeting. The ambulance driver has no choice but to return Frances to the hospital. (In another version, which Frances told Julia, she is simply deposited on the floor of the empty house, with Ross having failed to purchase the proper hospital bed. Whatever the specifics, it was certainly a traumatic event for Frances.) On another occasion, the pair went Christmas shopping, with Ross dropping Frances off. After she was finished, she waited for her husband out front. And waited. Ross had remembered some task he needed to do for the CSO, and by the time he returned, he found Frances, whose weak legs had buckled, lying on the sidewalk. "She said he did that kind of thing over and over again," said Julia. "But it was many years before she would tell these kinds of truthful things about our father."[22]

Ross understood that his organizing placed a tremendous burden on Frances, but he saw it as an inevitable consequence of having chosen the life of an organizer. This was an era in which gender roles tended to be quite rigid: men worked, and women stayed home to raise the children. It also certainly didn't help that his own father had been a poor role model. But even by the standards of the time, Ross could be cavalier in his disregard for Frances's needs—especially for someone who otherwise held progressive views of women. For Ross, however, pushing aside every other distraction, including the family, was simply what any good organizer had to do. "I didn't realize I was saying goodbye to family life—for life," Ross later said. "When you start organizing, that's it. You're not working any nine-to-five job anymore. You're not working just six days a week. That's the end of family life. I didn't know that. Not that that would have stopped me."[23]

In 1948, much of Ross's seven-day-a-week job was dedicated to voter registration and get-out-the-vote operations, first for primaries in June and then for the general election in November. The biggest test would come in 1949, when he anticipated that Edward Roybal would again run for city council. But these dry runs were important, because anyone who failed to vote in 1948 would be struck from the rolls and have to reregister the following year. As he had done in Casa Blanca, Ross tried to demystify the process for new voters, going so far as to borrow voting booths that people could use for practice. He also became a deputy registrar himself, a fact that was discovered by an investigator with the California Un-American Activities Committee, who noted, disapprovingly, that "when a loyalty blank was sent to him to sign, he failed to return it."[24]

By March 1948, reported the local newspaper *El Pueblo,* the CSO had registered 3,918 new voters. The article, "News of the CSO," noted that men's and women's divisions had been created—turning the drive into a tournament of sorts—with Matt "Cyclone" Arguijos* well out ahead with 1,025 voters registered.[25] During the drive, Ross created flyers urging people to get to the polls, using language that he would deploy in many future voter registration efforts:

> Remember—how we used to ask for street lights, bus transportation, playgrounds, sidewalks, street repairs, for help in getting equal treatment in housing and employment?

---

* Arguijos would eventually register 2,286 voters, far more than any other CSO activist. The second, third, and fourth slots were all held by women—Elisa Baker, Gerrye Overton, and Lourdes Tafoya—each of whom registered more than 500 people.

Remember—how they used to cup their hands to their ears and say, "Speak louder, please. We only hear about one-fifth of what you are saying?" That is because only one-fifth of us had registered and voted . . .
BUT TIMES HAVE CHANGED! WE CAN . . . WE WILL . . . WE MUST VOTE![26]

By the time Roybal announced that he was resigning as CSO president to run for city council, the CSO had become a political force in Boyle Heights and the adjacent neighborhoods of Belvedere and Lincoln Heights, where Ross had recently organized an additional CSO chapter. An estimated seventeen thousand new voters had been added to the rolls, earning mention in the liberal *Daily News,* which could always be depended on to churn out pro-CSO copy. Roybal would again face Christensen. This time around, however, the young health educator had a track record: as president of the CSO, he had been at the helm of a group whose efforts had led to new streetlights and sidewalks and that was working to hold police accountable for their long history of acting against Mexicans with impunity. In his speeches he called for the creation of a civilian police review board, a fair employment commission, and an end to housing discrimination. His was an ambitious and politically astute agenda, appealing not only to Mexican Americans but also to the district's African American residents, who faced similar challenges, and to the progressive Jews of Boyle Heights.

Two years earlier, Roybal had relied on little more than a ragtag group of family and friends. Now he had a grassroots machine. From the CSO's office at 2323 East First Street, on the corner of Soto Avenue, Ross managed the voter registration and get-out-the-vote operations, overseeing 150 precinct volunteers. With his usual fastidiousness, he created an individual 3x5 card for each of the ten thousand registered voters with Spanish surnames. In the run-up to the election, home visits were made, noting which people would need a ride to their polling place. On the day before the election, Ross learned that a mysterious Spanish-language postcard had landed in the mailboxes of Latino households in Boyle Heights. Next to an image of a stereotypical Mexican *charro*—or cowboy—red text accused Roybal of being a Communist. A phone team of eighty-five CSO members spent the day calling residents to counter the claim. On election day, as cars loaded with voters crisscrossed the district, the same phone team called each registered voter, multiple times. Others set up at the polls, passing along the names of no-shows to block walkers so they could be visited at home.[27]

During the campaign, Roybal had proven to be a skillful politician, emerging as a candidate whose appeal went far beyond the district's sizable

Latino minority. Christensen also suffered some obvious liabilities; Tony Rios, the steelworker and CSO activist, remembered photos circulating of the elderly council member asleep during meetings. Rumors swirled that he had a drinking problem. But the key difference between 1947 and 1949 was the ground operation, consisting mostly of volunteers on a shoestring budget. The average candidate for city council ploughed $15,000 into a race. The Roybal campaign spent just $5,500. In 1947, Roybal had received 3,350 votes. Two years later, he received 20,562 voters—a more than sixfold increase. He trounced Christensen, receiving more votes in Boyle Heights alone (12,684) than Christensen did in the entire district (11,948), with the highest turnout of any council election in the city.[28]

The election victory was a high point for Ross, who could justifiably claim to have helped dispatch the lie that Mexican Americans simply weren't interested in voting. It would also serve as a launching pad for the long political career of Roybal, who spent four terms on the city council and another thirty years representing Boyle Heights and East Los Angeles in the US House of Representatives. On the council he developed a well-deserved reputation for standing up for the marginalized, taking on abusive cops, pushing for fair employment legislation, and fighting on behalf of Latinos living in Chavez Ravine, who were eventually evicted to make way for Dodger Stadium. His was often a lonely and brave position, as when, in 1950—scarcely a year into his first term—he cast the lone vote against an ordinance requiring members of the Communist Party to register with the police, a position he took after consulting with the CSO. (Members of the CSO told him to vote against the measure "regardless of what it might do to his political future.")[29]

Ross and Roybal would always have their names linked in the historic campaign, and both found much to admire in the other. Thirty-five years later, at a celebration for Ross's seventy-fifth birthday, Roybal spoke in gracious terms. "The success that I have had has been due to the work that Fred Ross did in this community," he told the crowd.[30] In interviews, Ross was also quick to highlight his work with Roybal, who remained fiercely loyal to the CSO after assuming office. But while the campaign helped Ross refine his get-out-the-vote technique, it didn't tempt him to become more involved in electoral politics, and the lessons he took from the experience weren't all positive. On the night of the election, Ross, Roybal, and others gathered at a restaurant to follow the results. The first precinct to announce was downtown, which included Bunker Hill, where Christensen lived. It was a mostly white area and would prove to be the only precinct that Christensen would win. When the Bunker Hill results were announced, Ross recalled that Roybal and Roger Johnson both turned to him and complained that he hadn't done enough. "Remember when I told you that you were spending too much time organizing the Mexicans?" needled Johnson.[31] This casual swipe, after Ross had spent months pouring his energy into the campaign, left a mark.

Ross also felt that Roybal overlooked the grassroots work that had made the campaign victorious. Here is how Ross described, nearly four decades later, the scene after the full results had been announced: "We were in this big restaurant, probably about one hundred of us listening to radios. When he won, they had him come down to [the] TV station. His closing remarks were, 'I want to give full credit to my campaign manager, Roger Johnson.' There was a great silence in this room. 'How come my feet hurt?' yelled someone."[32]

In later years, Ross hinted that below the surface there was considerable tension between himself and Roybal. During one interview, Ross said that Roybal often "forgot" his first name in public, once thanking a "Frank Ross" in front of a crowd of CSO members during a celebration of a successful voter registration drive. Ross interpreted this as a none-too-subtle gibe meant to diminish his importance. Organizers, Ross concluded, "cannot avoid being somewhat threatening to existing leadership," because they are building a base of power that is potentially independent of the candidate, for which they may receive credit that the politician seeks. Even though Ross remained steadfastly in the background, he felt that Roybal regularly angled to take credit for work that Ross had done. "He wanted the backing of people, naturally," Ross said. "But he didn't want to kill himself to get it. On the other hand, I wanted to get the people and I was willing to kill myself to get them."[33]

The experience with Roybal helped clarify Ross's true passion: organizing people, who could then move politicians to do what they wanted. Although the Roybal campaign demonstrated that he had a nose for the work that actually gets people to the polls—the attention to detail, the multiple reminders, the refusal to take no for an answer—electoral politics, with the sole goal of putting someone in office, would never again be quite as exciting to Ross. Reflecting on the Roybal campaign in the mid-1980s, Ross concluded, "At the time, I wasn't as cynical about politicians as I am now."[34]

Bloody Christmas

IN THE FALL OF 1949, Ross received sad news: his first wife, Yvonne Gregg, had died in Santa Barbara at the age of thirty-seven. The cause was officially listed as pneumonia, though doctors determined that the cirrhosis of her liver was so advanced that she wouldn't have lived much longer, pneumonia or not. Alcohol abuse had shriveled the once boisterous and sturdy woman to painfully thin dimensions. On her deathbed she sported numerous bruises and a black eye, the result of a drunken car crash, for which she was facing a five-month jail sentence.

Yvonne's life had spiraled downward since she had divorced Ross and married Newton Young, the former navy sailor. They drank and fought, separated and reconciled, moving from one state to another in an illusive search for stable ground. After a bender landed Yvonne in a Utah hospital, the couple returned to California, staying with her parents in Ontario. For the nine-year-old Robin, who had been dragged along for the unhappy ride, the quiet house in Ontario, with two attentive grandparents, felt like paradise. Yvonne must have realized that she didn't have the capacity to provide a suitable home for her son, so when Young heard about a job in Santa Barbara, they left Robin behind. Yvonne died six months later.

Ross attended the funeral, where he greeted his son. Though Ross remembered to send birthday gifts each year, during the eight years that had passed since the divorce, he had apparently only seen Robin once. Ross learned that Yvonne had told her parents that Robin should live with Ross if anything happened to her. The family wasn't exactly prepared to take in another child. Ross was thoroughly consumed with his work, and Frances was still undergoing intensive physical therapy as she recovered from polio, forced to spend many days in bed. It was already a struggle to care for four-year-old Julia and two-year-old Fred Jr. But Frances pushed to take in Robin, despite objections from Ross's mother. "I finally won by saying 'of course it won't be easy,'" Frances wrote to her mother, describing the conflict. "Gib [Fred Jr.'s nickname] and Julie aren't easy, but it will be right. And the child is *Fred's son* and his mother is *dead*."[1]

In preparation for Robin's arrival, they moved into a four-bedroom home at 2610 Gleason Street. Located in the heart of Boyle Heights, the house was two blocks from the Community Service Organization office. They had little savings but were able to bargain down the rent to eighty-five dollars a month, with CSO members moving the furniture for free. Hobbled by polio, stretching an impossibly tight budget and welcoming a new family member were a lot for Frances to handle, but she was a gritty and proud woman, and she declined financial assistance from her mother. "What with one thing and another," she concluded in her letter, "I'm surprisingly fit."

It wasn't an easy transition for Robin. After visiting over Christmas, he moved in with his new family in February 1950. He arrived anxious and underweight, with sties on his eyes and boils covering his body, clearly traumatized by the death of his mother and his chaotic upbringing. In the first few weeks he refused to attend school, broke the arm of a three-year-old while roughhousing, and slammed the door on the head of the family housekeeper. "Fred and I have refused to become excited—outwardly," Frances wrote to her mother. Though it was difficult for her to get around, she took Robin to his weekly therapy sessions at Children's Hospital and was optimistic about the future. "Poor little Robin is so hungry for approval and loving," she wrote. "I know in six months he will be more grown up and we will feel very proud."[2]

After the Roybal victory and the gradual acclimation of Robin into the family, life settled down for Ross. With the election over, the CSO turned much of its attention to an issue members had been organizing against since the beginning: police brutality. At one of the first meetings Ross attended, people told of a war veteran who had been dozing in his car before being "suddenly awakened by two policemen who were using their flashlights as clubs and his head as target."[3] Another case brought to the attention of the CSO involved a cop who, while chasing a suspect, tripped and "accidentally" shot the man in the head. On the streets of East Los Angeles, the men in blue acted with impunity. In 1948, when seventeen-year-old Agustin Salcido was shot and

FIGURE 9. The Ross family on their front porch in Boyle Heights, circa 1952, soon to leave for Marin County. Left to right: Julia, Bob (Robin), Frances (in wheelchair), Ross, and Fred Jr. Courtesy of Fred Ross Jr.

killed by officer William Keyes, the CSO hired a private investigator. Officer Keyes, it turned out, had a history of shooting Mexican Americans. One year earlier, he had shot Joseph Gonzalez in the back; a year before that, Joaquin Lopez received a bullet through the head, leaving him paralyzed.[4] All three men were unarmed; Keyes never went to jail. Alongside the violence was the everyday indignity of being shaken down. On each corner, Edward Roybal recalled, "you'd see young men with their hands over a car and policemen going through their pockets, taking them in for no reason at all."[5]

For the city's political class, the Roybal victory was a message that the east side could no longer be ignored. Ross received a call from the office of Mayor Fletcher Bowron, who wanted to schedule a meeting with the CSO. Bowron, a Republican, likely expected to be on the receiving end of gratitude for traveling to Boyle Heights. Instead, members of the CSO used the opportunity to aggressively press him about police brutality. They demanded that investigations be launched into complaints they had filed, which the police chief had ignored. The mayor left in a huff, dismissing the problem, Ross later wrote, as limited to a few officers who were occasionally "a little over-exuberant" in their efforts to "keep hoodlums in order."[6] The CSO compiled long files and lodged a number of official complaints about abusive police activities but made little headway, swimming upstream against media coverage that linked Mexican Americans to crime. When white youngsters got together, they probably belonged to the same sports team; when Mexican American or black teens congregated, they were presumed to be members of one deadly street gang or another. The police saw their job, in the words of one scholar, as protecting whites from "inherently criminal racial groups," and the media obediently followed the police line.[7] People of color knew that police abuse was real and pervasive, but it would take a special case to crack the public shield of impunity that the Los Angeles Police Department (LAPD) enjoyed.

A few days after the Christmas of 1951, Ross pulled his car up to the office to find Maria Duran, a CSO leader, frantically motioning for him. There had been another beating. Ross rushed over to visit twenty-three-year-old Daniel Rodela, who was hiding out at his mother's house because he was worried, as he told Ross, that "the cops might return and finish the job." The young man was stretched out on an army cot, his body covered in bruises and his face a "pulpy mess" as he recounted what would soon become known as Bloody Christmas.[8]

Early Christmas morning, Rodela, his brother, and five of their friends had gone to a bar near downtown. Soon after they arrived, two policemen entered, searching for underage drinkers. Everyone in their group was of drinking age, but after inspecting their IDs, the cops still insisted they leave. The men refused, the officers attempted to physically remove them, and a fight broke out. The seven left without being arrested, but a few hours later cops showed up at Rodela's house, pulled him outside by the hair, beat him at a nearby park, and delivered him to the central city jail, where he joined his six friends.

Inside, a hundred cops were passing around bottles of liquor, getting a jump on Christmas celebrations. The festive mood turned ugly after a false rumor spread that one of the officers had lost an eye during the bar fight. Over several hours, fifty officers took turns entering the cells, savagely beating the defenseless men and slipping drunkenly in the pools of blood they created. They dropped knees on one victim's groin so many times that his bladder was punctured. Another, after being kicked in the temple, felt his head become temporarily paralyzed. The harshest punishment was meted out to Rodela, who weighed just 114 pounds. He suffered a broken cheek and a punctured kidney, and though he had been released from the hospital's prison ward, it was clear his wounds demanded more medical attention. Ross called CSO member Dr. Konstantin Sparkhul, who rushed Rodela to a hospital in Chinatown, where he was described as being "near death" and given two blood transfusions that saved his life.[9]

The next day, the headline of the *Los Angeles Times* read "Officer Beaten in Bar Brawl; Seven Men Jailed." The article described a "wild barroom fight" that occurred when the men "ganged up" on the two policemen. The photo included six men lined up at the central police station—Rodela was already in the hospital's prison ward—who appeared to be struggling to stand. One man cradled his arm, another had his shirt torn open; the face of the man nearest the camera was swollen and lopsided. They had been booked, the paper reported, on "suspicion of assault with a deadly weapon."[10] There was no mention of the jailhouse beatings.

This was the case that the CSO had long been waiting for, the type of unwarranted savagery that would repulse even the most law-and-order citizen. (It didn't hurt, either, that two of the seven victims were white.) Tony Rios, the future CSO president, in particular saw it as a watershed moment, emphasizing for Rodela how critical his role as a truth teller could be. But the excitement didn't last long. According to Ross, the attorney hired by the men, James Warner, was worried that highlighting the jailhouse beatings would cause the police department to launch a full-scale assault on the integrity of his clients. In a city whose press, with few exceptions, sided with the police, such a strategy could easily backfire. At the CSO office, Warner outlined his plan. He wasn't going to breathe a word about the beatings and would plead guilty on his clients' behalf and ask for leniency.

Rios was furious. Where Roybal tended to be more calculating—a useful trait for any politician—Rios often charged full speed ahead without always thinking about the consequences. But there was little that Rios or the CSO could do as long as the legal strategy was to pretend the jailhouse beatings had never occurred. When Ross tipped off a friendly contact at the *Los Angeles Daily News,* the reporter explained that he couldn't run anything until someone involved in the event actually went on the record.

The entire episode might well have been lost to history if not for what transpired several weeks later. On the evening of January 27, 1952, after attending a CSO meeting, Rios stopped by the Carioca Café in Boyle Heights. Sitting together at the bar were two visibly intoxicated men, who later wandered into the parking lot and began beating a construction worker. Rios and a companion, Alfred Ulloa, dashed outside to intervene, yelling for someone to call the cops. That's when one of the men pulled out a gun and threatened to shoot Rios. The pair of drunks, it turned out, were plainclothes vice cops. Rios and Ulloa were arrested, taken to the station, stripped, and beaten. During the assault, Rios kept his face unprotected, later telling an interviewer that he "wanted people to be able to see what the police had done."[11]

After being bailed out by Ross and Roybal, the thirty-nine-year-old Rios filed a complaint with LAPD's internal affairs. An investigator was soon at his doorstep. Think before you do anything rash, the investigator told him, pointing to a car parked on the street that was filled with cops. But this time the LAPD had beaten the wrong man. Rios went public with his accusations, debating a police lieutenant on a public access channel and using his case to make public the Bloody Christmas affair. Ross watched Rios perform from outside the studio's glass windows, immensely impressed. "The TV job of Tony's turns the tide," he wrote.[12]

The trial of Rios and Ulloa began on February 26, 1952. Both men were charged with interfering with the affairs of police officers Fernando Najera and George Kellenberger. Officer Najera, it seems, had a mighty short fuse: on the opening day of the trial, the *Los Angeles Times* reported that Najera had visited a movie theater the previous evening, become upset about a group "drinking and using abusive language," and stabbed a man. (The stabbed man, recuperating in a hospital, was charged with assault with a deadly weapon.)

Rios was a sympathetic defendant, with a long record of good deeds and a reputation as a civic leader. Ross drove CSO members to the courthouse to pack the room. Although the prosecution tried to paint Rios as some type of subversive, the ploy never took, as Rios was known as a staunch anti-Communist. And the bartender, withstanding a campaign of intimidation, testified that both cops had been drunk. The all-white jury needed only four hours to toss out the charges. "Jury Vindicates Rios and Ulloa" was the headline in the *Daily News,* whose reporter noted that the verdict "casts doubt on the stories of the officers."[13]

By now a lot of doubt was being cast about the behavior of the LAPD toward Mexican Americans. Roybal gathered fifty complaints of police brutality from the CSO and held a press conference, demanding action from police chief William Parker. After the beating of Rios, Ross had tried to solicit support from various groups to push for a serious investigation, but all declined: no one wanted to go up against the powerful police department. But the Rios verdict and Roybal's call for change broke the logjam, and a number of organizations finally voiced concern. No longer able to ignore the clamor, the Police Commission announced a public hearing into the matter.

The Bloody Christmas case had thus far been proceeding without any mention of the jailhouse beatings. But attorney Warner, sensing the swing in public mood, finally allowed the defendants to speak about what they had suffered. Judge Joseph Call, up to that point presiding over a fairly routine case, exploded with indignation. "The record in this case is permeated with testimony of vicious beatings and brutality perpetrated without cause or provocation long after these defendants were taken into custody," he announced, dismissing the charges against the defendants and demanding a grand jury investigation.[14] Suddenly, descriptions of the abuse were plastered across newspaper front pages. "They took us to separate cells in the isolation ward and then they started coming in every 15 minutes or so, five or six at a time, and beat us," said one of the victims.[15] The witness testimony during the investigation was so damning that even the conservative *Los Angeles Times* predicted that the officers would be indicted on brutality charges, a previously unthinkable development. Sure enough, eight officers were indicted for assault, five convicted, and one sentenced to more than a year in prison. It wasn't perfect justice—a concerted and obvious cover-up by the LAPD was largely ignored, and more abuses would follow—but it was the first time in the history of the LAPD that officers were found guilty of using excessive force.

The success of the Roybal campaign and the work against police brutality overshadowed a problem that would dog the CSO throughout much of its existence: funds were running out. By late 1949, Ross had started digging into his own pockets to cover the office rent and utilities, but after several months he had exhausted his savings. The CSO, which had so recently made history, was now teetering on financial collapse. At midyear in 1950, the organization's balance was just $38.60. A fund-raising drive netted only an additional $275. This was hardly adequate, especially in light of the imminent termination of Industrial Areas Foundation funding, which covered Ross's salary. Saul Alinsky had agreed to fund the project for three years, until December 1950, believing that by that time an organization ought to have become self-sufficient. As the deadline loomed, the CSO was anything but.

Part of the reason for the shortfall was the belief, shared by Ross, that the CSO shouldn't charge membership dues. The reasoning was that people would more readily pay for an organization once that organization had proved its mettle. The CSO had relied on funds from the IAF and the Jewish Community Relations Council of Los Angeles, but both funding streams were drying up. While there were periodic checks from liberal benefactors such as Seniel Ostrow, owner of the Sealy Mattress Company, and last-minute grants from labor unions, the organization limped along. Reliance on such funds hardly represented a long-term plan. Finally, the CSO outlined a new dues structure, starting at two dollars a year. While the proposal represented a start in the direction of sustainability, the rate could hardly be expected to fully pay for an organizer and overhead. Ross, with Alinsky's help, turned his attention to foundations to fill the gap.

Ross had heard that Roger Baldwin, the longtime director of the American Civil Liberties Union, was interested in supporting a nationwide Mexican American organization. Baldwin helped manage the Robert Marshall Civil Liberties Trust Fund, and Ross sent him a long proposal for expanding the CSO throughout California and into other southwestern states. He sent a similar proposal to the Ford Foundation. Neither responded favorably. Baldwin wrote to Ross saying that significant funds had already been dedicated to the National Farm Labor Union, a project headed by San Jose–based activist Ernesto Galarza, and thus far there was little to show for the effort. Baldwin, however, had a suggestion. "Your proposal is based upon a grass roots approach with slow organization by areas over a period of years," he wrote. "I think you should also consider the opposite approach; namely calling a national convention of all the existing agencies and leaders to form an association, and then follow it up with its own grass-roots works in the hand of the Mexican-Americans themselves."[16]

Ross considered such an approach a colossal waste of time. A large convention attended by agency heads was only bound to lead to one result: another convention the following year. His response began politely, as he still hoped for the funds, telling Baldwin that the idea of a national convention was "very sound." Then he tore it apart:

As you know, the Southwest Conference on the Education of Spanish-speaking People has been holding annual conferences for three years and nothing of importance has come of these. LULAC [the League of United Latin American Citizens] has been doing the same thing for many years with similar results. . . . I have been organizing Mexican-Americans steadily for the past 4½ years. In that period I have made many mistakes, but the most serious one was my assumption that civic-action organizations could be built by calling together representatives from various existing Mexican-American groups. . . . When this old-line leadership is called together with second generation people two things generally happen. They immediately attempt to remake the organization in the image of the groups they have known; and they engage in a fierce struggle for leadership among themselves.[17]

In arguing for pursuing a strategy from the bottom up, Ross was also taking a direct swipe at George Sanchez, a professor at the University of Texas who had organized the Southwest Conference on the Education of Spanish-Speaking People and had served as LULAC's president. Likely unknown to Ross, on Baldwin's desk was also a proposal from Sanchez. While Ross hoped to expand the grassroots CSO, Sanchez sought to pull together a group of experts who could provide advice to Mexican American organizations around the country. Sanchez preferred to keep the struggle in the courtroom and was leery of the CSO's street-level activism, once referring to the group as "trouble makers."[18] After waiting three months, Ross learned from Baldwin that the CSO had been passed over in favor of Sanchez's project. By the summer of 1951, Ross informed the CSO that he would be leaving within six months. "I am not surprised to hear of your continuing difficulties nor of your inevitable resignation," Baldwin wrote to Ross. "I wonder that you had the nerve to hang on so long. There certainly are other less burdensome opportunities open to a man with your experience, energy, and outlook."[19]

The failure to secure stable funding was certainly the major factor in Ross's decision to leave. While in Los Angeles he could go, as Frances called it, "off salary" for months at a time. "We spent all the savings we had, used war bonds," Ross later recalled. "We lived, but it was right down there at the bottom."[20] Frances ran a tight budget, but things were growing increasingly desperate, especially as her husband continued to spend $50 to $75 a month on CSO-related expenses. At their first house, the landlord threatened to evict them; at the second, when the house they were renting was put up for sale, they feared, again, that they would be sent packing. "These complications cannot be controlled so I refuse to fuss over them," Frances wrote. "We always shrug along somehow."[21] But it was a stressful way to live.

There were also hints that, without an election or specific cause, the CSO was growing stale. At one point, in a rare display of pessimism, Ross questioned the need to launch another house meeting campaign if the "membership meetings continued to be as dull as they have in the past."[22] It was one thing to land in a new neighborhood and build up a group from nothing. It was quite another to hang on to the initial bursts of optimism and excitement and turn that energy into a sustainable organization. That Ross leapt so enthusiastically into grant writing—the CSO expansion proposal he wrote for funders was eighty pages long—was perhaps a reflection of his feeling stuck at times, of his eagerness to move into new territory.

And there was another powerful force pulling Ross away from Los Angeles: Frances. She admired the work her husband was doing, championed his achievements to her mother, and fretted that people didn't recognize the effort he put in behind the scenes. She joined in the work, too, helping edit the CSO newspaper and attending organizational meetings, where members sometimes carried her up the steps. But she had grown tired of Ross's frequent absences and was frustrated by what Ross called his tendency to be in a "fog" while at home, so consumed by his thoughts about organizing that he was oblivious to the people around him.

There were moments when Ross seemed to be on the brink of change. After an electrocardiogram showed potential heart trouble, he cut back his hours. At the conclusion of the Roybal campaign, he told Frances that he realized his emphasis on work had made her life "horrible." A week after the conversation, he participated in Frances's physical therapy session. "It dawned on him I can't do it alone," she wrote to her mother. "It was a surprise to him to see how much weakness is left. If Fred remains human and you get to feeling well again, why don't you come down here for a visit."[23]

But the transformations never lasted. "Fred is being King and so [I] will have to jerk the rug from under him today or tomorrow," she wrote more than a year later. "Now that I am so nearly normal my *or else* will have teeth in it."[24] Decades later, Frances would tell their daughter, Julia, that she had made arrangements to move herself and the kids in with friends in

Healdsburg, a small town north of San Francisco. "She sat him down and said, 'I'm leaving you,'" Julia recalled, who had many long conversations with her mother about the relationship.[25] Whether the "or else" conversation referenced in her letter was the threat of divorce she later told her daughter about, by the end of 1951 Frances's optimism about her ability to change Ross was waning. And if he wasn't going to be around—either physically or mentally—then she wanted to move to Northern California, where she would be closer to her mother, who lived in San Francisco.

Word of Ross's resignation from the CSO reached Josephine Duveneck, president of the California Federation for Civic Unity. Based in San Francisco, the federation was a reincarnation of the California Councils for Civic Unity, and it needed to replace a departing executive director. The position held little interest for Ross, who had been mostly critical of such groups during his time in the Citrus Belt. But with money running out and Frances pushing to move, he had few other options. He accepted the offer on January 29, 1952, and in mid-March they drove up to Corte Madera, about ten miles north of San Francisco, where they had found a large but cheap house for sale. The quiet and picturesque town of two thousand was set in the foothills of Mount Tamalpais, a stark contrast to the bustling streets of East Los Angeles. If Ross felt like the move and the change of jobs was a retreat from organizing, he made sure to at least keep his options partially open. During discussions with Duveneck, it was agreed that "whatever time was available" after completing his regular assignments could be used to expand the CSO into Northern California.[26] Accustomed to working long hours and rarely taking days off, Ross would make plenty of free time.

NINE

Finding Cesar

ROSS ARRIVED AT HIS NEW San Francisco office on April 1, 1952, and dashed off a letter to the US Census Bureau requesting the number of "Spanish-Whites" for all California counties. His dream of turning the Community Service Organization into a statewide organization of Mexican Americans was still very much alive, even as he went about his official duties from behind a desk. Those duties included writing letters urging politicians to oppose various proposals—such as a US House resolution that sought to investigate tax-exempt organizations for "un-American and subversive activities"—and while Ross no doubt opposed such bills, he had little interest in playing the role of lobbyist, and even less interest spending his time in an office.

But he encountered a familiar problem: the California Federation for Civic Unity (CFCU) was broke. Two weeks into the job, Ross learned that the organization had just $433.12 in the bank. For the first month, Ross was told to spend "a minimum amount of work" on issues and instead undertake a fund-raising campaign.[1] CFCU president Josephine Duveneck helped as well, contacting civic unity councils to remind them to pay their dues. "If you could forward these to us within the next few weeks, it would be most help-ful," she wrote to the Sacramento chapter. "Our new director, Mr. Fred W. Ross, is prevented from undertaking the new program he had planned because he has to put in full time raising his salary from week to week."[2]

Ross neither enjoyed nor was skilled at raising money, though by early May he had evidently experienced enough success to allow for some time in the field. His attention turned to San Jose, which had a local unity council and a sizable Mexican American population. A CFCU board member gave Ross the name of Father Donald McDonnell, who ran church services out of a hall on the east side. When Ross arrived, he found McDonnell fixing the roof. "Seeing you up there all alone makes me wonder if your parishioners have deserted you," Ross called out. McDonnell grinned and came down to shake hands.[3]

"I had planned to try and set the Father afire," Ross later wrote, "but it didn't work that way. Before I had finished my rap he was all but jogging in place, wanting to know what he could do to help."[4] In McDonnell, Ross had found a bright and enthusiastic priest dedicated to working with the poorest of the poor. Two years earlier, McDonnell and three other priests—including his childhood friend, Father Thomas McCullough, who would later help Ross expand the CSO into Stockton—formed the Mission Band, dedicated to ministering to California's growing Spanish-speaking community. Still in his twenties, McDonnell had taught himself Spanish and visited farm labor camps, taking confessions and spreading a gospel that had plenty to say on the topic of social justice. Like Ross, he was trying to organize the unorganized, and he relied on similar tactics. As he wrote to San Francisco archbishop John J. Mitty, "The aim of our work is to bring the Church to the minority groups that are out of contact with the parish. The steps in the plan are: Mark out on the map the minority areas; find and train catechists and leaders to organize and conduct meetings in the home for prayer and instruction."[5] Mapping out minority areas, training leaders, and holding house meetings: the two men had virtually the identical organizational strategy. It didn't take long for Ross to realize he had come across an important contact.

He was amazed by McDonnell's energy. The priest would speed down bumpy roads in his jeep, taking him from one tottering shack to the next, calling out greetings and pushing open front doors without waiting for a response. At one stop he gathered together a group of several dozen people. "We all want to be healthy, don't we?" he asked. "And God wants us to be healthy. But we can't do it alone—we've got to work together. And how do we do it? We get organized." He motioned to Ross. "Here is our organizer."[6] Ross dove into the work, temporarily relocating to the Duveneck's house in Los Altos Hills, where the two would chat each morning over breakfast. "His working hours started around 4 o'clock in the afternoon, continuing until midnight or later when he crawled into the house and turned off the lights," Duveneck wrote. "I was excited to hear about the contacts of the previous evening and I think he liked to summarize what had taken place and point up his strategy for the next move."[7]

That his hours went so late was largely due to Alicia Hernandez, a nurse who ran a clinic out of a small room in McDonnell's church. Like McDonnell,

Hernandez was immediately supportive, accompanying Ross to dozens of house meetings and serving as both translator and agitator. During these meetings, Ross learned more about the issues facing residents of the east-side San Jose neighborhood of Sal Si Puedes. Without sewers, the area often flooded, turning the unpaved roads to impassable mud. In the spring of 1952, public health officials discovered 125 cases of amebic dysentery within a two-block stretch. In living rooms and at the parish hall, Ross outlined all that the CSO had accomplished in Los Angeles. Writing in his work journal, he recounted how he ended his talks. "Do you think such an org is needed here? Do you have probs? Am I needed?"[8] Momentum continued to build. On May 14, 1952, volunteers formed a temporary committee at the office of Claude Settles, a sociology professor at San Jose State University who belonged to the local unity council. Three weeks later, 150 people filed into the Mayfair Elementary School to formally launch the newest CSO chapter. *Sal si puedes* meant "get out if you can," but Ross— thanks to McDonnell and Hernandez—had found his way in.

Two days after the gathering at the school, Hernandez took Ross to 53 Scharff Avenue, a one-bedroom house in the heart of Sal Si Puedes. "To Cesar Chavez, not home, too late, back Monday at 8 PM," Ross wrote in his journal. Hernandez had grown close to Cesar's wife, Helen, who brought their four children to the clinic. On the following Monday, both Ross and Hernandez returned to the house, where the living room was now crowded with more than a dozen people. Ross went into his pitch, with Hernandez translating. Ross came away impressed. After the meeting, he wrote, "Chavez has real push, understanding, loyalty, enthusiasm, grassroots leadership qualities."[9]

Chavez had all of the characteristics Ross looked for in a leader. The twenty-five-year-old was plainspoken but sharp, shy but unbending. Born near Yuma, Arizona, Chavez grew up in an adobe home without electricity, which his father lost during the Depression. While Ross was getting settled at Arvin, the boy was swept into the westward migrant stream, his family chasing crops up and down California—picking plums in Gilroy, cutting grapes in Delano—finding any dry space to lay their heads: garages, labor camps, even barns. When he finished eighth grade, Chavez dropped out of school to work in the fields. The agony that Ross had experienced during his long day of carrot tying was, for Chavez, the reality of everyday life.

Despite his small stature—at the age of eighteen he was just five feet four inches and weighed 125 pounds—Chavez already showed signs of possessing an indomitable will. As a young teenager, he took charge of the family's work output, setting picking goals in the field and refusing to leave until they were met. His early departure from the classroom left his spelling riddled with errors, but it also kept his creative side intact.

That Chavez was so taken with Ross was ironic, given that he had initially wanted little to do with him. Five years after they met, Ross would learn that Chavez had at first taken him for a "phony do-gooder," with Helen having to insist that her husband stay home to meet the organizer. Later, once he had risen to become the leader of the farmworker movement, Chavez would recount their initial meeting with additional details, describing an attempt to scare Ross off:

> I invited some of the rougher guys I knew and bought some beer. I thought we could show this gringo a little bit of how we felt. We'd let him speak a while, and when I gave them the signal, shifting my cigarette from my right hand to the left, we'd tell him off and run him out of the house. Then we'd be even. But somehow I knew that this gringo had really impressed me, and that I was being dishonest. When the meeting started, Fred spoke quietly, not rabble-rousing but saying the truth. . . . The more he talked, the more wide-eyed I became, and the less inclined I was to give the signal. When a couple of guys who were pretty drunk at that time still wanted to give the gringo the business, we got rid of them. This fellow was making a lot of sense, and I wanted to hear what he had to say.[10]

This meeting that almost didn't happen would become part of the United Farm Workers' narrative, an inspiring origins story. In one version, which Ross told to several authors, he returns home to write "I think I've found the guy I'm looking for." How much of this story is an embellishment—like the made-up line from Ross—is unclear. If Chavez did attempt to play an elaborate prank on Ross, this fact was lost on Ross. Chavez's brother Richard, while acknowledging that they were certainly skeptical of Ross, later called the cigarette story "bullshit."[11] What is clear is that meeting Ross radically transformed Chavez, setting him down the path of an organizer. "I learned quite a bit from studying Gandhi," Chavez later said, "but the first practical steps I learned from the best organizer I know, Fred Ross. He changed my life."[12]

The week following Ross's meeting with Chavez, the CFCU board gathered at Duveneck's house to hear Ross report on the San Jose campaign. Teams of between eight and ten people were going door-to-door, he told them, encouraging people to register to vote. Four Spanish radio spots were pushing the same message. Ross was out with Hernandez every weekday, holding two house meetings a night. While some of the board worried that Ross was neglecting his other duties, most were enthusiastic. Duveneck in particular noted that fund-raising was difficult in part because of the "nebulous character of our work" and that San Jose represented something concrete they could point to.[13]

Ross did report one challenge. While twenty-five CSO members had volunteered to become deputy registrars, the ranking election official was only permitting one to become certified—and this individual was forbidden from leaving his voter registration table at an elementary school. Door knockers, then, had to interrupt someone's dinner, convince the person to register, and then cajole him or her into a waiting car that would take the person to the school. The operation was proving to be a logistical headache, and after fifteen days they had registered just three hundred people. When election officials had earlier thrown up barriers, the Los Angeles Central Labor Council had stepped in; Ross called on members of the council again, and after they alerted their counterparts in Santa Clara, the CSO was allowed five more deputy registrars and to register voters on the sidewalk.

As for Chavez, every spare moment he had was now dedicated to the CSO. He walked the blocks as a "bird dog," knocking on doors and talking through screens to direct the unregistered to a nearby deputy registrar. During this period he grew close to Herman Gallegos, who worked at a gas station in Sal Si Puedes. Gallegos was a recent graduate from San Jose State and had met Ross through Professor Settles, who had invited the organizer to speak about his work to a class on race relations. Like many who would join the CSO, Gallegos didn't need to be convinced that something was wrong—he simply needed some help in finding a solution. Gallegos had grown up in an adobe hut in a small mining town in Colorado, just a few miles from the infamous Ludlow Massacre, and moved to San Francisco when his father was diagnosed with the beginnings of black lung disease.[14] As a child he had lost his left leg after being struck by a train while playing in the rail yards. Having a prosthetic limb helped turn his attention toward school, and, ignoring the advice of a high school counselor to forget about college, he enrolled in San Francisco State. When two of his favorite professors were fired for refusing to sign loyalty oaths required of them under California's Levering Act, he joined the students in a walkout and transferred to San Jose.

After several weeks of pounding the pavement to register voters, the pair decided to run for leadership slots in the CSO: Gallegos for president and Chavez for vice president. The young men stayed up until three o'clock in the morning, nervously refining their speeches. "Cesar was agonizing, I was too," recalled Gallegos. Neither had spoken in front of a large crowd before, and they were going up against prominent figures in the community. "We were convinced these great speech makers were going to win," said Gallegos.[15] To their surprise, the pair of them won instead.

They approached Ross afterward. We can't believe it, they said. They didn't even think their speeches were all that great. They weren't, Ross told them. They didn't win because of a speech, he said—they won because they put in the work. People saw them knocking on doors. They saw them at the meetings. Anyone can give a speech. Not everyone will put in the work. For Gallegos, the episode was a classic example of Ross's teaching style: use real-world experiences to help people draw conclusions. "These little lessons were very, very informative," Gallegos recalled. "This is how he nurtured us. Not by lecturing us, but helping us to see for ourselves what made the difference."[16]

As the summer of 1952 turned into fall, the San Jose CSO focused on the upcoming election, registering four thousand new voters and raising alarms among Republican leaders, who noted the newfound activity on the east side. In the days before the election, the party announced that an "all-male squad" of poll watchers would descend on the east side, focusing on Mexican American neighborhoods. "The Democrats are moving in on these groups where the people don't know any better or are being taken care of in a financial way," one party leader claimed.[17] On election day, a number of newly registered voters were indeed frightened by aggressive questioning at the polls, which the CSO protested in the pages of the *San Jose Mercury News*. A week later, Chavez also fired off a letter of complaint to then attorney general—and future governor—Edmund "Pat" Brown, though no follow-up action was taken.

After the election, Ross briefly turned his attention to pulling together the CFCU's annual meeting, held in late November at the Asilomar Conference Center near Monterey. Participants filed into the main hall to listen to Thurgood Marshall deliver the keynote speech, titled "A Four Year Forecast for Civil Rights."[18] (It would be a momentous four years. In two years, the

Supreme Court would outlaw segregation in *Brown v. Board of Education.*)
By the spring, Ross had moved on to Decoto, a small Mexican American
settlement twenty miles south of Oakland, where he established the Alameda
County CSO. The *Oakland Tribune* covered the group's first meeting, running a story that included a photo of Ross, who was identified as both the
director of the CFCU and a field representative with the American Friends
Service Committee. The expanding CSO also received its first mention in a
national publication. "A People Comes of Age" appeared in the *Nation* on
March 28, 1953, recounting the origins of the group and its new effort to
"awaken" the thirty-six thousand Mexican Americans in the San Jose area.

Being recognized by a New York magazine must have been heartening for
Ross, and the formation of two CSO chapters in less than a year created a real
sense of momentum. But there was still the problem of money, hinted at by
Ross's multiple organizational identities. With CFCU funds dwindling,
Ross was now receiving separate checks from the American Friends Service
Committee, but these would likely dry up soon as well. That Ross was able
to cobble together a salary at all during this period was largely due to the
efforts of the CFCU's Josephine Duveneck.

Duveneck was a Boston Brahmin who came to the conclusion, after moving to California, that she was "healthy, over-privileged, and idle."[19] In 1924,
she and her husband had purchased Hidden Villa, a sprawling thousand-acre
ranch in the Los Altos Hills, which was soon an important gathering place
for radicals. The ranch's idyllic grounds sheltered Jewish refugees and returning Japanese Americans and became the site of the country's first interracial
summer camp. Duveneck was a member of the American Friends Service
Committee and likely first met Ross when he was helping resettle the
Japanese in San Francisco. A deep admirer of his ability to encourage leadership skills among people often ignored, she had been the person to originally
offer the CFCU job to Ross. And when funds ran low, it was Duveneck who
secured grants from the San Francisco–based Fleishhacker Foundation to
fund his time in San Jose and Decoto.

Ross used Hidden Villa as his base of operations when organizing in San
Jose, and while he could be skeptical of rich liberals—thinking their main
motivation was often simply to alleviate feelings of guilt—he had deep appreciation and respect for Duveneck, partially dedicating a short booklet he
wrote, *The Saga of Sal Si Puedes,* to "Mrs. Josephine Duveneck—who inspired
it." But while Duveneck had landed small grants to cover a few months here
and there, Ross needed something steady if he was going to pursue his dream

of seriously expanding the CSO. Which was when Saul Alinsky got in touch, offering money to do just that.

The answer to the CSO's money problem would come courtesy of a German Jewish immigrant, Emil Schwarzhaupt, who had arrived in Chicago in 1910 and quickly amassed a fortune in the liquor business. (Ironically, much of his wealth came after he sold his company to Schenley, which would be the first company that Chavez's farmworkers' union would target with a boycott.) Schwarzhaupt died on March 30, 1950, and in his will he stipulated that his estate—more than $3.3 million—be given away within twenty-five years, in accordance with his "conviction that in the long run society is benefited by having each generation solve its own problems."[20] A great admirer of the country that had allowed him to flourish, Schwarzhaupt wanted to help the foreign-born become active and assimilated citizens. Alinsky was coming off a rough fund-raising stretch when he learned, in 1953, that the Emil Schwarzhaupt Foundation had decided to grant the Industrial Areas Foundation $150,000 over three years, mostly for the CSO

The entrance of the Schwarzhaupt Foundation assured Ross a steady income for his organizing work. Over the next decade, the foundation would give more than half a million dollars to the CSO; for Ross, this meant a decent salary, paid expenses, and a brand-new 1954 Plymouth. His official start date was December 1, 1953; his salary $8,500, with another $4,000 to cover expenses. The assignment, to organize the CSO throughout California, had been his ambition for years, and in the months leading up to December he spent his time planning and dreaming, exchanging long letters with Alinsky. In August, Ross wrote that he was determined to avoid his earlier failures, which he attributed to a tendency to rush:

> The "hit and run" approach is a very dangerous procedure. The history of California's Citrus Belt is replete with examples of the wanderkind [sic] on the white horse who charged through the valley towns, supremely confident that the sheer beauty of his idea would weld the people fast for all time. . . . Such an approach is not only stupidly wasteful on the part of the person who employs it; it is productive of grave consequences for the future, because once a group gets started wrong and fails, it is triply hard to start it off again. It is far better to cover solidly two-thirds the ground, when time and staff are short, than skimp on the job and take a chance of leaving jerry-built establishments behind.[21]

Alinsky shared Ross's enthusiasm and analysis, writing that a "hit and run" approach is "like a skyrocket—a dramatic flash and then nothing." At the time, a number of Alinsky's IAF projects were fizzling out, and Ross's work out west promised to reverse that trend. "This action has been taken because of my personal and complete confidence, not only in your ability in the area of organization (which I regard as tops) but also in your character, intelligence and ideals," Alinsky wrote. "I share your feeling that you are about to get your teeth into what might well be one of the most significant organizational programs in the nation. I believe that I am not overstating the fact."[22]

TEN

On the Road

ORGANIZING IS OFTEN COMPARED TO running a marathon, but Ross was in no mood to pace himself. In the first six months of 1954, he put 15,754 miles on the new Plymouth, whose overworked engine would give out the following year. With census data as a guide, he mapped out a plan to take the Community Service Organization statewide: beginning in Salinas, he moved southeast until reaching the border town of Brawley, searching for leaders in small farmworker communities and the barrios of larger cities like Fresno and San Bernardino. He lived out of apartments and motels, staying at each location for a few months before moving on. It was an exhausting schedule—or would have been, for most people. What comes through in Ross's frequent reports to Saul Alinsky is not fatigue but enthusiasm. After working around the clock to build up the Monterey County CSO, Ross sped away to Fresno, arriving at 6:00 P.M. to hold a meeting that went until after midnight.

Within the year, Ross had established three new CSO chapters— Monterey, Fresno, and San Bernardino—following a similar pattern in each location. He arrived knowing a contact or two and expanded this circle during a month-long campaign of house meetings, after which the first mass meeting was held and a voter registration drive announced. Early on, Ross paid a call to the local Catholic churches, whose priests—thanks to Alinsky's friend Monsignor John O'Grady, head of Catholic Charities in Washington, DC—had already received instruction from the local bishop to provide whatever support Ross might need. He also made a point of popping into the office of the local newspaper, introducing the project in the most innocuous way and laying out the many supporters—including the church—that the CSO enjoyed.

Ross was aware of the delicate nature of his work. Seven years had passed since he had been labeled a Communist, but the mood in much of the country—and this certainly included California's more conservative inland regions—was still one of suspicion. The latest manifestation of McCarthyism was the McCarran-Walter Act, an immigration law that went into effect at the end of 1952. Jointly introduced by Senator Pat McCarran and Congressman Francis Walter, who would later chair the House Un-American Activities Committee, the legislation allowed the government to both keep out and deport any immigrants deemed "subversive to national security." The law was "grossly discriminatory," Ross wrote Alinsky, but it did have one silver lining: noncitizens fifty years of age and older who had lived in the country at least twenty years could now take citizenship tests in their native language.[1] The CSO had begun to offer citizenship classes in Los Angeles and San Jose, and the early response was overwhelming. Before hitting the road, Ross was able to convince Alinsky to pay a small salary to Eugene Lowrey, who had previously worked at the Immigration and Naturalization Service (INS) and was volunteering with CSO members in San Jose. Over the next several years, Lowrey would travel with Ross from one outpost to the other, setting up nighttime citizenship classes while Ross focused on house meetings and registration drives.

The reports Ross sent to Alinsky were filled with encouraging news. Before leaving San Bernardino, Ross summarized the group's accomplishments. Hundreds of people in that city were now attending bimonthly membership meetings. Two thousands doors were knocked on. Four thousand voters were added to the rolls. So many people had flocked to the eleven evening citizenship classes that the owner of the Spanish-language theater had to rearrange his screenings so as to have customers. The local newspaper reported on the CSO's activities in glowing terms. "Medal of Honor Winner Ends Drive," ran a *San Bernardino Sun* headline, the article noting that the CSO's four thousandth registered voter, Lieutenant Joseph Rodriguez, had been a hero in the Korean War.[2] After the 1954 election, the mayor, along with the area's state and federal representatives, joined the CSO, each paying the yearly dues of two dollars.[3] "The San Bernardino CSO has made a more vivid impression on both the minority and dominant community than any of the civic organizations in the history of the city," Ross concluded.[4]

He attributed part of the success to the dense concentration of Mexican Americans in the city. But another factor was certainly the draw of citizenship. In 1954, just as Ross was expanding the CSO, the INS launched "Operation Wetback," which would result in the deportation of more than one million undocumented Mexican immigrants within the year. Many barrios and colonias were suddenly crawling with immigration agents. In Parlier, a small farmworker town near Fresno, Lowrey held citizenship classes in the home of the local grocer. Many people, he reported, were "anxious to become citizens," but one evening, attendance was cut to zero. Lowrey learned that "immigration was in town and they were all afraid to leave their houses because they did not want to be questioned on the street." During a recent raid, a veteran had been stopped by an immigration agent and detained, despite furnishing his birth certificate and army discharge papers. "There are bound to be many instances of Mexican-Americans being pushed around in the search for wetbacks and the CSO is prepared to take action the moment any mistreatment or injustice is reported," Lowrey wrote, noting that the CSO planned to file complaints with the local congressperson.[5]

Countering the abusive treatment of people presumed to be "illegal" would be a recurring issue for CSO members. While the organization never publicly criticized the raids—its focus was on protecting the rights of Mexican Americans—the organization refused, unlike the League of United Latin American Citizens, to make citizenship a prerequisite to joining the CSO. It also waged a number of high-profile fights against immigration officials, who tended to treat Spanish speakers with contempt and often refused, in violation of the McCarran-Walter Act, to allow citizenship tests to be given in Spanish. Lowrey, who had worked for the INS for eleven years, understood and sympathized with people's distrust of the agency. "The Immigration Service is preparing to launch wide-scale wetback raids in the San Joaquin Valley," he alerted Alinsky, "and the traditional fear and hatred of the 'Immigration' is greater than ever."[6]

The mood of fear and hatred that was being reignited by the raids provided an additional incentive for eligible immigrants to become citizens—if nothing else, citizenship was as an additional measure of protection against overzealous agents. For Ross, the challenge was to use this enthusiasm for citizenship as a means to develop new leaders and build the CSO. Citizenship, of course, allowed people to vote, and with the vote came formal political power. But Ross wanted people to stick around. As he wrote to Alinsky, the CSO couldn't afford to "permit those who graduate from the classes and become citizens to slip through [its] fingers once their most urgent need is met."[7]

Because the CSO conducted citizenship classes at night, it enjoyed almost total autonomy from local school administrators; this autonomy allowed Lowrey and other volunteer teachers to turn the classrooms into organizing bases. They drilled an expansive definition of citizenship into the heads of students. Citizenship wasn't something you received after successfully completing an exam, they stressed, it represented the process of becoming an active participant in democracy. Classes were usually held the evening before the biweekly CSO general meeting, and a CSO leader would address the students, outlining a range of needed legislative changes—revisions to the McCarran-Walter Act, a statewide ban on employment discrimination—and insisting that people attend the next meeting to press invited legislators. "In this way," wrote Ross, "we are able to realize the dream of any organizer: personal, face-to-face notification of three-fourths of the membership that they are expected to be at the CSO meeting the following night. It works like a charm, believe me."[8]

The citizenship classes also allowed Ross to position the CSO in a light that even the most conservative factions could find nonthreatening: as an Americanization process that sought to assimilate Mexicans into the country. Carey McWilliams aptly characterized Americanization as "stupid, morose, and biased," and it indeed has a very complicated and checkered past.[9] Those clamoring for "Americanizing" foreigners often started with the assumption that such people were unintelligent, dirty, and primitive. But Ross deployed the word to help soften what some might see as the radical edge of the CSO: the development of Mexican Americans as political actors, who could wield real political power. Using the vocabulary of Americanization allowed the CSO to grow in places that could otherwise be hostile and earn the accolades of groups that tended to look upon most organizing activity as subversive.

From San Bernardino, Ross and Lowrey moved down to Brawley, in California's Imperial Valley. "As you know, Imperial Valley has long been known as the 'black hole' of California," Ross wrote to Alinsky. "In past years civil liberties attorneys, labor leaders, and other so-called 'do-gooders' have been ridden out of town on rails and subjected to ingenious kinds of persecution."[10] Because of the valley's well-earned reputation as a reactionary haven, Ross decided to initially focus on Americanization classes and eschew any discussion of voter registration. The heavy hand of Operation Wetback

FIGURE 10. A packed CSO meeting in Brawley, 1955. Ross is seated facing the crowd, second from left. Courtesy of Special Collections and University Archives, Stanford University.

was felt strongest in border towns like Brawley, and residents flocked to the citizenship classes. At one school, 310 students crammed into eight classrooms. Before long, the all-white members of the local American Legion presented the CSO with an American flag. It was only later that CSO members flexed their new political power, forcing officials to finally pave dusty roads, pushing the health department to hire a Spanish-speaking nurse, and electing the only nonsegregationist member to the school board.

In June 1954, Ross drove the family to Long Beach, where they rented a three-bedroom house across the street from the water. Frances and the three kids stayed through the summer, while another family rented their home in Corte Madera, an arrangement that allowed Ross, who was then organizing in San Bernardino, to occasionally visit on weekends.

The summertime arrangement was almost certainly Frances's idea. With the expansion of the CSO, Ross was hardly home, and when he did return to Corte Madera for a weekend he typically arrived late at night and exhausted, a bag of dirty laundry in the back seat. After years of physical therapy, Frances had regained much of the mobility she had lost to polio, but she still found the challenges of single parenting daunting. She also wanted more. Ambitious like her husband, she would soon enroll at San Francisco State University, earn a master's degree in clinical psychology, and go on to a distinguished career working with the mentally ill. For now, she had put her ambitions on hold, and hoped the summertime move to Long Beach would force Ross to share at least a small portion of the parenting responsibilities.

The biggest challenge for Frances was Robin. Now fourteen years old, he was still emotionally unstable and didn't feel close to either parent. "At the time we didn't get along that well—she was the evil-stepmother," he recalled decades later, about his early relationship with Frances.[11] He also felt hostility toward his father, first because Ross had left him behind as a toddler and, now that they had reunited, because he had abandoned him again, this time to pursue his organizing work. But because Ross was rarely around, most of Robin's anger was directed at Frances.

In September 1954, Ross drove the family back to Corte Madera, where Robin began weekly psychiatric sessions. It soon became clear that something more had to be done. "Another crisis has arisen in my home which requires my presence," Ross wrote to Alinsky in January 1955. Robin had "advanced toward Frances with mayhem in mind. Although scared to death, she managed to remain calm and stand her ground; and he caught himself just in time and went off shrieking insults and dire warnings." The psychiatrist was alarmed, thinking a violent outburst could be around the corner, and suggested a solution to Frances. As Ross told Alinsky, "They feel that if I were able to get back into my role as 'the father' and could spend two or three days a week around the house, being with him [Robin] and working with him, instead of just dropping in for a brief visit every three weeks or so—that his weekly treatments would be much more effective, the possibility of having these outbursts would be greatly minimized and Robin might very well eventually be able to adjust to his environment."[12]

That all depended on a big if: that Ross play the role, as he put it, of "the father." He told Alinsky that this "if" was akin to saying, "IF we get the Fund For the Republic grant," referring to a long-shot grant they no longer expected to receive. As much as Robin might have benefitted from his presence, Ross would not sacrifice his organizing. He was blunt in his self-assessment: "As you can see, I've got to take some kind of action in order to save my home. Ever since this thing has happened I've been constantly worried for fear something might happen to Frances or the other children with the result that my mind has been constantly jumping back and forth from the work to the home situation. I've been a failure as a father for a long, long time; and if I don't get this thing settled somehow, I'll be a washout as an organizer."[13]

Because Ross was not likely to be home for extended periods of time in the near future, Robin's psychiatrists suggested a private school, Stillwater Cove Ranch School, located on the Sonoma coast ninety miles north of San Francisco. Ross took a break from organizing to drive Robin to the school, which went through sophomore year and whose thirty-five boys mostly came from troubled or broken families. At Stillwater they lived on an isolated ranch overlooking the ocean, spending their days shooting guns, riding horses, and trapping game, forming what came to feel like an extended family. The school was extremely expensive: $165 a month (about $1,500 today). Ross apparently had to borrow money to afford the tuition, but it would prove to be a wise investment. Years later, Robin—who now goes by Bob— would say that the year and a half he spent at Stillwater Cove saved his life.

It is hard to miss the striking similarities between Ross and his oldest son. Ross had grown up with a father who was first distant and then absent. He had been out of control as a young teenager. For the second semester of his freshman year, Ross's mother, not knowing what else to do, transferred him to a private boys' school on the coast. Robin grew up with a father who was either distant or absent. Robin had been out of control as a young teenager. For the second semester of his freshman year, Robin's parents, not knowing what else to do, transferred him to a private boys' school on the coast. Though hard to miss the similarities, it's likely that Ross did. His thoughts were on Brawley, where he had been holding a house meeting drive when his work was interrupted. He could accept—he had accepted—being a failure as a father. He would never accept being a failure as an organizer.

.   .   .

There was one person who could match Ross's dedication. During the voter registration drive in San Jose, which lasted three months, Cesar Chavez had taken just one day off—and that only at Ross's insistence. The volunteers were "mostly college guys who always had to go to meetings or go study," Chavez recalled. "I couldn't understand why they didn't find it [voter registration] as important as I did."[14]

Ross could teach the nuts and bolts of organizing: make reminder calls before every meeting; practice your pitch before knocking on doors. But one can't teach *will,* the seemingly involuntary need to do whatever it takes to succeed. This will is complimented by a sense of urgency, which, in an excellent organizer, practically radiates from the body. Ross had immediately recognized that urgency in Chavez—"Chavez has real push," he wrote after their first meeting—and so, before leaving the Bay Area, Ross arranged for the young man to receive a small stipend to continue working with the CSO in Decoto. This was Chavez's first full-time organizing job, and it wasn't an easy assignment. He looked like a teenager next to Ross and had to prove that he wasn't, as Ross put it, "just a young, dumb kid."[15]

Chavez was young, but he had learned a lot in the short time he had watched Ross. The tall stranger initially made his work seem easy and natural, but Chavez quickly reconsidered. "Right away I began to see that organizing was difficult," he said. "It wasn't a party. I began to see all of the things that he did, and I was amazed—how he could handle one situation and have a million things going in his mind at the same time."[16] With the San Jose voter registration drive, Chavez had surprised many with his abilities, but his confidence faltered when he attempted to organize a new chapter in Oakland. A local Catholic priest had set up the first house meeting. Chavez arrived and sat in the corner of the living room, silent and petrified. Finally a woman spoke up: "Well, it's getting late. I wonder where the organizer is." Chavez finally gathered the courage to speak, holding a meeting that was, in his estimation, a "disaster."[17] Without Ross as a guide, he was so nervous that he couldn't keep his thoughts together. But his nerves finally settled, and by the end several people had promised to hold additional house meetings.

As he began to gain confidence, Chavez proved to be an unusually close student of people. After any event, Ross insisted on sitting down and analyzing what had happened. Chavez would lie awake at night, reviewing the day's meetings. What jokes had people laughed at? What avenues of conversation had sparked some resistance? What worked? What didn't? Small-scale human interactions fascinated Chavez, just as they fascinated Ross. Chavez refined his techniques as the house meetings in the Oakland campaign continued, gaining confidence but still worried that the first mass meeting, held at a local parish, would be a bust. Chavez arrived early, fearing the worst. But before long the church was overflowing. Afterward, he raced to the phone and called Ross to report the great news. There was now no doubt about it: he was meant to be an organizer.

Ross believed that good organizers were extremely hard to come by, and he lobbied Alinsky to hire Chavez, who went on the Industrial Areas Foundation payroll on March 15, 1954, at a salary of thirty-six hundred dollars a year. Chavez would follow the Ross pattern of spending a few months in a location, organizing a CSO chapter, and moving on. By the summer, after finishing in Oakland, Chavez had moved his family from San Jose to Madera, a farming town in the San Joaquin Valley. "I have had house meetings every night since I arrived," he wrote to Ross, soon after settling in. "Saturdays and Sundays and I'm booked solid to a day prior to our general meeting."[18] Like Ross, he prioritized the CSO program over any other considerations, with an almost fanatical devotion. Two days before Christmas, Ross called up Chavez, who had moved the family to Bakersfield, to see how he was doing. Only then did he learn that Chavez was completely broke. Ross wired him fifty dollars. "I later learned that if he hadn't received the $50 there would have been no Christmas dinner, no presents for the kids and wife, nothing," Ross wrote to Alinsky. "So you can see, he's *really* giving his all to the program, and I mean *all*."[19]

The Richard's Hotel was a budget boardinghouse in Stockton, popular with migrant farmworkers who appreciated the generosity of proprietor Alicia Chavez, known to occasionally offer free rooms to people who couldn't pay. Alicia lived at the hotel with her twenty-five-year-old daughter, Dolores Fernandez, who by the summer of 1955 was divorced and raising two young daughters. One day, a friend who owned a nearby drugstore called the hotel, warning the mother and daughter that "two Communists"—who turned out to be Ross and Eugene Lowrey—had descended on the city to organize Mexicans, using what he called "cell-type" techniques.[20]

It was the first time that Fernandez, who would soon become Dolores Huerta through a second marriage, had heard of the CSO. The young woman had worked a string of unsatisfying secretarial jobs and had recently returned to the University of the Pacific, where she hoped to earn her teaching credential. Not long after the warning phone call, a teacher invited her to a house meeting. Unlike Chavez, she wasn't immediately taken with Ross, whose organizing claims seemed far too ambitious. He appeared, as she later put it, "slightly *loco*" when he mentioned that the CSO could bring hundreds of people together for meetings. But she was struck by Ross's frank discussion of topics like police brutality. "He kept hitting all these ugly things that people sort of wanted to forget," she recalled. As a teenager, police had frequently stopped Huerta and her friends without cause. One of her secretarial jobs had been at the sheriff's office, where officers laughed about slapping drug addicts across the face. But these were the sorts of problems, she said, "that you didn't go around having meetings to talk about."[21]

Huerta, a registered Republican, was also preoccupied by the possibility that Ross was a Communist. She attended the house meeting with two friends. Afterward, they grabbed drinks at a Stockton nightclub and debated his background. The following day she gave Ross's name to an FBI contact she knew through the sheriff's office. He told her Ross was clean. At the first CSO meeting, Huerta found that it was as crowded as Ross had promised. Huerta didn't need any more convincing. She signed up to register voters on Tuesday nights. When someone dropped out of a Wednesday slot, Ross asked Huerta to cover. Never one to go halfway, Huerta was soon registering voters six nights a week. She would become the chapter's first secretary.

Like Chavez, she would observe Ross closely, gleaning bits of wisdom here and there. Once, after welfare benefits were denied to a man left paralyzed by a stroke, Huerta went to the welfare office and spoke to the caseworker. After the caseworker refused to let the man reapply, Huerta visited Ross and asked him to intervene. Instead, Ross told Huerta to return to the office and ask to speak to the supervisor. Huerta was skeptical—she wasn't accustomed to rocking the boat, yet—but she followed Ross's advice, and the man received his benefits. As with Chavez, Ross played the role of an older and reassuring figure, giving the young woman an extra nudge of confidence.

Not that she needed much of a nudge. Huerta had a way of careening through life as if she were a football player covered in pads, running straight into challenges with a complete lack of fear. Though she was a small person, "small" was the last word anyone who had been in her presence would use to describe her. "She's a real fire-brand," Ross wrote to Alinsky, noting that Huerta "does more work for the CSO than all the rest of the Stockton leaders put together."[22] But unlike Chavez, she didn't have the temperament of an organizer. She was not one to stay in the background, and she certainly wasn't patient. "Her main fault is a tendency to take on too many CSO responsibilities and programs, fly off in all directions at once, and as a consequence bog down on some of them from time to time," Ross continued. (In his unpublished book, the chapter about Huerta is titled "Woman in Motion.")

Ross worked with Huerta to improve her focus, and he cut her off during frequent outbursts, saying, "Dolores, you're not thinking—you're feeling."[23] For Huerta, Ross showed that one could channel righteous anger at injustice into a steady and relentless force that was calm and methodical, without getting exasperated at every roadblock. And while it was clear that only so much of this calm style would rub off on Huerta, it didn't really matter: *too much* energy and passion was a problem Ross could work with. It was obvious that she was totally committed to the CSO and unafraid. Ross also noted, early on, that she was particularly interested in doing something about the "field worker" problem.[24]

The Stockton chapter was as feisty as Huerta. Ross believed that a group needed "fighting issues," and Stockton had more than its fair share. Located on the northern edge of the San Joaquin Valley, the diverse city was surrounded by fields of nearly every fruit and nut one could imagine. Each week seemed to bring a new tale of cops beating some unfortunate young man. Much of the abuse occurred on the city's skid row. When they needed extra workers, growers would head to the area, ordering people to get into the van for a day's work; if they refused, police were on hand to haul them to jail. Border patrol agents prowled skid row, harassing anyone who looked Mexican and demanding proof that the person wasn't "illegal." When the CSO sent a letter of complaint about this practice, an INS investigator from San Francisco visited. In his work journal, Ross described the encounter: "He asked for our identification, and we asked for his. He asked if we were Citizens of US and we turned the same question on him, and informed him that of course we didn't have to answer any of these questions.... He said we'd started out wrong by working in Skid Row with all those unrespectable people. We told him we were not concerned with respectability in this instance, that they were human beings and as such had rights, and that our job was to help prevent contravention of those rights."[25]

At the time, it was unusual—to say the least—for a group of Mexican Americans to demand proof of citizenship from a federal investigator with the immigration office. The historian Lawrence Goodwyn, a leading scholar of the American Populist movement, wrote that any democratic movement depends on participants who have attained "a high level of personal political self-respect" and who therefore refuse to be resigned or intimidated.[26] Over its lifetime, the CSO amassed a long list of tangible accomplishments— registering hundreds of thousands of voters, electing a handful of politicians, forcing city officials to pave streets and crack down on police brutality—but what many members recalled, decades later, was their transformation into individuals with too much political self-respect to be ignored or abused.

And so the CSO was built, with Ross and Chavez crisscrossing the state to find people who were ready to fight. In March 1954, CSO members had traveled to the Asilomar Conference Center on the Monterey Peninsula to

FIGURE 11. Founding convention of the national CSO, March 1954. Ross is at center, wearing a plaid shirt. To his right is Edward Roybal; to his left, Herman Gallegos. A mustachioed Cesar Chavez stands in the first row, second from right; Saul Alinsky is at far left. Courtesy of Walter P. Reuther Library, Wayne State University.

celebrate the organization's national founding convention. At the time there were five chapters. Edward Roybal gave the keynote speech. "We have been socially and politically ostracized," he told the delegates. "We have said that this is the cross we must bear. Now we are no longer going to say that this is the cross which we have to bear. This is the convention in which we are now going to fight back and we are not going to stop.... We are now beginning this great organizational drive throughout the Southwest."[27]

By the middle of 1955, the CSO had grown to eleven chapters and could legitimately be called a statewide organization. Its strength was beginning to be felt in Sacramento as well. Two years earlier, the CSO had visited the state capital to push for a law providing pensions for elderly noncitizens. At the time, the CSO was relatively unknown, and the bill was killed in a committee of the State Assembly. By the summer of 1955, the proposal easily passed the Assembly, though it ultimately died in the Senate. (The proposal was the CSO's primary legislative demand and would finally be passed, after an eight-year campaign, in 1961.)

At its current rate of growth, Ross wrote Alinsky, the CSO would have active chapters in every sizable Spanish-speaking area in the state within the year.[28] Which, as it turned out, would present a whole new set of challenges.

ELEVEN

Growing Pains

AT A CONFERENCE IN 1947, while employed by the American Council on Race Relations, Ross gave a presentation on "neighborhood organization." With less than a year of organizing experience under his belt, he had already settled on some of the core principles that would guide him for the rest of his career. One: "Don't give them the idea that you are there to 'help' them." Two: "Find out from them what their problems are. Don't *tell* them what these problems are, or what they should do about them." Three: Prove they will work. "A long-winded conversation can be considerably shortened if you will find out whether the individual is willing to carry out a work assignment. Those who make excuses are generally not good membership material."

"Mr. Ross concluded reluctantly," wrote the note taker, "for he had not had time to cover the portion dealing with 'how to keep the organization going once it is started.'"[1]

It was a case of being saved by the bell. Ross had little to say about the topic, as his record would reveal. A few years later, he assessed this failure in a letter to Cruz Nevarez, who had been active in San Bernardino's unity league. "Remember the Unity Leagues in San Bernardino, Redlands, Casa Blanca, El Modena, and San Diego? Where are they now? Where were most of them six months after they were organized back in 1946?" Ross acknowledged that he had made many mistakes, most obviously that of "trying to do the job *too fast*."[2] Instead of remaining in a community for only a few weeks, he would spend at least several months building up each Community Service Organization chapter, which would allow it to stand on its own.

That was the hope, anyway. Building stable chapters proved more difficult than Ross anticipated. Some chapters were sturdy. In Stockton and Bakersfield, leaders drove the work. But other seemed to begin to unravel the moment Ross or Cesar Chavez left town. By December 1954, Ross had already observed this phenomenon, ending the year with a "coordination drive" to try and reinvigorate the chapters he had left behind. His report to Saul Alinsky was upbeat. "In the course of the last six weeks, time and again I have been impressed with the stability of the various CSO's I visited and with the intense enthusiasm (CSO fever) of the majority of the leaders," he wrote. "Cracks that were beginning to appear in the foundations of some of the organizations have been pretty firmly cemented. Tired leaders have been given a shot in the arm and discouragement has been replaced with hope in many, many cases."[3]

But Alinsky had reservations. While the CSO was certainly growing, the growth was uneven, and there was little sign that the organization was becoming financially sustainable. Los Angeles, the flagship chapter, was in such dire straits that the Industrial Areas Foundation loaned the group $1,200 to keep its citizenship classes afloat. Alinsky believed that an organization should only need three years of outside funding before it became strong enough to support itself. Or at least this is what he confidently told foundations; his record with the CSO and other IAF-sponsored groups argued otherwise. For the CSO, year three was coming into focus, and yet little progress had been made in this regard. An IAF board member expressed concerns, which Alinsky relayed to Ross. But Ross pushed back, writing that such a critique overlooked the remarkable level of work going on "under the exclusive supervision of volunteer leaders."[4]

Someone without Alinsky's experience might have taken this claim at face value. But his work in the Back of the Yards neighborhood of Chicago had convinced him that a strong organization needed not only volunteers but also the resources to afford paid staff. It was certainly laudable that the CSO involved hundreds of volunteers, but it still relied on paid organizers—and at some point the money that paid the organizers was going to disappear. During a CSO executive board meeting in 1955, Alinsky laid out the matter in stark terms. They had one of two roads to take: continue to grow without worrying about the finances, which would cause the CSO to "destroy itself," or launch a "consolidation" program of the existing chapters to stabilize the organization.[5] Once the newest CSO chapters were established—Ross was organizing one in Stockton and Chavez another in Hanford—the consolidation phase must begin.

Thus began a pattern that Ross and Chavez would follow, with several interruptions, until each left the CSO. The duo covered old ground, returning to chapters and often turning around a dying organization in a matter of weeks. After a short stay in Brawley, the paid membership jumped from 100 to 346; in Los Angeles, from 100 to 347; in Bakersfield, from 89 to 423. "From a trickle . . . interest in the CSO services swelled to a stream by the end of our third week in Sacramento; and by the time we left the leaders were wringing their hands in wondering how they were going to take care of all the problems of all the people," Ross reported to Alinsky.[6]

Problems were good: they meant the CSO was responding to real people with real issues. The Bakersfield chapter forced the city to install a sewer system in the barrio. In Fresno, members convinced the city to strip the license of a crooked labor contractor and won back stolen wages for farmworkers. Chapters waged numerous battles against election, welfare, and immigration officials, finally forcing racist bureaucrats to treat Latino clients with respect. They investigated complaints of police brutality and elected members to school boards, city councils, and boards of supervisors. This was all to the good: if the CSO was going to support itself, it needed dues-paying members; to attract dues-paying members, it needed to gain a reputation for taking up the good fight. Along with bumping up membership dues from two to three dollars a year, Ross and Chavez launched a "service program" in chapters, staffed by volunteers who could perform various tasks—translating documents, helping file immigration papers—for a fee.

Returning to chapters also meant lighting a fire under leaders who had grown complacent. Without the guidance of Ross or Chavez, the shrunken membership often coalesced around a clique that had grown to like the status quo, as it allowed them to do little more than give speeches. The service program, Ross hoped, would force these leaders, however reluctantly, into action. "At first, we felt a little guilty about building up this intensive service program in the various chapters, and then leaving the leaders holding the bag," he wrote. But he found that "once we have initiated the program and the people are aware of its value, they force the leaders to continue with it after we have gone. The leaders know that if they let the people down on *this* program the people will walk out en mass [sic]. Then there will be nothing for the leaders to lead."[7]

Over the years, the Emil Schwarzhaupt Foundation provided more than half a million dollars in grants to the IAF in support of the CSO. At the same time, the foundation was also funding a curious organization run out of a schoolhouse in rural Tennessee. The Highlander Folk School, founded by Myles Horton in 1932, had become an important civil rights incubator in the segregated South, a place where blacks and whites sought refuge to study and strategize, think through problems and imagine solutions. "What is too big for one person to handle can be figured out by all of us together," Horton once said. "We will have a new kind of school—not a school for teaching reading, writing and arithmetic, but a school for problems."[8] Among the students at Highlander was Rosa Parks, who would return to Montgomery and, several months later, refuse to relinquish her seat on a bus.

Horton was less an organizer than an educator, interested not in building organizations but in developing people who, given the encouragement, could begin to dismantle an unjust system. Carl Tjerandsen, executive secretary of the Schwarzhaupt Foundation, was a college dean of education and was enthusiastic after visiting Horton in Tennessee. When he returned, he encouraged Alinsky and Ross to create an educational component within the CSO. Ross was initially hesitant. He believed in what he called "on the spot" leadership development: people learned by taking action and evaluating the results, not by holding discussions behind desks. But Tjerandsen offered additional funding, which neither Ross nor Alinsky cared to turn down. Beginning in 1956, Ross helped train leaders to run what they called "educationals," which were structured but open meetings for members to discuss issues in more depth. It didn't take long for Ross to realize their value. Dolores Huerta, who ran educationals in Stockton, described the process:

> You try to crank up your brain. You ask questions to get back to what is basic. You start with: "What's hurting?" and push on to: "What's wrong?" and "Why?" You might have an educational on: "What is a meeting?" "How is it different from a get-together?" "What about parliamentary procedure?" "How does it help?" "What is binding about a meeting?" "Why do we have majority rule?" We might meet on: "How does this happen?" "Who does it?" "What are the duties of officers?" We held an educational on: "What makes a leader?" We ended up saying that it has nothing to do with oratory, clothes, education. Rather, it is one who works for the people. Therefore, even a farm worker can be a leader.[9]

The typical CSO meeting was packed with agenda items, which at times gave average members little chance to participate meaningfully. The educational meetings, on the other hand, were a chance for everyone to speak their mind and tackle complicated subjects together. The first educational Ross witnessed occurred in Stockton, where the city was soliciting support for an urban-renewal project in a Mexican American neighborhood called Goat Valley. Many were initially behind the project, but skepticism grew as they discussed the motives of the project's supporters, which included the Chamber of Commerce. Together, the CSO chapter's members sifted through planning details, discovering that most residents of Goat Valley were too poor to receive any compensation for the homes they would lose. In the end, it was decided that the CSO would oppose the proposal. (Despite their efforts, the project would go through.)

The educationals also had a democratizing effect on chapters, a consequence that leaders didn't always appreciate. Ross believed that many chapters floundered because leaders were attracted to the CSO for less than honorable reasons—"glory, recognition, power"—and forgot about the needs of rank-and-file members, who, ignored and disillusioned, dropped out.[10] By insisting that the people could solve their own problems, educationals encouraged members to trust their own voices and intelligence. As occurred in Stockton with the urban-renewal fight, members also gained expertise that made them less inclined to sit quietly while leadership did nothing. In his lengthy report on the CSO, Tjerandsen quoted two unnamed chapter leaders who were unhappy with the results. "Now our meetings last twice as long because these people have suddenly become little authorities on their subjects," one complained. "Some of the questions that they raise don't show the proper respect for the officers," said another.[11] Such sentiments were precisely the evidence that turned Ross and Alinsky into believers in educationals.

Alinsky had made his name organizing in Chicago by pulling together a community-labor coalition—the Back of the Yards Neighborhood Council—that transformed what had been a narrow union struggle into a movement that galvanized an entire neighborhood. Ralph Helstein was the leader of the United Packinghouse Workers of America (UPWA), which represented employees in Chicago's slaughterhouses, and over the years he and Alinsky had become close friends. The pair often discussed the possibility of forging a CSO-union alliance in California, and they made at least one initial attempt when Helstein hired Tony Rios in December 1954 to organize in the Imperial Valley.[12] But the short-lived project evidently never took off.

In the summer of 1958, a new possible collaboration emerged, focused on Oxnard, a city located on California's Central Coast. In Oxnard, Helstein's union had won a number of union elections but was making little headway in securing contracts, and he was, he told Alinsky, searching for a "new look."[13] Ross attended a meeting called by Helstein at the Fairmont Hotel in San Francisco, along with Ernesto Galarza of the National Farm Labor Union and Father Donald McDonnell of Sal Si Puedes, where they shared their thoughts on why campaigns in the field had thus far failed. Soon after, Helstein and the CSO had an agreement: the union would provide the CSO with twenty thousand dollars to organize in Oxnard, hoping that the group's work would create a community-labor partnership that could force growers to the table. Slotted to lead the Oxnard effort was Cesar Chavez.

Chavez arrived in Oxnard several months later, launching an intensive voter registration campaign that was impossible to ignore. During house meetings, he heard many locals complain that they were unable to get work in the fields. The problem, they complained, was the *bracero*—or Mexican guest worker. Sixteen years earlier, Ross had been sent to inspect labor camps in anticipation of the arrival of these guest workers, in what was advertised as a temporary measure to fill a wartime shortage. But once growers had access to a steady supply of relatively docile workers—who could be sent home if they complained about pay—they had no intention of giving it up. The largest bracero camp in the country, in fact, was located in Oxnard.

By law, braceros were only to be used in fields when growers couldn't find local workers. But Chavez soon learned that growers—in collusion with government officials—found easy ways to get around this requirement. He took unemployed workers to the Farm Placement Service office in Ventura, where they were given referral cards and sent to the labor camp. But when they arrived at the labor camp, Hector Zamora, head of the Ventura County Farm Labor Association, said the jobs for the day had already been filled. The workers returned to the camp early the next morning, referral cards in hand. Zamora sent them away: they needed new cards, which meant another lengthy trip to Ventura. Back and forth they went, the days turning to weeks, collecting cards but no jobs. All along, Chavez kept meticulous records. Organized labor often contended that guest workers both displaced local workers and depressed wages. Chavez's extensive paper trail provided irrefutable evidence.

With the odds stacked against him, Chavez worked around the clock, striking out in every direction. Workers sent letters of protest to Governor

FIGURE 12. Cesar Chavez in Oxnard, far right, November 1958. Ross returned from a visit amazed at what Chavez had been able to accomplish. Courtesy of Walter P. Reuther Library, Wayne State University.

Edmund "Pat" Brown, demanding he fire Edward Hayes, the head of California's Farm Placement Service. They wired telegrams to US labor secretary James Mitchell, requesting an investigation. CSO members staged a march through town, which ended with individuals publicly burning their referral cards. The noise grew too loud to be easily dismissed. Government officials attended CSO meetings and listened to the complaints. Investigators finally visited the fields. The head of the state's employment services, John Carr, came to Oxnard to interview Chavez and the workers.

It was an exhausting schedule. Along with the endless trips to and from the fields and labor camps, Chavez had organized a chapter of 650 members, whose meetings were filled to capacity. Ross had always known that Chavez was talented, but after spending a weekend in Oxnard, he concluded that Chavez was operating on a different level entirely. "That thing could be the story of stories," he wrote Alinsky. "It's utterly fantastic. That damned CSO office is like a small auditorium, jammed with rummage sale junk and people from 5:30 AM until midnight, 7 days per week and Cesar killing himself. . . . He already has the most powerful movement in the state going there."[14]

Contractors, seeking to avoid further protests, began to show up at the CSO's office early in the morning to pick up workers. Wages started inching upward. The same government that had once ignored Chavez's complaints now quickly returned calls and sent investigators into the fields, demanding that growers hire locals. What had been a nonstory—the growers' abuse of the bracero program—was now receiving television and newspaper coverage. But as the yearlong project came to an end, Chavez registered his worries with Ross. The CSO money had allowed him to hire an assistant, with whom he wasn't overly impressed. He criticized the union organizers as well, feeling they weren't willing to put in the real work needed to keep the movement going. "I'm very much afraid," Ross wrote to Alinsky, "from what I saw and heard from him [Chavez], that unless UPWA organizers are really forced by Ralph [Helstein] to do some organizing, our dream of building a union through CSO help will go aglimmering."[15]

The concerns were prescient, as Chavez learned when he returned to Oxnard a year later. The money from the union had run out, and he was now living in East Los Angeles, where he had become the national director of the CSO. In this role, he continued to keep a close eye on the Oxnard chapter, and what he saw wasn't encouraging. The meetings, once crowded with hundreds of people, had dwindled to several dozen. Through the campaign, contractors had been forced to hire workers directly at the CSO office. On his visit, Chavez arrived at the office early in the morning, when workers were usually being dispatched, and found it locked. The union office was closed as well. The workers were huddled on the street, keeping warm by a fire. Others gathered by the train tracks or the dump. One worker, who recognized Chavez, reminisced about "el susto que les dimos a los rancheros"—the scare they had given the growers. Later, when the CSO office finally opened, Chavez asked a board member where everyone had been, mentioning the workers he had found shivering in the streets. Those are just drunks, he was told. Anyone willing to work hard could make it fine. Chavez listened, enraged. "En donde dejaste los huevos?" Chavez asked, walking away. *Where did you leave your balls?* "The CSO and the union leaders at that moment became, in my mind, the worst foes of the people," Chavez wrote to Ross.[16]

For Chavez, Oxnard had provided proof that farmworkers could be organized, even in the face of great odds. (*Conquering Goliath* is the title Ross chose for his book about Chavez in Oxnard.) But it also provided proof that such efforts could quickly be undone, due to forces outside of the organizer's control. Chavez had done everything within his power to build an organization of farmworkers, only to watch the union and CSO let it all go to pieces. "Some board members are so lazy that they will not help," he fumed to Ross.

"Everything is left up to the organizer and the board members just come around like big shots giving orders and taking the credit. At the general meetings everybody gets up and tries to outdo the next man, but when the time comes to get into action they don't move."[17]

The most important lesson Chavez took from Oxnard was the need to retain control. "I'll never want to work with anybody else on another project unless it's Fred Ross," he wrote, "otherwise I'll go at it alone."[18]

TWELVE

The Life and Death of the CSO

ROSS HAD ONCE ASPIRED TO write a great American novel, and while at Arvin he had penned a number of poems inspired by his experiences with Dust Bowl migrants. Several of these appeared in print, including "Cotton Fever," which was published in the May 1941 issue of the *Saturday Review of Literature*. In 1942, he submitted a collection of his poems for the James D. Phelan Award in San Francisco, earning an honorable mention. Among Ross's fans was William Rose Benét, the founder of the *Saturday Review* and a Pulitzer prize–winning poet. He was enthusiastic about Ross's poems and his potential. "I've heartily recommended them," Benét wrote to a colleague. "I'm glad to recommend his work to any publisher."[1]

Despite this minor critical success, Ross had long since stopped writing poetry, though his love of literature remained intact. The basement of the Corte Madera house was overflowing with his books; among his favorite authors, whom he returned to again and again, were William Faulkner, John Steinbeck, and Ernest Hemingway. But organizing had pushed out any time to write, aside from the work journal he kept for Saul Alinsky, where no detail was deemed too insignificant to record. (A typical entry: "Went to Winter School at 7 PM and got tables at entrance and set up paper to record names and addresses of all who attend.")[2]

Now he was given the breathing space to write something more substantial: a book about the Community Service Organization. Both Ross and Alinsky felt that the CSO had been unfairly overlooked by the media and hoped that the publication would spark new interest, while also serving as a final report to the Emil Schwarzhaupt Foundation. A recent example of this slighting was the group's voter registration work in 1960, largely paid for by the AFL-CIO, in support of John F. Kennedy's presidential campaign. The effort had been a rousing success. The union funds allowed the CSO to hire additional staff, and in short order more than 100,000 new voters in California were added to the rolls. In a press release, CSO president Herman Gallegos applauded the "grueling, day after day efforts of over 500 CSO deputy registrars," who had put in more than 120,000 hours.[3] Yet the CSO received barely a mention for its efforts. Part of the problem, Alinsky told Ross, was the group's name. "I can't help thinking that regardless of the ineptness of any public relations handling on the part of the CSO people it would almost take a genius to get dramatic publicity for as drab and non-distinctive a name as CSO," he wrote. "Even a guy with the name of Joe Smith has a name with more individual identity than the CSO."[4]

Alinsky's *Reveille for Radicals* had put the spotlight on his organizing project in Chicago, the Back of the Yards Neighborhood Council. Perhaps a book by Ross would likewise raise the national profile of the CSO. After all, despite its ups and downs, it was undoubtedly the most powerful Mexican American organization in the country—and yet almost nobody had heard of it. Ross was excited about the assignment, which he began in 1960, but it would soon prove both physically and mentally taxing. He had had back surgery in 1950 to fuse several weakened vertebrae, but he still dealt with chronic pain, which he attempted to lessen by sleeping with a piece of plywood under his mattress and another plank beneath the seat of his car. Sitting for long stretches of time aggravated the injury, so Ross was often forced to write while standing up, using the fireplace mantel in the living room as a table. Other times he wrote while lying flat on his back, a posture that did little to improve his already atrocious handwriting. (Alinsky's exasperated secretary once volunteered to buy Ross a typewriter so that she would never again have to decipher his scrawl.)

The second challenge was the writing itself. Good organizers must be students of people's fears, hopes, and motivations. But Ross's subtle reading of people didn't translate onto the page, which he filled with two-dimensional characters who spouted phrases like, "We're getting pretty tired of this no-action stuff!"[5] He likely realized that he was failing to capture the drama or complexity of his organizing work. He began to walk around the house, muttering about "this damn book." His output slowed, as he wrote and rewrote and rewrote some more. Back in Chicago, Alinsky waited for the pages, growing increasingly impatient. "I have read your letter, with your optimistic notation that you will have finished the book by the end of June," he wrote in January 1961. "I accept this regardless of all evidence to the contrary."[6]

By April, Alinsky was growing exasperated. "Dear Son," he wrote, "Job never had to put up with you!":

> From your letter I gather that you are averaging one half of one page (double space big margins) per day, which at your salary figure boils down to $12.00 a word which, I must admit, makes you the highest paid writer in the history of literature. I didn't raise a question about the lack of a CSO in San Diego.... Perish the thought that I am suggesting you ought to go down to San Diego and organize it. This would mean a reduction of your prodigious writing efforts to just one line a day and we would have to delay anticipated publication date from 1966 to 1982.[7]

More than a year later, Ross still hadn't turned in what he had promised. "Let us remember," pleaded Alinsky, "that you are not out to compete with the time Gibbons spent in doing *The Rise and Decline of the Roman Empire*."[8] (Historian Edward Gibbon spent fifteen years writing his monumental multivolume book, *The History of the Decline and Fall of the Roman Empire*.) But despite his best efforts, Ross just couldn't seem to complete the book. "You had better finish it while you still have a CSO kicking around," Alinsky wrote in the spring of 1962, "unless you want to title it *The Life and Death of the CSO*."[9]

As Alinsky's letter suggested, the CSO was floundering. That fact was made plain in November 1962, when Ross took a welcome break from writing to embark on a road trip that crisscrossed the valleys of California, covering eighteen hundred miles in ten days. In the passenger seat was Carl Tjerandsen of the Schwarzhaupt Foundation, who was eager to get a firsthand look at the organization the foundation had invested in so heavily over the previous decade. The results weren't encouraging. Of the thirty-four CSO chapters listed on the group's letterhead, they visited twelve—and one imagines Ross chose the strongest of the group. Of the twelve, Tjerandsen found that only six were healthy. The rest had either collapsed completely or were plagued by leaders who, as Tjerandsen wrote in his field notes, didn't want to "rock the boat."[10]

Like Ross, Tjerandsen saw a class dynamic at work, reporting that the weak chapters were often led by college graduates, while the "liveliest CSO's have unskilled workers as presidents."[11] While financial problems still plagued the organization, Ross was hopeful that the Stockton chapter, which was raising money through its service center, provided a model for the future. Another positive note was sounded by Chris Hartmire, head of the California Migrant Ministry, a small Protestant group within the National Council of Churches that was dedicated to serving farmworkers. Hartmire had come under the spell of the quietly charismatic Cesar Chavez and told Tjerandsen that the organizing trainings his staff had received from Ross and Chavez had been "revolutionary."[12]

The long road trip must have elicited complicated feelings in Ross, triggering both warm memories and sadness in knowing that, after having given every ounce of his energy to the organization, it was in a tailspin that he seemed powerless to stop. By the end of 1962, the CSO's total paid membership stood at just 2,432. As funding from the Schwarzhaupt Foundation was set to expire, the organization had made no progress toward financial sustainability.

A major blow to the CSO had occurred earlier that year. On March 18, 1962, Chavez resigned as the group's national director. A decade had passed since Ross had recruited the shy twenty-five-year-old to the path of organizing, and the student had grown into a skilled teacher who chafed at the limitations set by the CSO's board. Like Ross, he harbored an instinctive distrust of the middle class, and he felt that the CSO had lost its way by treading a path to respectability. Chavez was also adamant that the annual membership dues needed to be raised to put the organization on a more secure financial footing. But CSO members, led by Tony Rios, the national president, dragged their feet whenever the question of raising dues was brought up, arguing that it would cause membership to drop.

Chavez had another explanation for such reluctance, writing to Alinsky that "the leaders know full well that if dues are increased they will have to produce for the membership."[13] A month later, Chavez was steaming after a meeting with Rios and other CSO officers, in which they again resisted an increase in dues. "It seems strange, Sol [sic]," he wrote to Alinsky, "that so many of these people insist on having this patronizing attitude towards the membership. Sometimes I wonder if they want an organization, or just a 'show-case' group to say 'look at what we are doing for those poor, poor people.'"[14]

Such tensions had spilled into the open at the CSO's annual convention in the spring of 1962, held at the stately De Anza Hotel in the border city of Calexico. The theme of the meeting was "Our Next Objective—Justice for the Farm Workers!" This was exactly what Chavez wanted to pursue, but on his own terms, without feeling tied down by others whose vision conflicted with his own. As members debated yet again whether the CSO should raise annual dues from three to five dollars, accompanied by the usual infighting, Chavez stood up to announce his resignation. It didn't matter that, earlier in the day, the CSO had approved a plan to form a "Farm Labor Committee" or that a wealthy private citizen, sympathetic to farmworkers, had agreed to donate fifty thousand dollars for the cause. Chavez wanted freedom. Money would come, if it came, later. The impact that Alinsky had on Chavez is often exaggerated, but in this regard—the need to not be constrained by funders— one can clearly see his influence. Back in Chicago, Alinsky's office blackboard had just one line written across it: Low Overhead = High Independence.[15] Chavez left the CSO virtually penniless and with an impossible goal in mind, but he was now free to make his own mistakes.

Though Ross had dedicated fifteen years of his life to the CSO, his loyalties were to his onetime student. Ross shared Chavez's dream of building a union of farmworkers, a constituency that would always occupy a special place in his heart. It was with farmworkers at Arvin that Ross had first lived among the poor, and it was at Arvin that he had first observed an organizing campaign in action. Ross had studied farmworker history and knew how quickly growers and the law could destroy a strike. He knew the odds of success were long. But he had also been amazed by what Chavez had accomplished in Oxnard. If anyone could bring a union to farmworkers, Ross believed, it was Chavez.

Still, the departure of Chavez was difficult for Ross to witness, with Dolores Huerta recalling that her mentor was in tears at one point. Though the tension was principally between Rios and Chavez, it spilled over to Alinsky and Ross as well. Rios and Alinsky had a contentious history. Rios tended to view the irreverent organizer as something of a meddler who sought to make decisions and set conditions from Chicago. These tensions originally flared in 1955, when Alinsky hired Rios to organize CSO chapters in Arizona, a stint that proved short-lived after Rios refused to file expense reports or even explain his activities. Relations were smoother between Rios and Ross. Their long and productive history dated back to the founding of the organization, and both men appreciated the other's dedication and sincerity. But Ross's allegiance to Chavez was clear, and the CSO convention drove a wedge between Ross and Rios. "My major worry about Rios-CSO developments is its effect on you," Alinsky wrote. "I know that regardless of everything I have told you, you probably feel embittered, and very hurt. If it be of any consolation to you, the affection which I now enjoy from the Back of the Yards Council is at a lower stage than that which you enjoy from Tony Rios."[16] Soon after the convention, Ross came down with a stomach ulcer. "So now I have *all* the attributes of a good organizer, except ability and an organization," he wrote to Chavez.[17]

By this time, Chavez had moved with Helen and their eight kids to Delano, a grape-growing town in the San Joaquin Valley, where they eked out an existence on unemployment and whatever wages Helen earned in the fields. The prospect of launching a farmworker union was daunting, enough to freeze any sensible person in his tracks. So Chavez broke the project into pieces, just as Ross had done when planning the expansion of the CSO. Chavez and Helen sat down with Huerta to divide up the territory, circling every farmworker town and labor camp on a map of the San Joaquin Valley. To begin, Chavez conducted a farmworker census, creating registration cards to collect names and ask workers what they considered to be a fair wage. When Ross learned of Chavez's plans, he immediately wrote to Alinsky, asking that the Industrial Areas Foundation fund Chavez at the rate of six hundred dollars a month for the census.[18] Alinsky, however, didn't believe farmworkers could be organized, and he rejected the request, adding that his "getting involved in any form would promise plenty of trouble."[19]

Alinsky was far from alone. Plenty of people thought Chavez had signed up for an impossible mission. Ross harbored no such doubts—or if he did, he successfully concealed them from Chavez. The endeavor also played on Ross's romantic side, the side that had been in awe of the farmworker organizers who had descended on Arvin during the Depression, taking on the entire sordid agribusiness industry without fear. Lonely and doubting himself, Chavez leaned heavily on Ross in the months after he left the CSO. The pair exchanged frequent letters, with Ross offering unconditional support and faith in Chavez, often inserting ten or twenty dollars—"units of supply," he called them—to help pay for food and gasoline. "You have no idea how much your letters pick me up," Chavez wrote in May 1962, adding that he doubted the organizing would take off without "the special 'Ross' touch."[20]

In reply, Ross noted that he was nearly finished with his book, and so it was "getting closer and closer to the day when you'll no longer have to rely on *mi sombra* [shadow] to handle house meetings."[21] But while Ross visited often, he wouldn't end up joining Chavez during those early years. Ross later wrote that he offered to work for Chavez for free during the period, evidently content to survive on Frances's salary; she had earned her master's degree in clinical psychology and was a rehabilitative counselor at the Lighthouse for the Blind in San Francisco. Chavez evidently rebuffed Ross's offer, though why he did so isn't exactly clear. Perhaps Chavez felt that he had to embark on the journey alone. Or perhaps he wasn't comfortable asking Ross to work for free, knowing that it would cause significant financial stress for his family. Robin (now Bob) had left to attend the University of California, Davis, but Ross's two other children, Julia and Fred Jr., were still in high school and living at home. Chavez was certainly aware of how much his mentor had already done to help, from spearheading fund-raising drives to prodding CSO members to assist with the farmworker census. When Chavez wrote to Huerta about money problems, he instructed her not to tell Ross about his family's pitiful finances. "I'm very serious about not letting Fred know," he reiterated, "because he gets worried and we are not really that bad off—we have something to eat now."[22]

Slowly, through sheer perseverance, Chavez began to make inroads. "I left Stockton at 2:30 AM and arrived in Delano at 6:30 AM," he wrote to Ross. "Saw a small crew on the road in Tipton and stopped over long enough to register them."[23] The CSO connections proved to be a great help, especially in Bakersfield, where member Dave Burciaga—who championed Chavez's work—organized a series of house meetings. By August, Chavez calculated that he had covered 14,867 miles in eighty-six days.

The founding convention of the Farm Workers Association (FWA) was held in Fresno on September 30, 1962. "I wish I could come down for your big blow up with the FWA," Ross wrote. "But I can't, while I'm still on the IAF payroll, as you know."[24] Despite Alinsky's objections, Ross soon reconsidered, booking a ticket and writing to Chavez that he would come—"if they let stinking *gabachos* [white guys] in!"[25] After the convention, in which Chavez was elected general director, Ross wrote a congratulatory note. "Well, *viejo,* you've really done a fantastically wonderful job! I know there's a long way to go, but with that marvelous *maña* [cunning] of yours, and judging by the glory I saw pouring from the eyes of the farm workers sitting around that table all afternoon, and with luck, you'll make it. I'm absolutely sure of it."[26]

The excitement that Ross felt at the launch of the Farm Workers Association was tempered by his obligations to the CSO, which were feeling more and more like drudgery. After hearing Tjerandsen's pessimistic report from his road trip with Ross, Alinsky announced a change of plans. If funding from the Schwarzhaupt Foundation didn't come through for 1963, Ross was to relocate to Chicago, where he would work on another IAF-sponsored project, the Temporary Woodlawn Organization (TWO).

The Woodlawn neighborhood, located in the shadow of the University of Chicago, was engaged in a battle with the school over a proposed urban-renewal plan. It was "the hottest project going," Alinsky wrote; as opposed to the long-ignored CSO, the activities of TWO received widespread coverage by the national press.[27] Under the direction of TWO, residents of the African American neighborhood organized rent strikes, tackled overcrowded and segregated schools, and filled forty-six buses on a trip to city hall, where more than twenty-five hundred people registered to vote en masse. One of the important behind-the-scene movers was Nicholas von Hoffman, a skilled organizer with the IAF who had become something of a second son to Alinsky. Hoffman was everything Ross was not. Brash, abrasive, and cocky, the thirty-three-year-old wore expensive suits, wanting to look "like a super pimp."[28] When suspicious blacks asked him why he was an organizer, von Hoffman answered, "Well, if it works, I'm going to get rich and famous and powerful."[29] But despite the flash and bravado, von Hoffman was a tireless worker—so tireless, in fact, that by the end of 1962 he had burned himself out. Alinsky hoped to bring on Ross as a replacement.

It would have been an intriguing and challenging experience for Ross, and one wonders what he might have accomplished in a big and politically complex city like Chicago. But just as he made preparations to leave, his mother, Daisy, fell ill. "Mother has 20 per cent chance recovery from operation for cancer," he wired Alinsky on November 28, 1962. "Will probably know in 72 hours. If unable [to] come [to] Chicago Saturday will wire you."[30] Daisy would recover, but Ross would never leave for Chicago. He spent several weeks at his mother's side, and by the time Ross returned to Corte Madera, the Schwarzhaupt Foundation had agreed to fund a final year of work.

And so it was that, once again, Ross returned to the CSO chapters, trying to figure out a way to make the organization financially solvent. The strategy in 1963 wasn't different than before: convince chapters to open service centers, which would charge fees for various forms of assistance. Now that both Chavez and Huerta had left, Ross was collaborating with Gilbert Padilla, who had been recruited to the CSO by Chavez nearly a decade earlier. The son of migrant farmworkers—he had been born in a labor camp—Padilla worked his way up to a position as a dry cleaner in Hanford, about thirty miles south of Fresno. In 1960, Chavez hired Padilla to run Stockton's service center, and

Ross, who appreciated the young man's drive and passion, selected him to work on what would be the final attempt to get the CSO on its feet. The pair spent the year trying to convince chapters to increase their yearly dues to twelve dollars, along with recruiting and training members to run the service centers. In his reports, Ross tried to end with positive news—possible breakthroughs, new members recruited—but his upbeat tone wasn't enough to hide the true state of affairs. When he visited the once mighty San Jose chapter, just four people attended the membership meeting.[31] And whatever progress he made came after weeks of dedicated work. "You are able to get things rolling again, but how much of this depends on *you?*" Tjerandsen wrote. "Obviously you will not be able to remain in touch with the situation indefinitely."[32]

The answer would come soon enough, as the CSO continued to lose momentum after Ross departed.

There were several explanations for the demise of the CSO. Padilla, who held multiple positions with the CSO over nearly a decade, put much of the blame, paradoxically, on the CSO's most important legislative triumph: the passage, in 1961, of a state bill providing pensions for elderly noncitizens. Many of the CSO leaders were elderly, and Padilla felt that these members left the group fat and happy. "They got their pension," he said. "So why should they come back?"[33] This criticism was echoed by Chavez, who felt betrayed by the departure of the older members.

The pension critique was related to a more fundamental one: the CSO had become dominated by middle-class members who didn't want to work particularly hard and felt most comfortable with a group that played it safe. Ross had seen this dynamic at work numerous times. The classic example was Fresno. "How one chapter went to hell" is how Ross began his report on the city, which can stand in for his thoughts on why many chapters lost their way. The center of Ross's critique was that people who had risen above their neighbors, whether through "accident of birth or opportunity," rushed to the CSO and replaced any organizing campaigns with "cream puff programs":

> No matter how glibly they prate about the need for "Mexican Unity," their real drive is toward identification with the dominant community, and of avoiding, at all cost, anything which could conceivably impede that process. . . .
> As against the desk-thumping delegation or the demonstration, you take the approach of the "consulting agency," the channel between the minority and dominant community. As such you count on invitations to serve on every

committee designed to talk an issue to death in the county. Or you set up a fancy scholarship program. To be sure, you are only able to provide help to an infinitesimal number of students but, since everyone loves kids, you hardly fail to enhance your prestige in the eyes of the overall community.[34]

This is the identical critique that Ross made of groups like the League of United Latin American Citizens that he had found when he first began organizing in the Citrus Belt. The longtime leader of the Fresno chapter brought in people from the professional class—doctors, policemen, lawyers—who were happy to, as Ross once described, "meet, seat, eat, and repeat (or retreat)." A similar dynamic played out in Salinas, where by the early 1960s, the CSO leadership was drawn from not farmworkers but labor contractors.

Chapters with a more working-class membership typically fared better. In Hanford, for example, the leadership was made up primarily of farmworkers and manual laborers. Even in 1963, when most of the chapters were floundering, Ross reported that Hanford was going strong: "They are constantly in there slamming away at City and County bodies and officials, demanding their rights, fighting police brutality, protesting, denouncing, eliminating discrimination and injustice.... Things were especially lively when I was there. They took on the Police Dep't on a brutality case, got the offending officer punished, and brought out over 100 members to meet with the Chief and administered a verbal thrashing."[35]

There was also, of course, the problem of money. The CSO, like nearly every organizing group save labor unions, could never find a way to pay for itself. Perhaps, given more time, the service-center model could have brought in enough money to sustain the chapters. But focusing exclusively on the group's money woes sidesteps a bigger issue, which is that by the early 1960s the CSO lacked an overarching mission—and it was this vacuum that the middle-class moderates filled. For fifteen years the organization had fought to get streets paved and stoplights installed. They had cracked down on abusive cops and disrespectful bureaucrats. Tens of thousands of people became citizens; half a million voters were added to the rolls. More work remained to be done, of course, but the CSO had largely accomplished what it set out to do: provide Mexican Americans with a political voice.

Ross would later take immense pride in having helped build the CSO, and indeed the leadership that emerged from the organization was extraordinary. Cesar Chavez, Dolores Huerta, and Gilbert Padilla would cofound what became the United Farm Workers. A young lawyer active with the CSO in the city of El Centro, Cruz Reynoso, would serve as the first Latino on California's Supreme Court. Herman Gallegos helped create and then lead what became the National Council of La Raza. In the political arena, Edward Roybal's election served notice that the country was entering an era when Latinos could no longer be ignored. And the fearless Tony Rios helped expose the abuses of Bloody Christmas, finally offering evidence that police could be held accountable. These were the headliners—but behind such individuals were the thousands more men and women who remained largely anonymous but who were crucial in building the strongest Mexican American organization of its period.

But while Ross would later spend hours fondly reminiscing about the CSO and its accomplishments, that was the long perspective—and it was a perspective that Ross lacked as he attended his final CSO convention in March 1964. The three-day affair was held in Oxnard, where the fruits of Chavez's earlier organizing had long since been wiped away. The organization was by now a shell of its former self, with Ross covering his own expenses on the trip, as the IAF money had run out a month earlier. He no longer had a formal role to play with the group, and so he remained silent as Tony Rios proposed a motion, which passed, that forbade the CSO from accepting "outside services" from groups like the IAF in the future. "At this point, I'm happy to say that the CSO is little more than a bittersweet memory," Ross wrote to Alinsky. "May it fade entirely and soon!"[36]

PART THREE

Organizer as Teacher (1964–1992)

THIRTEEN

Poverty Fiasco

IN EARLY 1964, ROSS AND SAUL Alinsky sat down with leaders of the
United Presbyterian Church in San Francisco. By now, funds from the Emil
Schwarzhaupt Foundation had been exhausted, and the men were casting
about for their next project, proposing to set up an organization in San
Francisco's Mission District loosely modeled after the Temporary Woodlawn
Organization in Chicago. Alinsky had brought along two friends to the
meeting, Dave Ramage and George Todd, who both worked out of the
Presbyterian Church's New York office.

The Presbyterians weren't ready to move on San Francisco, but Ramage
and Todd made a counteroffer. The Presbyterian Church owned one hundred acres of land in Guadalupe, Arizona, the result of a bequest from a
missionary in the 1920s. Several miles outside of Tempe, Guadalupe was an
unincorporated village, home to Mexican Americans and Yaqui Indians,
though the two groups didn't get along particularly well. The Yaquis had
originally lived in Sonora, Mexico, but were driven from their lands by dicta-
tor Porfirio Diaz, with many enslaved and sold to the owners of sugar planta-
tions. Others retreated north and settled in Guadalupe in 1907, glad to be
free but suspicious of their Spanish-speaking neighbors. Ramage and Todd
held out hope that an organizing project would encourage better cooperation
between the two groups and lead to some long-overdue improvements to the
village. "We've got a big problem out there," Ross was told. "One of the worst
rural slums in America, and the Church owns half of it."[1]

Ross arrived in Guadalupe in April, quickly realizing that it was unlike
any community he had organized. Many of the homes were made of mud and
straw, some without running water. Only one out of ten residents was
employed; those who worked typically spent their days in the fields earning

just seventy cents an hour. There were no streetlights, sewers, or paved roads; no doctors, libraries, or mailboxes. The water that came from the faucet was often cloudy with sand, and sometimes filled with worms. Many residents were illiterate. With a population of 4,000, only 182 were registered to vote.

It was, in short, exactly the sort of place for Ross. He followed the pattern established with the Community Service Organization: holding house meetings in English, Spanish, and this time Yaqui; recruiting and training a group of deputy registrars (four Yaqui Indian and two Mexican American); and launching a voter registration drive. Initially, some Yaquis refused to sign anything—a wise move, given their history—but Ross was able to persuade the chief, who had a loudspeaker perched on his roof, to announce his blessing of the project. In three weeks they registered more than five hundred people. On May 20, 1964, with eighty-five people in attendance, the Guadalupe Organization was established.

Key to the effort were Lauro and Margarita Garcia. Four years earlier, the couple had moved their eight-by-twenty-eight-foot trailer to a dirt lot in Guadalupe, while Lauro, a Korean War vet, attended Arizona State University. Soon after arriving, they became involved in local affairs, fighting against the county's attempt to shut down the village's only health clinic, which had become infested with rats and cockroaches. After the Garcias helped repair the building themselves, they forced the county to double the number of clinic offerings. Both were instinctive activists. Early on, Margarita told Ross that he looked familiar. It turned out that she had served as treasurer of Sacramento's CSO chapter in the 1950s.

In the run-up to elections in November, Guadalupe residents met with their county, state, and federal representatives. The first politician was on the phone when they entered his office and showed little urgency to end the call. After learning of their voter registration efforts, he told his secretary to hold all phone calls and listened attentively. Each meeting began with a list of demands; each meeting ended with the group explaining that they would "advise the Guadalupe voters by newsletter, every two weeks until election day, as to whether or not they [the politicians] had delivered."[2] The organization also invited candidates to a town hall meeting, attended by hundreds of people on a scorching summer night outside Guadalupe's aging elementary school. Within weeks, every demand was in the process of being met. Streets were paved. Stop signs, traffic signals, water mains, and streetlights were installed. Each house was given a mailbox. The county agreed to fund a local deputy sheriff. The cultural anthropologist Margaret Mead observed Guadalupe that summer and was initially confused by what she encountered. "At first, it was hard for anyone . . . to see what Ross was doing, because he just seemed to be talking with anyone who would stop and talk to him," she wrote. But after three months, she found the progress "almost unbelievable."[3]

Another visitor that summer was Ross's sixteen-year-old son, Fred Ross Jr. It was Frances who had suggested that their youngest son join his father, hoping the experience would lead them to develop a stronger bond than Ross enjoyed with his two other children. When he was home, Ross didn't speak much about his work, though his son had a vague sense that his dad "was helping poor people." In Guadalupe, the high school student spent his days mimeographing postcards to remind people about meetings and teaching English classes. At the town hall meeting, he was amazed by how quickly the two communities had put their differences aside and how people who once appeared shy were now standing up in public and peppering politicians with questions. "That is where it crystallized for me how significant the work was," said Fred Jr.[4] While Bob and Julia would remain distant from and often frustrated with their father, his youngest son would follow in Ross's footsteps, joining the United Farm Workers in 1970 and dedicating his life to organizing.

Ross's contract to work in Guadalupe was only for five months, but the short period left a lasting impact on the community. With money from the Presbyterian Church, he hired Lauro as a staff person for the Guadalupe Organization. The following year, the organization received nearly sixty thousand dollars in federal funds from the Office of Economic Opportunity to begin a credit union, host legal clinics, open a dental clinic, and train community health workers. In 1971, the Guadalupe Organization filed a class-action lawsuit against the Tempe school district, arguing that it dumped Yaqui and Mexican American youth into special-education classes simply because they weren't proficient in English. As a result, children in Arizona now must be assessed in their native language.[5]

After witnessing the slow decline of the CSO, the success at Guadalupe served as a pick-me-up for Ross. But his stay in Arizona was interrupted with somber news from Southern California: his mother's colon cancer had returned and spread. He flew to Los Angeles to see Daisy, who was now in a nursing home. Ross and his mother had a close, if complicated, relationship. Daisy viewed her oldest son's lifestyle with bewilderment, finding it hard to see why this smart and handsome man had elected to live out of motels and help Mexicans he hardly knew. (Daisy never entirely grew out of the prejudices

FIGURE 13. Ross and sixteen-year-old Fred Jr. in Arizona during the summer of 1964. Courtesy of Fred Ross Jr.

that had caused her to pull her son from an integrated school.) She had hoped Ross would take up a more respectable and lucrative career. Ross's younger brother, Bob, had amassed a small fortune operating a gas station and car wash; he lived with his wife in a sprawling house in Beverly Hills and drove a Lamborghini. That was a life Daisy could understand, and a career she could explain to friends.

The political differences between Ross and Bob (and Bob's wife, Blanche) had caused them to grow apart, but Ross's bond with his mother remained strong. There was, however, still an undercurrent of anxiety in the relationship. The scars from being sent away to his grandparents never fully disappeared, and Ross was in some sense trying to prove his worth to Daisy until the end. In his unpublished autobiography, Ross noted that the "theory" that Daisy loved Bob more was "pretty generally accepted," even by his mother. But everything had changed during her first bout with cancer, two years earlier. "I rarely left the hospital for several weeks," he wrote. "This so impressed her that she did a reevaluation of the whole relationship, and confided to my brother that 'Frederick is an absolute saint!'"[6]

Daisy had beaten the odds earlier, but this time it was clear she had no hope for recovery. Ross spent several days by her side, until she passed away on July 17, 1964, at the age of seventy-nine. When he returned to Guadalupe, the local Franciscan father conducted a funeral mass to honor Daisy. Hundreds of Yaqui Indians and Mexican Americans filed into the adobe church, packing it to capacity. Ross, still grieving, was deeply moved by the turnout.

Guadalupe had been the ideal setting for the Ross approach, a small, self-contained, rural community. "I had been in Guadalupe less than a week when it became apparent that, with luck and a lot of work, it would be possible to wind-up with a near-classic demonstration of mass-organization here," he wrote.[7] His next assignment would take him to Syracuse, where such a neat and tidy campaign would be impossible.

Ross was brought to the city by Warren Haggstrom, a professor of social work at Syracuse University. During his graduate work, Haggstrom had developed what would become a lifelong fascination with community organizing. His family had lost their small Minnesota farm during the Depression, after which he worked as a farm laborer; he later joined the Marine Corps and attended college on the GI Bill. His interest in organizing deepened after reading Alinsky's *Reveille for Radicals,* and the professor traveled to Chicago to observe the fruits of Alinsky's work. In Syracuse, Haggstrom was developing a reputation as a rabble-rouser. He had recently been arrested at a protest against urban renewal—organized by the Syracuse chapter of the Congress on Racial Equality (CORE)—and had begun teaching organizing courses to his graduate students.

While Ross was in Guadalupe, Haggstrom had visited and told him about a possible job opportunity. In addition to being a professor, Haggstrom was a consultant for an organization called the Crusade for Opportunity, a social-service agency in Syracuse that was hoping to launch an organizing project with funds from the federal government's new "War on Poverty." There was reason for Ross to be hesitant. The Crusade for Opportunity had previously been named the Mayor's Commission for Youth, and many of its members had either been selected or approved by Syracuse's Republican mayor, William Walsh. During his first trip to Syracuse, Ross laid out his concerns to Ben Zimmerman, head of the Crusade, but received assurances that group members were committed to creating an "autonomous" organization that wouldn't be swayed by city hall. In their proposal for government funding, the Crusade had written of building an "Action Area Neighborhood Association" that would "determine its own policies and agenda."[8]

It took an immense amount of naïveté about political power to imagine such a scenario, and Ross read over the proposal with a skeptical eye. "Do you really think you're going to get away with this?" he asked Crusade leaders. All heads nodded. Ross asked what might happen if the group picketed a slumlord who turned out to be a Walsh-appointed board member. They told him he would simply have to educate the board member. Ross pushed back: "No, I'm not going to educate them," he said. "The people that are going to educate them are the people themselves. The board members would be telling me, 'Why do they have to do this right now? Why can't they wait? They're just being very unreasonable about this.' Well, that's because they don't understand the people and they don't understand the problems. They don't understand why it is that the people have to act right now instead of next month or next year or never, probably. And they never will understand until the people force them to understand."[9]

Ross was dubious about the project, but he didn't have many other options. He wanted to remain in California and work with Cesar Chavez to build a farmworker union, and had offered his services for the modest rate of fifty dollars a week. But Chavez had used what little money he had raised to hire

Dolores Huerta. Frances had recently left her job at the Lighthouse for the Blind; Julia was attending the University of California, Berkeley; and Fred Jr. would soon begin his senior year in high school. Ross could no longer work for free. In August he flew back to Syracuse to join the staff of the Crusade, where he was to direct its "community development" program. In typical Ross fashion, he set to work on a voter registration campaign, focusing on the city's African American residents. In the South at this time, in what became known as the Mississippi Freedom Summer, thousands of volunteers were doing the same. They were arrested, beaten, and sometimes killed; homes and churches were firebombed. Still they persisted. But in Syracuse, once Mayor Walsh caught wind of the registration drive—with any new voters likely to be Democrats—he pressed Zimmerman, the director of the Crusade, to stop work. The project was abruptly cancelled, Haggstrom was fired as a consultant, and the entire program was placed under "surveillance." It was but a small taste of the controversy to come.

After a vacation with Frances in Mexico, Ross's preferred getaway from the pressures of organizing, he returned to Syracuse in October 1964. (Frances would join him in February, with a family friend moving in to watch Fred Jr.) The aborted voter registration campaign made it clear that any "autonomous" project would need independent money. With the cooperation of the Crusade, Ross decided to forego organizing and instead raise money that could eventually fund a separate nonprofit organization sponsored by, but independent of, the Crusade. Ross wasn't a great fund-raiser, but he had some success, especially with churches that were impressed with the results of his short stay in Guadalupe. After two months of fruitful meetings, he submitted a list of names to the Crusade for a potential board for the semi-independent group that he hoped to launch. Having learned how quickly one could step on political toes in Syracuse, Ross chose the names with care, seeking individuals who could be trusted to withstand the inevitable political pressure that would soon develop.

But here, again, he faced resistance. Zimmerman objected to several of the names, arguing that certain members of the Crusade board would never accept them. The individuals he had selected, Ross recalled being told, were "fuddy-duddy ministers way out there in left field, and Haggstrom, who's way farther out in left field." For Ross, this was the last straw. "They [the Crusade board] were going to try and control the [new] board by getting the people on it that they wanted," he told an interviewer the following year. "Not people that would stand up, but people they could control. So they could have their cake and eat it too."[10] Haggstrom had also lost faith in the Crusade as a potential organizing vehicle, seeing it as too deeply connected to the mayor.

Meanwhile, officials at the Office of Economic Opportunity (OEO)—the federal agency tasked with implementing a number of antipoverty programs—were eager to find a "Community Action" project to fund. Community Action would soon become the most controversial arm of the War on Poverty, for good reason. Unlike traditional top-down approaches to fighting poverty, Community Action was to be bottom-up, free from the control of local or state government. Its goal, in a phrase both militant and illusively vague, was to achieve "maximum feasible participation" among the poor. Nurturing such involvement, it was hoped, would strike at the heart of poverty by both encouraging civic participation and ensuring that the most glaring barriers to breaking free from poverty would be addressed.

Haggstrom notified Sanford Kravitz, a social worker running Community Action at the OEO, that Syracuse University was interested in developing its own organizing program. Kravitz's response was immediate and enthusiastic. Sargent Shriver, head of the OEO, was impatient to begin funding such projects, and Kravitz told Haggstrom to cobble together a proposal as quickly as possible. The speed of the proposal's acceptance was remarkable. Over a weekend in late November, Haggstrom ironed out details with officials from the OEO in Washington, DC. On December 7, 1964, he submitted the proposal. One week later, the federal government announced approval of its first Community Action project, making a grant of $314,329 to Syracuse University.[11]

The proposal, which Ross helped draft, and which highlighted his work in Guadalupe, called for the creation of a Community Action Training Center (CATC). Ross would lead "field instruction," supervising sixteen participants each semester who would be pulled from two streams. The first would be social-work graduate students who studied with Haggstrom. The second, selected by Ross and Haggstrom, would be civil rights activists who received a stipend but no degree. (Participation in the program did, however, keep them out of the Vietnam-era draft.) Both groups would go into Syracuse's three predominantly African American neighborhoods and hold house meetings, forming neighborhood groups that would merge into a citywide "organization of organizations," modeled after Alinsky's work in Chicago. As the CATC got up and running, students attended classes on social action when they weren't out knocking on doors, and they browsed books in the center's library, filled with titles like Hannah Arendt's *On Revolution* and Mohandas Gandhi's *Story of My Experiments with Truth*. Once a month, Alinsky stopped by as a visiting lecturer, and each week the CATC hosted a prominent organizer who shared his or her experiences. Syracuse suddenly felt like it was at the center of something radical and groundbreaking.

Perhaps no one better exemplified the protest mood of the time than Danny Schechter. While at Cornell University, Schechter had become involved with the Northern Student Movement, an affiliate of the Student Nonviolent Coordinating Committee (SNCC), rising to become its communications director. He landed in Syracuse fresh off a stint organizing rent strikes in Harlem, enthralled by the energy of the movement but hoping to learn more about the craft of organizing. "By the end of 1964, a number of us were thinking we needed a new strategy—that protest wasn't enough," he recalled. "If the civil rights movement was going to institutionalize and keep going, we needed to have some sort of strategy and tactics."[12] That certain segments of Syracuse might not appreciate a bunch of young radicals descending on their city to practice "strategy and tactics" became clear when Schechter was arrested, minutes after arriving, for driving a car with an expired registration. The five hundred dollars' bail was waived after Ross arrived at the courthouse and explained Schechter's connection to the university; the district attorney advised Schechter to get a haircut before his hearing.

Schechter was one of the eight nonstudent organizers recruited for the CATC. Most earned thirty-five hundred dollars a year, but two slots were funded at eight thousand dollars, given to those who had accumulated the most arrests during their activism. Like many in the group, Schechter, who would go on to become an acclaimed media analyst and documentarian, was independent, bright, and instinctively antiauthoritarian. He drew connections between the widening war in Vietnam and African Americans living in slums, and he recoiled at what he felt was Ross's narrow worldview, where all focus was placed on neighborhood issues.

But perhaps Schechter's biggest problem with Ross, which was shared by other members of the New Left in Syracuse, was his authoritarian approach. As an organizer with the CSO, Ross had spent much of his time listening and offering guidance. But when teaching a roomful of young people how to be organizers, he was much less interested in their input. He had a program that he expected them to follow, and he became upset when they deviated from it. Many bristled at this top-down approach. As Haggstrom later wrote, certainly thinking of Schechter, "The discontented students began commonly to ask: 'Isn't it inconsistent to build democracy in the community when we do not have democracy in our own structure?'"[13] Some began to call their teacher "Boss Ross."

Despite this early tension, the CATC project began promisingly. The students fanned out across central Syracuse, each assigned to a turf, and formed six groups by May 1965. One of those turfs, the 477-unit James Geddes Homes, was assigned to Bill Pastreich, a second-year social-work student. Pastreich knew nothing about organizing, having stumbled into the program on the recommendation of his girlfriend, a fellow graduate student. At first, Ross conducted house meetings while Pastreich observed and took notes, but Pastreich was soon operating alone, following the "rap" that Ross had taught him: "When we met people, we'd say, 'There are three kinds of power. There's the power of money—and we aren't ever going to have that. There is the power of numbers—and we're going to have that at the first big meeting. And there's the power of the vote—that's what we're going to get to work on right after the meeting.' That's what you said. You said the same fucking thing to everybody."[14]

Unlike Schechter, Pastreich appreciated the rigid structure—and even found it to be liberating. "I loved it from the beginning," he said. "I loved that you had something to say to all these people. You could knock on the door and actually *talk* to people."[15] As a student, Pastreich was quiet and reserved. A year earlier, he had attended a protest against urban renewal, picked up a picket sign, and marched in a circle for an hour, too shy to utter a word. But he blossomed under the tutelage of Ross, who both demystified the process of organizing and made it feel like the most urgent vocation in the world. After six weeks of organizing, Pastreich turned out 135 people to the group's first meeting.

Public housing residents had plenty of reasons to be upset. Floors were falling apart, paint was peeling, and refrigerators and stoves needed to be replaced. Trash pickup was irregular, with garbage frequently left to rot in the streets. But the mayor, well aware that the public housing complexes were becoming organizing strongholds, mounted a counteroffensive. In early March, Pastreich was arrested on the grounds of the James Geddes Homes by a security officer and charged with trespassing. During the trial, it became clear that the city was upset that Pastreich was on the property in the cause of "soliciting ideas." Pastreich was eventually acquitted, but the arrest was only the opening shot. The following month, Syracuse Housing Authority commissioner Charles A. Walker wrote a four-page letter to President Lyndon Johnson asking that the federal funds for the Syracuse project be cancelled, as it would "ultimately cause serious trouble" and create "a division between the races."[16]

An investigator with the OEO was dispatched to Syracuse, and Mayor Walsh and Syracuse University chancellor William P. Tolley met to iron out any "misunderstandings." The meeting did little to repair relations. In June, the *Syracuse Post-Standard* ran a series of breathless articles that described the evils of the Syracuse project, relying on a single source: Housing Authority director William McGarry. Readers learned, per McGarry, that Syracuse students were behind a "ghastly war against law, order, and respectability" and engaged in "a class struggle in the traditional Karl Marx style." Vigilante demolition crews had been formed, marauding through the housing developments, smashing windows, breaking elevators, splintering doors, and "urinating and defecating in the hallways." McGarry was hysterical, claiming that the campaign was "perhaps one of the most diabolical acts ever perpetrated on a community by an institution of higher education."[17]

Behind the wild rhetoric was this: tenants in several housing complexes had formed organizations and were demanding repairs, along with direct meetings with city officials. And that is precisely what they got. Initially rebuffed, they held pickets and a sit-in at the lobby of the Housing Authority headquarters, forcing the first face-to-face meetings between public housing tenants and housing officials in the city's history. Soon, five hundred old refrigerators and stoves were replaced, the floors were fixed, and garbage service was improved. Playgrounds were built outside public housing complexes. People were registering to vote. That June, when Mayor Walsh traveled to Washington, DC, for a congressional hearing, he testified that Syracuse had become the scene of "social experiments of the most dangerous type."[18]

Pressure from the mayor didn't particularly bother Ross, nor did the drumbeat of negative press. Both were indications that the power structure felt threatened, which was a positive development. And while Ross was the architect of the CATC project—the students were essentially following the organizing blueprint Ross had used to build the CSO—he had a knack for keeping his name out of the press. Almost all media accounts characterized

Syracuse as an Alinsky project—which heightened the controversy, and which Alinsky no doubt enjoyed—with Haggstrom also making frequent rebuttals to public criticism. To help relieve pressure on Syracuse University, a separate organization was spun off from the school several months into the project, called the Syracuse Community Development Association, which took responsibility for the organizing.

Ross wasn't overly concerned about the mayor, but he was growing increasingly upset with the tendency of organizers to take on leadership roles within the various neighborhood organizations. As Ross told a reporter for the *Syracuse Herald-American,* "We try to beat into them that they are enablers rather than leaders."[19] Not everyone was accustomed to playing a behind-the-scenes role, which for Ross was a nonnegotiable tenet of the vocation (except, as revealed later, when it came to Cesar Chavez). The issue came to a head after a protest at the Syracuse welfare office. Pastreich, who had worked as a welfare case manager in New York City, learned that families needed clothes for Easter. In New York, each family on welfare was supposed to be allocated a certain amount of money for clothing, though this rarely occurred. Based on that past experience, Pastreich took a delegation to the Syracuse welfare office and demanded money for clothes, and the flustered workers cut a check on the spot. When news of the victory spread, other groups converged on the welfare office. "It was a classic protest—three hundred people raising hell," recalled Pastreich.[20]

Ross hadn't been told of the protest and was outraged when he learned that several organizers were at the forefront, chanting and yelling and leading the action. One of the organizers, Bruce Thomas, had been a leader with Syracuse CORE and traveled to Mississippi during the summer of 1964. "He was much more a leader than organizer," said Pastreich, who would later work with Thomas in the welfare rights movement. "He was tough, he had been in jail, he could sing: he was the movement dream guy."[21] But for Ross, Thomas was too eager to strike a dramatic pose in the limelight, which was exactly where Ross thought an organizer didn't belong.

A second major conflict in the CATC project was over Ross's emphasis on discipline. Part of the problem was that some people simply weren't prepared to work as hard as Ross wanted them to. Others felt that the joy and spontaneity they had experienced in the civil rights movement—with its singing and dramatic direct action—had been replaced by an ascetic older man who seemed to approach organizing with the cold rigor of a schoolmaster. It was one thing to get swept up in the movement, quite another to spend night after night holding house meetings, repeating the same pitch. Still others felt constrained by Ross's insistence that they focus, laser-like, only on local issues and not talk to leaders about issues like the Vietnam War. For young radicals like Schechter, it was simply impossible to ignore the context of the times. "He had an ordered methodology in a very disordered period," recalled Schechter. "A bunch of people were emotional and upset about what was going on—the Vietnam War, the assassination of Malcolm X—and so it's not surprising that some of us went off the reservation."[22]

Ross thought that focusing on larger issues like the Vietnam War would sap organizational energy (and, no doubt, lead to more scrutiny from the government). He was also skeptical of the New Left's organizing claims. He later described an encounter with Tom Hayden of Students for a Democratic Society (SDS), who came to Syracuse in 1965 to speak about his work in Newark. Originally based on college campuses, SDS had launched the Economic Research and Action Project (ERAP) in 1963, sending members to organize in neighborhoods around the country to help build an "interracial movement of the poor."[23] In Newark, Hayden formed the Newark Community Union Project, which would focus on issues of immediate concern to local residents. The group's official slogan was "Let the People Decide," with organizers dedicated to the notion that they would provide "no direction," lest they be guilty of manipulating poor people.[24] Ross was unimpressed:

> He talked and he talked, and he talked. It seems like they had an old house over there [in Newark].... I said, "Well, what kind of organization is it? What do you do at the meetings?" "Well," he said, "it's just sort of a continuous meeting, and we had a big room, and people come and go, and every once-in-a-while the spirit would move somebody, and he or she gets up there and talks about a problem, and if it seems like it's important, well, we try to get some kind of consensus." ... So I said, "Well, how many problems have you worked on." [And he said] "Well, we haven't worked on any yet, but we're getting there."[25]

This was likely an unfair description of what transpired, but it does shed light on how Ross viewed much of the New Left. For Ross, organizing was a craft—a craft he had honed over decades and that he considered the most important vocation in the world. Hanging around a house in a ghetto, where you talked politics and held long meetings, might have been participatory and exciting, but it wasn't organizing people for action. (In fact, according to one participant, those involved with ERAP would quickly develop "a deeper sense of the extreme slowness" of community organizing, with most of the projects never getting off the ground.)[26] Even worse, from Ross's perspective, was that the same people not willing to do the work somehow expected to be in the middle of dramatic fights that resulted in victory. As Alinsky told *Harper's* in an interview that summer, echoing Ross's thoughts, "The problem with those kids is that they always want the third act—the resolution, the big drama. They want to skip the first act, the second act, the tediousness, the listening. Actually, you do more organizing with your ears than with your tongue."[27]

That was how Alinsky and Ross felt, at least. Students like Schechter had a different take: while the world was imploding around them, they were spending too much time trying to get the City of Syracuse to put up a new stop sign or paint some apartments. Those efforts were all fine and good, but the severity of the larger crises affecting the country demanded a more militant and unified front, where poor people could band together and act on concerns beyond their immediate neighborhoods. Students also questioned how Ross put their energies to use; as one faculty observer of the CATC project reported, "Ross's insistence on matters such as constitutional construction and Robert's Rules of Order bored them."[28]

Civil rights workers were risking their lives in the South. The Free Speech Movement had won a resounding victory in Berkeley. Neighborhoods like Watts in Los Angeles were going up in flames. This was not the time to create another bureaucratic organization or try to elect the same weak-kneed Democrats who were waging war on Vietnam. It was time to demand more. It was time to disrupt. Years later, Frances Fox Piven and Richard Cloward's influential and challenging book, *Poor People's Movements,* put forth a critique that students like Schechter likely would have embraced. The authors' central thesis is that, in times of social unrest, organizers too often focus on trying to channel that energy into the creation of formal organizations instead of escalating the conflict:

> During those brief periods in which people are roused to indignation, when they are prepared to defy the authorities to whom they ordinarily defer, during those brief moments when lower-class groups exert some force against the state, those who call themselves leaders do not usually escalate the momentum of the people's protests. They do not because they are preoccupied with trying to build and sustain embryonic formal organizations in the

sure conviction that these organizations will enlarge and become powerful. Thus the studies that follow show that, all too often, when workers erupted into strikes, organizers collected dues cards; when tenants refuse to pay rent and stood off marshals, organizers formed building committees; when people were burning and looting, organizers used this "moment of madness" to draft constitutions.[29]

In retrospect, it's clear that Syracuse in 1965 was not one such moment. The organizing efforts of the students had allowed them to connect with people who were certainly unhappy and proved eager to fight back, but this was not revolution. And Ross was certainly not someone comfortable with the sort of chaotic, sometimes violent protest described by Piven and Cloward. For Ross, the purpose of the organizer was to build stable organizations that could advocate for change, typically in an orderly and respectable fashion. He did not share the New Left's alienation, nor their sense that something was "sick" in the country. If he "fought the system," he did so by encouraging people to make demands on that system, not by burning it down. Having organized during the height of the Red Scare, Ross was constantly alert as to how actions might appear to ordinary people, and he had little patience for what he considered New Left theatrics. Thirty years had passed since he had been a wide-eyed college student, and he was unable to see the world through their eyes, if only to better reach them.

The conflicts between Ross and some of the students burst into public view that fall, when Schechter and two other organizers traveled to Newark for an SDS conference, bringing along several leaders from Syracuse. The trip to Newark happened to be on the same weekend as an organizing meeting in Syracuse. For Ross, the Newark trip was a complete betrayal. He moved quickly, assigning the three organizers to an additional level of supervision, which they immediately protested by going on strike. Ross dropped them from the program, with Haggstrom issuing termination notices. Ross had been concerned that the trip to Newark would be diversionary, but Schechter reported that the effect was the opposite: the leaders, having connected with people in Newark facing similar challenges, returned energized. (Indeed, seven community leaders signed a letter protesting the firings.) But from Ross's perspective, the organizers had failed to follow his instructions and had to go. In response, the fired students organized a picket line in front of the CATC office, filled with "neighborhood people" who were "singing freedom song and carrying signs protesting dictatorship and imploring the administrators within to 'Practice What You Preach—Democracy.'"[30]

That was how Schechter would describe the scene in the fall 1965 issue of *Studies on the Left*. His article was titled "Reveille for Reformers" and took broad swipes at Alinsky (and Ross) for adhering to rigid organizing structures and refusing to adapt to the changing times. "The younger organizers resent a paternalistic and dogmatic approach," Schechter wrote. "They are anxious to help people draw connections between their minor concerns and broader issues. They are interested in building consciousness as a part of building organization. The Alinsky approach, stressing narrow self-interest, tends to limit any broad vision." Schechter concluded that much of the CATC project was a farce. "For all its talk of 'building power,' of change through conflict, the Syracuse experiment is basically an effort to provide therapeutic experiences to 'deprived people,' to give them a sense of motion which might satisfy some immediate psychic needs but will do very little, given the structural nature of poverty, to change their lives."[31]

The article was clearly written in anger, penned in the immediate aftermath of Schechter's firing, and while he would remain hurt by his dismissal, his position had softened by the time he wrote a follow up several months later. Though he was still critical of the project's lack of ideology and vision, he wrote that radical organizers had much to learn from Alinsky and Ross, who had put together "impressive organizations through hard and clever work" and whose skills "can be very useful to serious organizers."[32] (Schechter would eventually come to consider Ross an "underappreciated force" and would host Ross on his popular Boston radio show in 1977 to promote a United Farm Workers campaign.)

As internal dissension grew, the political forces aiming to shut down the Syracuse project—and other Community Action programs across the nation—gathered momentum. This was, it should be noted, a bipartisan affair: no mayors wanted independent groups of poor people organized in their city. Chicago mayor Richard Daley was the most powerful critic. At one point he called Bill Moyers, then the White House press secretary, and launched into a tirade. "What in the hell are you people doing? Does the president know he's putting M-O-N-E-Y in the hands of subversives?"[33] A group of big-city mayors, led by San Francisco's John Shelley and Los Angeles's Sam Yorty—both Democrats—accused Community Action of "fostering class struggle," with Walsh chiming in that the poor in Syracuse were "being urged to storm City Hall."[34]

The public face of Community Action was Sargent Shriver, who directed the Office of Economic Opportunity. Shriver was a tireless visionary, responsible for the creation of the Peace Corps, Head Start, VISTA, and Legal Services for the Poor. As the head of Johnson's War on Poverty, he initially struck a confident tone in the face of the backlash. "We have planned a community action program, emphasizing action," he told a US House panel in April 1965. "When we see disputes at the local levels, we think we are getting what Congress intended."[35] But Johnson, whose sensitive political antennae had caused him to be leery of the program from the beginning, was starting to feel the heat.

In September 1965, Ross traveled to Washington, DC, to meet with Sanford Kravitz, who managed Community Action and reported to Shriver. Ross returned to Syracuse and informed his colleagues that Kravitz was "impressed with the controversial nature of our program."[36] But that controversial nature would, in the end, prove to be the CATC's downfall. In October, at a sit-in at the welfare department to demand back-to-school clothes, eleven people were arrested, including two CATC organizers. Much was made of the fact that the $293 used to bail out the arrestees originated from the federal government. Mayor Walsh once again called for President Johnson to defund the project and even used the opportunity to link the CATC to a skyrocketing teenage crime rate, a preposterous claim that was nonetheless broadcast in all seriousness across the front page of the local newspaper.

By now, Ross wanted out, and he privately announced his plans to resign. Soon after, the OEO announced that any Syracuse groups seeking Community Action grants would have to apply for funds through the Crusade for Opportunity. This was precisely what Mayor Walsh had publicly demanded, and it represented a complete retreat from the original purpose of Community Action. In response, the neighborhood groups in Syracuse formed a People's War Council against Poverty, with a delegation of twenty people traveling through the night to confront Shriver at his Washington, DC, office in what was described as a "verbally explosive" meeting.[37] A smaller group flew out to Texas, where they pitched a tent near President Johnson's ranch and were promptly arrested. Ross had no hope that the government would ever fund real organizing and played little role in the campaign to try and pressure the OEO to reverse its decision. On January 28, 1966, the *Syracuse Post-Standard* announced on its front page that Ross had resigned his position as field director and would be returning to California.

Ross never wrote about Syracuse. He felt that the entire episode had been a debacle. The few times he spoke publicly about the period, he did so disparagingly. "They [the students] wanted to tell me how to organize. It was awful," he told a reporter in 1976.[38] In another interview, he said that he considered the students to have been civil rights organizers "who wanted to demonstrate all the time" and that if they wanted such training, they should "get it from Martin Luther King's people."[39]

This sweeping characterization was unfair: along with mass demonstrations, the civil rights movement had a deep tradition of grassroots organizing and local leadership development. Ross himself had witnessed this type of work up close. In the spring of 1965, he had traveled briefly to Mississippi to survey voter registration activity and speak to civil rights organizers, a trip that had been arranged by George Wiley, a onetime chemistry professor at Syracuse who had left academia to become a national leader with CORE. (Wiley later founded the National Welfare Rights Organization.) In the South, the Deacons for Defense and Justice, an armed group of African Americans, escorted Ross, and when he returned he told Fred Jr. that he was deeply impressed with the bravery of the civil rights workers.[40]

One of the visitors who traveled north to speak to Syracuse students during the CATC project was Bob Moses of SNCC, an exemplar of the civil rights organizing tradition. Moses had spearheaded Mississippi's Freedom Summer and placed a strong emphasis on voter registration. When he spoke in Syracuse about his experiences in Mississippi, Moses was characteristically modest. "I guess the essence of what I learned in that first, say, four- or five-month period was that it was possible to stay in a community and do some kind of work," he told the students. "It's possible to get people to come to meetings. It's possible to get a few young people to work with you."[41]

Moses had been deeply influenced by Ella Baker, the brilliant organizer and civil rights leader. Baker shared Ross's distrust of flashy mobilizations and spent her life encouraging strategies that put more emphasis on the development of local leaders. But there were also significant differences between Ross and organizers like Moses and Baker. Moses was afraid that too much organizational discipline could lead, in the words of one scholar, to "suffocating the spirit."[42] Baker also argued for a flexible approach and felt, according to her biographer, that it was important that youth activists be given the freedom and autonomy to "make their own mistakes."[43] Her vision had room for many strategies; as one close associate recalled, Baker emphasized that there "are many legitimate and effective avenues for social change and there is no single way."[44] Ross did not share this view. He saw disciplined organizing—and, in particular, *his* method of disciplined organizing—as the best way to achieve social change.

In Syracuse, this discipline had broken down. In correspondence with an editor at the publisher Random House, Ross characterized the project as a "poverty fiasco." After the relative freedom with which he had been able to operate in California, he had suddenly found himself squeezed from all sides. Student radicals thought he was reformist. The mayor called him and the CATC Marxists. The press was overwhelmingly hostile. The OEO monitored developments closely, even sending an investigator to check in on the program.

Ross was accustomed to having only one person looking over his shoulder: Alinsky. He was also used to operating on a shoestring budget. At Syracuse, for the first time, he was making serious money: $19,000 for the year, the equivalent of $143,000 in 2015. Another perk of the position was free tuition for Fred Jr., who had enrolled in Syracuse University as a freshman in the fall of 1965. But Ross cared little about money. In the end, Syracuse became an example of how much money the government could waste while pretending to help and empower the poor. As he wrote to Chavez, who had asked Ross for advice on how much to charge for a "consultation fee" on a project:

> My advice to you is to be sure and include a whopping figure in the budget. . . .
> There should be no problem about this, since I'm confident he [the client] is
> fully aware that every "advisor of the poor" who is worth his salt has a solid
> battery of participant observers, analysts, field interviewers, and such other
> out and out con-men and fee-fakers as the poverty-traffic will bear in his
> entourage. Have you heard Alinsky's description of the poverty program? A
> guy is taking a leak. The first full flow is all the dough that goes to us consult-
> ants, specialists, social workers, etc. And you know that last little drop that
> you always shake off (or ought to)? Well that's what goes to the poor.[45]

Yet the nine-month Syracuse experiment wasn't a total failure. More than one thousand children received money for clothes from the local welfare agency, public housing units were fixed up and additional security officers hired, playgrounds were built, and a supermarket was forced to hire African American employees. The CATC project was defunded and became a national news story—with widespread coverage in *New York Times* and Associated Press stories—precisely because it was, to some extent, doing what it was designed to do: encourage poor people to become leaders and more fully participate in the democratic process.

But those accomplishments were little solace to Ross. He had ignored his instincts, walking into a project that he hadn't wanted to do in the first place, and he paid the price. As he saw it, he was returning to California—where the once mighty CSO had largely dissolved—having little to show for his year and a half in Syracuse and without any work prospects. He felt, he wrote, like "a thing of no use, no worth. . . . In a word: nothing."[46]

FOURTEEN

David vs. Goliath

WHILE ROSS HAD LITTLE TO show for his time out east, the same certainly couldn't be said for Cesar Chavez during the same period, whose fledgling farmworker association was quickly gathering momentum as it confronted the juggernaut of big agriculture. From the beginning, he emphasized that his new organization was not a union—though a union was, of course, what he had in mind. He feared that workers would associate a union with strikes, and strikes with failure. When he began taking membership cards into the fields of Delano, the possibility of a strike was the first question on people's minds. "Everyone but everyone wants to know if this means 'strike' and I have been saying—no strikes, unless we know we'll win," he wrote to Ross in the spring of 1962.[1] Like Ross, Chavez was a student of agricultural history, and he knew that the history of the fields was replete with strikes that were easily crushed by growers and law enforcement. Instead of sparking a flash that could quickly be extinguished, Chavez had spent the last three years organizing in the Ross tradition, holding small house meetings where he won workers to his cause. A big strike was a possibility, of course, but somewhere down the road, once the association had built more power. This was a historic project, and Chavez was going to take his time.

That was the original plan. Grape workers, impatient for a raise, had other ideas. On September 8, 1965, roughly a thousand Filipinos refused to go into the fields of Delano. Earlier in the grape season, the workers, members of the Agricultural Workers Organizing Committee, an AFL-CIO affiliate, had struck in the Coachella Valley, resulting in a pay hike. Now the workers expected the same rate when the harvest shifted to Delano—$1.40 an hour, plus 25 cents a box. News of the strike quickly spread through the town, posing a dilemma for Chavez: he didn't feel his organization was ready to strike, but he couldn't very well let his members serve as strikebreakers, which would drive a deeper wedge between Filipino and Mexican farmworkers. On September 16, Mexican Independence Day, he stood in front of hundreds of farmworkers gathered inside a church, where they pledged to join their Filipino brothers and sisters. Chants of "¡Viva la huelga!"—long live the strike!—bounced off the walls.[2]

The strike soon turned into a boycott, and the boycott into something that felt like the stirrings of a movement. Chavez solicited outside support, offering "a floor to sleep on and three meals a day," and a stream of young Bay Area radicals, some fresh from the victory of the Free Speech Movement in Berkeley, descended on the sleepy farmworker town.[3] Others fanned out to cities across the country, urging people to boycott Schenley, a high-profile liquor brand that owned a local vineyard. Walter Reuther of the United Auto Workers visited and pledged his support, along with five thousand dollars a month in strike funds. Senator Robert F. Kennedy arrived in Delano to participate in a hearing on migratory labor, drawing cheers after he advised an overzealous sheriff, who admitted to arresting people whom he believed "might" break the law, to spend his lunch hour brushing up on the Constitution. When the hearing concluded, farmworkers began a three-hundred-mile march to Sacramento, timed to arrive in the state capital on Easter Sunday 1966 and put pressure on Governor Pat Brown to mediate an agreement between Schenley and the farmworkers. Carrying signs that read "Peregrinación, Penitencia, Revolución"—Pilgrimage, Penance, Revolution—the group passed through rural communities along the way, led by a man hoisting a cloth banner of the Virgin of Guadalupe.

Ross followed the news of the march closely from Corte Madera, feeling bittersweet. In his absence, the man he had mentored was leading a movement of farmworkers—Chavez's great dream realized—while Ross sat on the sidelines, seemingly unneeded. As the pilgrimage wound its way north, Ross filled his hours listening to classical music and moping around the house.

It was Frances who finally insisted they join the march as it arrived in Sacramento. Relations between husband and wife had reached a low point in Syracuse, and it was a mark of progress that they were again living together. Frances had traveled to Syracuse four months after Ross arrived and initially found the city "very attractive."[4] But the trip proved to be a disaster. If Ross had promised to carve out space for her, the demands of the Community Action Training Center project, especially as it generated controversy, soon consumed his time. Frances's isolation was compounded by the weather. The winter of 1965 was one of the harshest on record in Syracuse, with a massive blizzard and temperatures dipping to twenty-six degrees below zero. Frances suffered from two common postpolio symptoms—weakened muscles and an increased sensitivity to cold—and spent much of her time trapped inside, unable to navigate the icy streets or tolerate the frigid weather. She cut the trip short, returned to Corte Madera, and evidently contemplated divorce. Saul Alinsky wrote to her in May, regarding Ross, urging that "nothing of any final nature be done by correspondence."[5]

When Ross returned to Corte Madera, he tried to patch things up, but his efforts didn't go well at first. "My mom wouldn't speak to him," recalled Julia, who was living with her mother after dropping out of college. Ross stayed elsewhere—probably a friend's house—knowing he wasn't welcome, but one day he stopped by to chat with Julia on the front porch. "That's the only time I have ever seen him emotional, and irrational," she said. "He told me he was traumatized. He really was falling apart. I told him I thought he needed some counseling help. But mostly I counseled him. I said, 'Dad, what did you expect?'"[6]

Ross had weathered personal crises before, but Frances's rejection came at a time when his organizing work was also stalled, and it was likely this combination that made the rejection sting. He was a failure as a husband, father, *and* organizer. After several weeks, however, Frances softened and allowed him back home. Ross knew that she had developed a "phobia" of his organizing work, since it meant he was never home.[7] So it was a mark of Frances's dedication to her husband that, seeing him depressed, she convinced him to attend the tail end of the farmworker march to Sacramento.

On the day before Easter, she dragged him to Our Lady of Grace School in West Sacramento, where a crowd of two thousand people filed into the hall. Chavez surprised Ross with a hug from behind. He looked exhausted, Ross noted, with "deep, purple smudges" under his eyes, but their reunion was nonetheless joyous.[8] Chavez had good reason to be tired. He had been walking for weeks, his feet so blistered that at times he was forced to hobble along with a cane. But he also had good reason to be in high spirits. During the march, he had received a call from a lawyer representing Schenley, who said the company was ready to negotiate. At first Chavez thought it was a prank; when it became clear that the offer was genuine, he dashed off to Los Angeles and returned with a commitment from Schenley to negotiate a contract. Four years after its formation, what was now called the National Farm Workers Association (NFWA) was on its way to becoming a union.

FIGURE 14. Ross and Chavez during the DiGiorgio campaign, 1966.
Courtesy of Jon Lewis/farmworkermovement.us.

Chavez ushered Ross up to the stage at the school and recounted how Ross had recruited him on that fateful evening in East San Jose. Ross looked out at the energetic crowd, filled with idealist teenagers and veteran farmworkers, all waving the dramatic flag of the union: bright red, with a black eagle at its center. Fifty-five years old, fresh off what felt like a defeat at Syracuse, Ross hadn't been sure where to put his energy. Now he knew. "I had been bound for this union," he later wrote, "ever since Cesar had started it."[9]

There was little time to celebrate the Schenley victory. On Easter Sunday, the march to the capital surged to ten thousand supporters of what was being called, simply, *la causa*—the cause. Now that Schenley had capitulated, Chavez, described by the *New York Times* as a "calm little 38-year-old," told supporters that it was time to shift their boycott to DiGiorgio, the largest grower in California.[10]

After the march, Ross joined Chavez for a meeting held near Fresno to discuss the union's next steps. Technically, Ross was there as a consultant, researching the union's death-benefit plan for a migrant organization in Arizona. But the assignment was just an excuse to rejoin Chavez, and he quickly put it aside, participating in the strategy session and agreeing to train organizers for the DiGiorgio campaign. Having finally made some progress in repairing his relationship with Frances, he would now spend most of the year far from home.

DiGiorgio was proving a canny opponent. When the Schenley agreement was made public in the spring of 1966, DiGiorgio announced that it, too, would welcome a union, provided that it came by means of a secret-ballot vote between different unions. To the general public, such an election might sound like a fair and democratic solution. But because farmworkers had been excluded from the National Labor Relations Act of 1935—which established ground rules for union elections and punished employers for breaking them—there was little reason to trust the company's offer. Already, DiGiorgio was stating that one of the unions on the ballot would be the Kern-Tulare Independent Farm Workers, a "union" that was actually led by labor contractors and growers. DiGiorgio was just as hostile to unions as it had been back when Ross was at Arvin, though the company had transformed in other ways. Its founder, Joseph DiGiorgio, spoke broken English and built his empire from scratch. Now his nephew Robert was in charge, and Robert had business in his blood, not farming. A graduate of Yale, he lived not in farm country but in San Francisco, where he served on the board of the Bank of America. Robert moved to diversify the company, turning it into a major producer of canned fruits and juices, and it was these DiGiorgio brands, with names like TreeSweet and S&W Fine Foods, that made it such an appealing target for a boycott.

Ross was impressed with the leadership team Chavez had attracted. Along with Community Service Organization stalwarts like Dolores Huerta and Gilbert Padilla, the Migrant Ministry under Chris Hartmire had essentially become an arm of the union. Hartmire assigned the Reverend Jim Drake to Chavez, and Drake soon developed a reputation for being an "important invisible person," making major contributions—it was Drake who proposed a grape boycott—while remaining, like Ross, in the background.

Another deep thinker who landed at the union was a chubby mustachioed man named Marshall Ganz. Ganz had grown up in Bakersfield and dropped out of Harvard to travel to Mississippi during Freedom Summer in 1964, rooming with Mario Savio, who would launch the Berkeley Free Speech Movement soon after. Ganz was the son of a rabbi and finely attuned to notions of justice and equality, though he had never given a second thought to the plight of California farmworkers. When he returned to Bakersfield, just after the strike was launched, he found that he saw his hometown anew, with what he called "Mississippi eyes."[11] When he first met Chavez, the farmworker leader was reading *The Gathering Storm* by Winston Churchill. Chavez told Ganz that he was studying Gandhi and to understand Gandhi, he needed to understand Gandhi's chief opponent. Like many who would find their way into the movement, Ganz was immediately drawn to Chavez, seeing him as both a quietly inspiring figure and a strategic genius.

Chavez knew that DiGiorgio represented the greatest test the union had faced, and he put Ross in charge of the campaign. Early negotiations with the company to establish election rules didn't go well. During the first meeting, Chavez received a phone call and learned that a DiGiorgio guard had pointed a gun at picketers. In a brave if reckless move, one of those picketers, twenty-six-year-old Ida Cousino, had walked up to the guard and announced that she was making a citizen's arrest. A DiGiorgio supervisor knocked Cousino to the ground and a melee broke out, with one picketer receiving thirteen stitches. Chavez hung up the phone and broke off the negotiations. He and Ross traveled back to Delano, where Ross watched as Chavez castigated the picketers for participating in the brawl. When the farmworkers pled their case, arguing that they had to protect "the honor of women," Chavez grew frustrated. "You don't become any less a man by refusing to strike back," he said. "Being able to take it and hold our anger in, we gain our manhood." The workers finally agreed that they had made a mistake, while Cousino sat silent, staring at the ground. "I wanted to go over and comfort her," Ross wrote, "but the moment the meeting was over, she was gone."[12] Ross's writings rarely exhibit such touches of personal tenderness, but it is clear that Cousino, whom he described as having "deep, dark eyes," had caught his attention.

A major challenge for Ross and his team of about thirty organizers—made up of farmworkers and a handful of Anglo volunteers—was simply reaching the workers. DiGiorgio won a court injunction that barred picketers from public roads, where they could at least shout messages with bullhorns, and began bussing in employees from a remote labor camp so that organizers couldn't meet them in town. For its part, the union sent "submarines," or covert organizers, into DiGiorgio's crews to build support, and two supervisors peeled off into the Chavez camp. Then two farmworker leaders, Amelia Cadena and Antonia Saludado, came to Chavez with an ingenious tactic. The judge had said farmworkers couldn't picket DiGiorgio—but was there any reason they couldn't hold a vigil? Richard Chavez worked through the night to convert the back of his brother Cesar's old Mercury station wagon into a shrine to Our Lady of Guadalupe, which they parked at the entrance to the DiGiorgio ranch. Soon, hundreds of workers were gathering there for prayers each day.

Despite such strokes of creative genius, the union faced a difficult task. Without an agreement for ground rules—and negotiations with the company were making little progress—DiGiorgio was free to fire entire crews of union supporters. Then the Teamsters showed up. DiGiorgio brought the Teamsters Union in as a "responsible" alternative, and Teamsters cards, handed out by foremen, flooded the fields. On June 22, DiGiorgio suddenly announced that it would hold an election in three days and that it would bar striking workers from participating. These were clearly unacceptable terms, and the NFWA scrambled to mount a counterattack. Huerta and William Kircher, organizing director of the AFL-CIO, flew to San Francisco and interrupted what Joseph DiGiorgio had hoped would be a triumphant press conference. In Delano, the NFWA campaign to win over workers turned into a boycott operation, with organizers instructing farmworkers to refuse to participate in the union election. On election day, Ross stood outside the polling station and watched as the first truck of workers pulled up. Half remained seated, refusing to vote. Another truck drove up and parked, with someone inside hoisting up the NFWA flag. It drove away without a single worker exiting. By the end of the day, nearly half of the eligible workers had not voted, with the Teamsters receiving the votes of the vast majority of those who did.

Everyone claimed victory: the Teamsters because they had received the most votes, the NFWA because so many workers had chosen not to participate. The NFWA again pressed Governor Pat Brown to intervene, as the union had asked with the Schenley strike. The governor had not been on hand to welcome the marchers to Sacramento—instead, he had spent the day at Frank Sinatra's vacation home in Palm Springs—and many saw his absence as a slap in the face of farmworkers. One such group was the Mexican American Political Association, which announced that it would only endorse

Brown if he investigated the DiGiorgio election. This was a real threat: Brown had faced a serious primary challenge from Los Angeles mayor Sam Yorty and now confronted an even stronger opponent, Ronald Reagan, in the general election. Brown bowed to the pressure and called for an inquiry led by Ronald Haughton, a respected arbitrator. After two weeks of interviews, Haughton declared the election invalid and recommended a new election set for August 30, 1966. Under his proposal, the new election would include all workers who had been on the payroll when the strike was launched and would allow organizers equal access to the workers. Boycott activity must cease. The NFWA members voted to accept the terms. All attention shifted to the election.

From the beginning of the strike, the growers' line had remained the same: farmworkers were satisfied with the way things were. Given the option of joining a union, the farmworkers would reject Chavez and his band of young radicals and outsiders. The DiGiorgio election represented the first chance for workers to officially express their preference, publicly and in a process that all sides agreed was fair. The importance of the election from a public relations perspective, therefore, was hard to overstate: nearly a year into the strike, workers would validate one side or another. This fact wasn't lost on Chavez. "I knew that if we lost this one, we would lose the union, because the public wouldn't have supported us after that," he later said. "We hadn't established credibility with the public."[13]

Ross's first task was to establish order and discipline in an environment that was bubbling over with enthusiastic but unfocused energy. His team met three to four times a day in the Pink House, a small bungalow on Delano's west side that had become the union's headquarters. They jostled for space in the living room, interrupted by a steady procession of farmworkers, journalists, religious leaders, and film producers, who stepped over arms and legs on the way to a rear bedroom that served as an office for Chavez. For Ross, the interruptions at times felt "very close to maddening," especially as the summertime temperatures soared. "But what can you do," he acknowledged, "when there is only one way in and out, and you are clogging it?"[14]

Ross worked the group hard. The first meeting of the day was at eight o'clock in the morning; the last often wrapped up after midnight. If anyone had anticipated that organizing would be a laid-back affair, he or she quickly learned otherwise. Ross went around the circle, demanding detailed reports

FIGURE 15. Staff gathering at the Pink House during the DiGiorgio campaign, 1966. Ida Cousino is seated second from left, wearing a bandana. Courtesy of Jon Lewis/farmworkermovement.us.

from each organizer, his clear voice cutting through the buzz of the room. Whom had they met with? What did the worker say? What did *they* say in response to the worker? Why did they say that? What might they say next time? Along with his unrelenting attention to detail, Ross stressed the need to be honest. If a meeting hadn't gone well, he told the team, don't pretend it was a success. Share the difficulty, and the group would try to find a solution together. Organizers soon learned that Ross was expert at sniffing out tall tales. "When some of them began to sound too optimistic, I had them give examples, tell exactly what the workers said," he wrote. "Often this showed it up as something less than a complete success story."[15]

The list of eligible workers ran to fifty pages. Repeating the strategy employed during Edward Roybal's city council campaign in Los Angeles, Ross created a 3x5 index card for each worker. Organizers were given new cards each morning, which they returned at the end of the day with additional scrawled notes. With these notes and the lengthy debriefs, Ross assigned a category to each worker: anti-union, neutral, pro-union, or unknown. Many of the anti-union workers were clearly out of reach. "I will not join your Communist outlaw bunch," wrote one angry DiGiorgio employee, blaming the conflict on "you foreigners and agitators with your ungodliness."[16] Ross told the team to focus on converting the neutral workers, as well as on those whose views they didn't yet know.

Ross's team, mostly farmworkers, was highly motivated but untested. Ross turned the campaign into a boot camp of sorts: many of the graduates went on to become among the union's most skilled organizers. They fine-tuned their raps and role-played interactions, searching for messages that best resonated with workers. During the lunch hour, they traveled to DiGiorgio's forty-five-hundred-acre Sierra Vista Ranch, where workers lived in one of six segregated camps. Much of the lunchtime action occurred at the "bullring," a grassy area next to the packing shed that offered the shade of a large walnut tree. Ross issued strict instructions to focus on winning over workers and avoid getting sucked into shouting matches with the Teamsters. Sometimes his message was heeded, sometimes not. More than a few organizers returned to the afternoon debrief red-faced and hoarse.

The election rules stipulated that organizers could also visit workers during the evening, and it was in these meetings—held away from the screaming Teamsters—that the most critical work took place. Here was where organizers like Eliseo Medina first shined. Medina, a baby-faced twenty-year-old who looked like he still belonged in high school, was ten when his family moved from Mexico to Delano. He spoke no English and spent his summers in the vineyards. But he quickly caught up with and then surpassed his peers in school; he left after the eighth grade, when told that Mexicans ought to stick to vocational classes. When the strike began in 1965, Medina had broken open his piggy bank to pay his dues. In 1966, he had visited Huerta hoping to land a union job with Schenley. Instead, she told him to stop by the Pink House to help with DiGiorgio. By the time Medina arrived, Ross was alone in the house, having already sent the team out for their visits. He initially told Medina to return the next morning, but the young man was so eager to get started that Ross gave him the address of a labor camp in Wasco, twenty miles south of Delano. When Medina returned for the evening debrief, his list of supportive workers led the pack. Medina was clearly a natural organizer, and Ross soon learned that he matched this talent with an uncommon work ethic.

"I was thirsty for knowledge," Medina recalled. "I just couldn't get enough. I'd come in early, get more cards, and head back out."[17] He watched closely as Ross queried each organizer during debriefs—asking for more information, searching for weaknesses in the story, using individual examples to reveal lessons to the group. Like many, Medina was impressed by Ross's emphasis on discipline and his high expectations for rookie organizers. But this insistence on accountability was combined with the freewheeling feel of the meetings, in which people bounced ideas off each other as they searched for solutions together. Like everyone on the team, Medina put in impossible hours, but his enthusiasm for organizing only grew—even after a Teamsters organizer slugged him in the face. "I was just blown away by the atmosphere of the movement, and what I was learning." He would later join the union's executive board and, after leaving the United Farm Workers, would become a major force in both the labor and immigrants rights movements.

Another dedicated organizer was Ida Cousino, the picketer who had attempted to make a citizen's arrest of the armed DiGiorgio security guard. Together, Ross and Cousino studied maps, reviewed index cards, and visited the fields to talk to workers. At some point they also became a couple. They tried to hide the relationship, but Delano was a small town, and there was little room for secrets or privacy in the charged environment of the campaign. Cousino and Ross had met at the rally held in West Sacramento during the march to the capital, and the attraction seems to have been immediate and strong. While Cousino knew that some of the other volunteers didn't like Ross, thinking he was "too bossy" and square, she found him to be an inspiring figure. "I could see what he was doing and had a lot of respect for him," she said. "Strategically, he was one of the brightest people I've met—and he really cared for these people."[18] During their rare moments alone, Cousino would read through Ross's manuscript of his CSO days, which he lugged around in the trunk of his car, or listen as he regaled her with past organizing exploits. Though he was more than twice Cousino's age, he was still fit, attractive, and showed no signs of slowing down.

It's harder to know Ross's thoughts on the relationship, because while he dropped hints in his writing—uncharacteristically pausing to describe Cousino's eyes or noting that he felt the need to comfort her—he never acknowledges that the relationship was anything but professional. Not that it's difficult to imagine why Ross might have been drawn to Cousino, a striking younger woman who was deeply committed to organizing farmworkers. But the brief affair was certainly out of character for a man who always seemed in control of his emotions and who apparently never had relationships with other women during his many years on the road. Ross told Cousino that he and Frances had separated, but this is far from clear. More clear is that once Frances learned of the relationship, she began divorce proceedings against her husband, though he evidently convinced her to hold off.

Shortly after the DiGiorgio campaign concluded, Cousino was told to leave the union by Chavez, and Ross and Frances eventually patched up their marriage.

Several weeks into the DiGiorgio campaign, Ross felt they needed something new. Back at the Arvin labor camp, during the cotton pickers' strike, workers had looked forward to the *Tow Sack Tattler* each week, which featured calls to join the strike alongside humorous gossip and crude drawings by Woody Guthrie. For DiGiorgio, Ross came up with *El Mosquito Zumbador*—the Buzzing Mosquito—a daily bulletin with a cartoon mosquito in which DiGiorgio became the butt of every joke. New issues were mimeographed each morning, and organizers grabbed a stack before heading out to the vineyards. The mosquito was a symbol of the union: persistent, pesky, and impossible to kill, buzzing about the heads of the clumsy giant DiGiorgio and the corrupt Teamsters.

July saw the arrival of Alinsky, who had been subpoenaed by the California State Senate to participate in a "fact-finding" hearing in Delano. The fact the Senate hoped to find was that Chavez was a Communist, which it could do by linking Alinsky to Communism and Chavez to Alinsky. He arrived at the crowded high school auditorium in Delano and told the senators that while he was immensely proud of Chavez, he had nothing to do with the union, since he hadn't spoken to Chavez in years. Someone then asked Alinsky if he was a Communist. He replied, Ross thought, with the air of someone flicking off a flea: "I want to point out that I am not now, and never have had any connections with either the John Birch Society, the Ku Klux Klan, the Minute Men, the Communist Party, or the DiGiorgio Corporation."[19]

The room exploded into applause, but the truth was that Alinsky didn't hold out much hope for Chavez. Farmworkers were simply too hard to organize. "It's like fighting on a constantly disintegrating bed of sand," he told a journalist.[20] Huerta once accompanied Ross on a visit to ask Alinsky to financially support the union. She remembered Alinsky saying that he didn't want to contribute to a lost cause. Ross, who was fiercely loyal to Chavez, replied: "Well, you have before. You supported the Abraham Lincoln Brigade in the Spanish Civil War."[21] But no money from Alinsky was forthcoming, and it was hard to fault his pessimism. Chavez was attempting to make history, going up against not only a powerful company but a powerful union.

Each of the Teamsters' organizers earned at least twenty thousand dollars a year. Members of the team supervised by Ross, in contrast, earned the going rate for farmworker volunteers: five dollars a week, plus room and board. One week before the DiGiorgio election, the NFWA and Agricultural Workers Organizing Committee merged into the United Farm Workers Organizing Committee (UFWOC) under the auspices of the AFL-CIO. This decision upset some people close to Chavez, who felt that traditional unions were plodding and reactionary, but it brought in an additional ten thousand dollars a month.

Not that any of the money found its way to the volunteers. For virtually no money, Ross demanded total commitment, and it mattered little to Ross whether you were a young Anglo or a veteran Mexican farmworker. Nick Jones was a student radical from North Dakota who arrived with a bushy beard. Ross told that him that his scruffy looks were hurting the cause and demanded that he ditch the beard. Jones protested, but was clean-shaven two days later. Marcos Muñoz was a twenty-five-year-old farmworker who had bravely walked out of the fields and into the union, not knowing where the money for his next meal would come from. Ross never had a firm command of Spanish, and Muñoz spoke almost no English. But the farmworker was still able to get his message across to Ross: *All these meetings are pointless. And what did Ross know about farmworkers, anyway?* Ross explained to Muñoz that the meetings were not optional. And it was true: Ross wasn't a farmworker—he was an organizer, and if Muñoz wanted to organize, he needed to be at the meetings. Jones would later rise to direct national boycott operations, while Muñoz would run the successful boycott operation in Boston, where he insisted, to Ross's delight, that volunteers meet every day.

One month before the election, Ross finally received the complete list of eligible voters from DiGiorgio, along with their last known addresses. Thus far, the campaign had focused on finding workers in the Delano area, but the comprehensive list allowed Ross to begin a dragnet operation, sending organizers to search for workers across California, Texas, and even Mexico. The task seemed almost impossible: by definition, migrant farmworkers don't often stay in one place for long, and some workers' names could be maddeningly common. And who would bother driving hours just to lodge a vote for the union? But Ross's no-excuses ethos was contagious. Campaign staff tracked down more than 250 eligible workers; journalist Ronald Taylor of the

FIGURE 16. Reviewing the list of eligible workers for the DiGiorgio election, 1966. Dolores Huerta is far left, Ross center, and Chavez second from right. Courtesy of Jon Lewis/farmworkermovement.us.

Fresno Bee reported that one worker came from the state of Jalisco, traveling three thousand miles to vote.[22]

On election day, Ross spent his time rushing between the Pink House and the Sierra Vista Ranch, subsisting on coffee and cigarettes. He had slept little during the final week, and not at all the night before, powered in part by dextroamphetamine, a stimulant he and others were popping to ward off fatigue. He had taken care of every detail, or so he thought. Even when the AFL-CIO loaned the union a dozen organizers, Ross had considered their approach "too casual" and assigned his own staff to duplicate the work.[23] Still, he couldn't escape the sinking feeling that he had missed something critical. At one point he heard a report that a DiGiorgio supervisor was inside a roped-off area meant only for voting workers. Ross arrived and charged in, shouting at the supervisor for a few moments before realizing that he was an election official. His nerves were frayed.

When the voting was over, the box of ballots was driven to San Francisco to be counted. Back in Delano, before announcing the results, Chavez called Ross up to the stage and began by reading off the votes among the mostly white shed workers: UFWOC 43, Teamsters 94. But it was a different story in the fields, where 530 workers voted for the UFWOC and just 331 for the Teamsters. The room erupted with cheers, the crowd lifting Chavez on their shoulders and carrying him around the room. Many shouted with joy. Others were crying. For Ross, the victory was a perfect example of how an opponent's strength can turn into a liability. While the farmworker organizers had crisscrossed the Southwest in search of workers, the Teamsters sipped beer poolside, confident that they would prevail. "Well, they made the mistake that powerful groups usually make," Ross said. "They underestimated the strength of the opposition. [They] underestimated our willingness to work and to win."[24]

But that work had left Ross completely spent. The morning after the election, before the results had come in, he joined Jim Drake and Chavez at a Delano hotel to plan for the upcoming union election at DiGiorgio's ranch in Arvin. As Drake and Chavez talked strategy, Ross slipped out of the chair and lay down on the floor, falling into a deep sleep.

FIFTEEN

Don't Buy Grapes

ROSS WOULD SERVE AS THE farmworker union's organizing director from 1966 to 1968, a two-year period that he considered one of the high points of his career. It was a time of excitement and experimentation, where each victory led to an even greater challenge, with Ross zipping around the country to help organize strikes, boycotts, and voter registration campaigns. Approaching sixty years of age, he showed no signs of slowing down, playing the role of an energetic elder to a movement that quickly took over his life.

But first, rest. Given a few days off after the DiGiorgio election in Delano, Ross headed to the beach, catching up on sleep before returning to open a union office in the small town of Lamont. This was the base for another DiGiorgio campaign, focused on the company's operations in nearby Arvin. Ross and Marshall Ganz toured the area, stopping by the old migrant labor camp that Ross had managed during the Depression. The health clinic was no longer in operation and the manager's house, where Ross had once found Woody Guthrie asleep on the grass, was in ruins. It felt, Ross wrote, like he was visiting a "psychic cemetery," though there wasn't much time to reflect.[1] Hoping to continue momentum, the union sought to force DiGiorgio to hold another election for Arvin workers before the harvest ended that fall of 1966.

DiGiorgio, stung by the Delano defeat, was reluctant to grant the union another chance to extend its power. So Ross again turned to Governor Pat Brown, who had brokered the first election agreement. A delegation of workers traveled to Brown's house in Los Angeles, asking that he intervene. They were told that any problems they had should be directed to the company. A few days later, with the season nearly over, Brown's noncommittal response gave Ross an idea. Might the governor sign a letter, addressed to the DiGiorgio workers at Arvin, explaining that workers who desired an election ought to take the issue up with the company?

Brown was heading into the final weeks of a campaign against political newcomer Ronald Reagan and was difficult to track down. Fortunately, Ignacio Lopez, the onetime muckraking journalist whose friendship with Ross dated back to the 1940s, worked in the governor's Los Angeles office, and he was eventually able to persuade Brown to sign off. Read narrowly, the bilingual letter was relatively innocuous, simply telling workers to bring up workplace issues with their employer. But it also could be read as a call to action, addressed to individual farmworkers from the most powerful figure in the state. "After Brown signed them [the letters]," Ganz wrote, "organizers mailed them special delivery from post offices in Arvin, Lamont, and Bakersfield. Just after the letters arrived, organizers darted from home to home, inviting committee members to an emergency meeting to decide how to respond to the governor. After two hours of late-night deliberations, they decided to 'follow the governor's advice.' They would leave before dawn the next day, drive the 300 miles to DiGiorgio's headquarters in San Francisco, and insist that DiGiorgio agree to an election."[2]

In Syracuse, Ross hadn't been comfortable with the New Left's confrontational style, but it didn't take long for him to acclimate to the direct-action tactics of the union. Ross and the farmworkers arrived in San Francisco's staid financial district on October 18, 1966, to find it converted into a spectacle of protest and theater. Atop a flatbed truck, members of El Teatro Campesino—a street-theater troupe founded by Luis Valdez—performed skits, while hundreds of supporters walked picket lines in front of DiGiorgio's headquarters. Farmworkers took the elevator to the top floor and sat down on the floor of Robert DiGiorgio's office, refusing to leave until he promised elections. They were escorted out by the police and arrested. They returned, this time with local labor leaders, and were arrested again. Meanwhile, the crowds grew larger, and DiGiorgio finally agreed to hold an election in ten days. When the Teamsters Union agreed to step aside, the United Farm Workers Organizing Committee (UFWOC) easily won the second election of its young career.*

* The union changed its name four times over the years: first it was the Farm Workers Association, then the National Farm Workers Association, then the United Farm Workers Organizing Committee, and finally, the United Farm Workers. The UFWOC officially became the more familiar UFW in 1972. For simplicity, I refer to the union as the UFW from now on.

The Arvin campaign marked the first time that Ganz worked alongside Ross. Unlike many who flocked to Delano eager to help, Ganz had previous organizing experience under his belt, having spent the summer of 1964 in Mississippi with the Student Nonviolent Coordinating Committee. That summer had been transformative for Ganz, filled with "a lot of heart and a lot of presence." But he had never encountered anyone who approached organizing with the discipline and rigor of Ross. "I understood it [organizing] as a calling there," he recalled about Mississippi, "but we weren't very long on craft."[3]

Ganz would become one of the union's most skilled organizers, and he considered Ross an important mentor. But theirs was a rocky beginning. "I had no use for Fred," he recalled. "It was like, 'Who the hell is this guy telling us what to do?' We have to be here at this time, count all this bullshit. We were young guys who thought we knew what the hell was up." His insubordination got to the point that Cesar Chavez called him back to Delano and explained that if Ganz wanted to be an organizer, he would need to follow Ross's instructions. One of the lines Ross drilled into people's heads was "If you can't count it, it didn't happen." How many people came to the meeting? How many walked the picket line? Organizing could encompass many activities, but at bottom it depended on getting people in motion, which took a lot of work—and a system. Ganz came to see Ross, above all, as "an excellent craftsman," and he noticed a change at the union when Ross arrived. "When I came to work with the farmworkers," he said, "there was a whole shift after Cesar brought Fred in, to introduce us to the fact that, 'Hey, this isn't just like being cool and going around talking to people.' There is a real craft here. Numbers matter. You had to count things. You had to engage in ongoing learning. Strategy was not something you had, but something you did. That whole disciplined focus, learning-oriented approach was just extraordinarily important."[4]

And there was a lot to learn. In the late 1960s, the UFW was still a young organization with only a few victories and long odds against its success. Trying to do what had never been done before, and inspired by Chavez's creative and unorthodox thinking, organizers invented the rules as they went, searching for soft spots in the dragon that was big agriculture. And the softest and biggest spot of all was the boycott.

Ironically, the boycott, which would become the union's most powerful weapon, was a direct consequence of earlier efforts meant to keep farmworkers powerless. During the Depression, Congress passed the National Labor

Relations Act (NLRA), which granted workers the right to form unions and bargain collectively. It was a landmark achievement in the fight for labor rights, but in order to garner support from southern politicians, President Roosevelt was forced to exclude farmworkers and domestic workers—the two occupations most often held by African Americans—from NLRA protections. But since farmworkers didn't enjoy a formal right to unionize, they also weren't limited by the restrictions placed on the NLRA by the Taft-Hartley Act of 1947, which included a ban on secondary boycotts. Secondary boycotts—in which a union not only tells people not to buy a particular product but, for example, also says not to shop at stores that carry the product—was a tactic that most unions couldn't use but that the farmworkers exploited with enthusiasm.*

Ross had not been involved in the original boycott against Schenley, but he was quick to appreciate its power. Once the Arvin election concluded, he took a team to San Francisco to lead a boycott against the union's newest target, winemaker Pirelli-Minetti, focusing on liquor stores. Within months they had convinced 450 stores in the Bay Area to pull Pirelli-Minetti products; by the summer of 1967, the company signed an agreement with the UFW, while the Teamsters agreed to abandon efforts to organize farmworkers (a promise that would prove to be short-lived). That summer also saw the launch of the UFW's biggest boycott to date, against a company called Giumarra. Five years earlier, Chavez had left the Community Service Organization to settle in Delano with a crazy dream. Now the scrappy union was taking on the largest grower of table grapes in the country.

The Giumarra boycott intensified in January 1968, when Mexican and Filipino farmworkers, along with a handful of Anglo volunteers, boarded a donated bus in Delano to begin a cross-country trip to New York City. Shivering in the unheated vehicle, they wrapped themselves in sleeping bags

---

* The solution to one early snag in the boycott tactic is indicative of the creative minds that Chavez attracted. Among the DiGiorgio employees were nine individuals who shelled peanuts in a shed and thus technically not agricultural workers. Growers argued in court that the UFW could no longer hold secondary boycotts, because its membership included these shed workers, who were covered under the NLRA. The union's new lawyer, twenty-six-year-old Jerry Cohen, knew little about the technicalities of labor law but had the rebel's belief that laws were made to be bent. The UFW created a new union, the United Peanut Shelling Workers of America (membership: nine), and was once again free to boycott whomever it pleased.

and blankets, singing countless rounds of "De Colores" to keep their spirits up and their blood moving. (Despite such efforts, one volunteer came down with bronchitis.) After the weeklong journey, they woke at the Seafarers' union hall in Brooklyn—the temporary headquarters for the boycotters—and were called to a meeting. "Standing there in front of us with his signatory brown clipboard and yellow legal pad, notes all scrawled over it, Fred gave us our marching orders," wrote volunteer Ed Chiera.[5]

New York City was a key market for Giumarra, and Chavez's strategy was to overwhelm the grower with a show of force. Ross was in charge of the boycott operation, whose original group included veterans from the DiGiorgio campaign like Eliseo Medina and Marcos Muñoz. They rose well before sunrise, picketing the Hunts Point Terminal in the Bronx from four to eight o'clock in the morning, when cargo was unloaded from ships. Afternoons were spent at the Seafarers' hall, where boycott volunteers telephoned produce brokers, pretending to be concerned citizens and urging them to stop purchasing Giumarra grapes. It was hard to judge the impact of the calls, which often resulted in brokers' unleashing a string of profanity, though volunteers took solace in knowing that at least they were tying up the lines and preventing additional orders from being placed. Other crews visited stores to urge owners to drop Giumarra grapes, a suggestion that, if rebuffed, was reinforced by roving picket lines dispatched by Ross. The day ended with an evening meeting at nine, in which they would review the day's activities and go over the next day's assignments. Early signs were promising. "We began to look around the markets at one point and we didn't see too many Giumarra labels on the grape boxes," Ross recalled a year later.[6] But the union soon learned it had been outfoxed. Other grape growers were sharing their labels with Giumarra, which made it impossible to boycott a single company. Through cooperation, growers hoped they had rendered the boycott unworkable. Instead, Ross proposed a dramatic escalation: expand the Giumarra boycott to one that targeted all California table grapes.

This was a risky move. The union thus far had picked off one company after another, building strength as it went along; it was hardly clear that it was ready to confront an entire industry. Indeed, Chavez was initially skeptical, worried about the possibility of lawsuits. But Ross and Dolores Huerta lobbied hard for a total boycott. For the campaign to be successful, Ross knew it needed to have a clear message. New York City had become a mess, with boycotters spending much of their time simply trying to figure out the latest maneuvers of the growers. "Don't eat grapes" was a clear message. In May 1968, Chavez took to the *Today* show, announcing the boycott.

In February, Chavez had made another important announcement: he had stopped eating entirely. While boycotters in New York City were scrambling to clear shelves of grapes, morale back in Delano was suffering. Nothing seemed to have changed. The strike had largely collapsed and the once bois-terous picket lines had disappeared. Though Chavez espoused the need to keep the struggle nonviolent, frustration was growing in the ranks. Talk of violence began to circulate.

One of the greatest challenges in organizing is getting through the inevitable flat points, those moments when momentum stalls and victories are forgotten. Sensing that such a moment had arrived, and taking a page from Mohandas Gandhi, Chavez gathered his supporters and announced that he had begun fasting as a means to recommit the union to nonviolence. Then he walked out to Forty Acres, an uninspired plot of land the union had purchased near the city dump, and settled in. Within the union, reactions to his declaration were mixed. Some felt it was inspired; others thought it was a gimmick, or egotistical. Ross was in Brooklyn when he heard the news, still struggling to figure out a strategy to beat Giumarra. His first thoughts were of Chavez's health. "I think Fred probably loves Cesar more than anybody in the world—maybe even more than his wife and children," recalled Huerta, who had also relocated to New York.[7] During the evening boycott meeting at the Seafarers' hall, a stricken Ross announced the fast, asking people to write letters of support to Chavez.

The twenty-five-day fast would become a pivotal period in the UFW's history. Supporters threw up tents on Forty Acres to be close to their leader, and a nightly mass was held, which soon attracted an overflowing crowd. Farmworkers waited in lines to visit the man who was sacrificing his very body for their cause. Martin Luther King Jr. sent a telegram of support. Toward the end of the fast, Ross arrived in Delano. Some organizers weren't comfortable with the religiosity of the fast, but Ross, an agnostic, spoke at the nightly mass without hesitation. When Saul Alinsky called to express his embarrassment at the public spectacle that Chavez had created, Ross coun-tered in the language both men understood. The fast was a stroke of organ-izing genius. Chavez had united the farmworkers and established himself as their leader. According to Huerta, who was also on the call, "Saul was at a loss for words."[8] (If so, this would have been a first.)

FIGURE 17. Ross speaking at the nightly mass in Delano during Chavez's fast, March 1968. Courtesy of Walter P. Reuther Library, Wayne State University.

The fast elevated Chavez—only moderately well known when it began— to a figure of national importance. For Ross, already fiercely loyal to Chavez, it further confirmed that the young man he had found in Sal Si Puedes was a truly historic figure, operating on a higher plane than anybody else. Soon after the fast concluded, the writer Peter Matthiessen visited Delano to profile Cesar Chavez for the *New Yorker*. He interviewed Ross, whom he described as a "bony man with an air of tired but indomitable honesty," asking who might eventually replace Chavez. Ross stared back at Matthiessen and replied, "Nobody."[9] Ross, of course, was not alone in this sentiment: for most people, it was impossible to imagine the UFW without Chavez at its helm. But Ross's confidence in Chavez had now transformed into unconditional fealty, making it impossible in later years for Ross—the one person Chavez might have heeded—to challenge his former student when he took the union down what would prove to be a very destructive path.

Chavez broke his fast on March 10, 1968, surrounded by thousands of people who had descended upon Delano for the occasion. Seated to his right was

Robert F. Kennedy, who sported a union button on his lapel. The forty-two-year-old senator from New York broke bread with Chavez, pledged his support for the union, and within a week announced that he was running for president. Chavez ordered the boycott operation to shift its focus to supporting Kennedy's campaign in California, with Ross directing the work in Los Angeles.

Without Los Angeles, Kennedy couldn't win California. And without California, Kennedy had little hope for the presidency. After President Lyndon Johnson shocked the nation by declaring he wouldn't seek reelection, two Democrats—Kennedy and Eugene McCarthy, a surging antiwar candidate—were left to fight for the nomination. Ross once half-joked that leading voter registration drives had been "the story of my life," and he again returned to task, walking the same streets of East Los Angeles he had haunted while helping put Edward Roybal into office nearly two decades earlier.[10]

Joining Ross for the first few days of the campaign was his youngest son. Fred Jr. had transferred from Syracuse to the University of California, Berkeley, and traveled south to work on the campaign during spring break. Father and son arrived "bright and early" to visit Tony Rios at the CSO's national office and stop by the Kennedy campaign headquarters to pick up a rental car. "So after taking a lot of the afternoon *talking* about voter registration Dad was getting pissed off. (You know, typical phonies who sit on their asses and blab about working)," Fred Jr. wrote to his sister Julia. Ross and son took four CSO voter registrars on a door-to-door canvass, quickly registering forty new voters. "By the end of four days of Fred Ross in town, 1000 new voters had been registered," Fred Jr. proudly reported. "He is really incredible. The little people remember him from 10 or 20 yrs ago. I ran into one old guy who looked down and out and was bitching about work conditions, etc. So I asked him if he was registered to vote and he said hell yes, why I was a deputy registrar in the first Roybal campaign."[11]

After this initial burst of energy, the UFW set up headquarters at the Church of the Epiphany in Lincoln Heights, which had recently served as a base for the walkouts of thousands of Chicano high school students. Ross sent teams of organizers into the streets with a mission: find people in each precinct who would agree to be captains. Each precinct captain would then go door-to-door to register others while also turning his or her house into a temporary campaign headquarters. "An organizer tries to turn each person she meets into a temporary organizer," was one of Ross's organizing axioms. With temporary organizers spread out across the city, the campaign registered eleven thousand people in twenty days.

On June 4, 1968, Kennedy carried the state, largely because of his strong results in Los Angeles, where he swept the Latino precincts by huge margins. He took to the podium at the Ambassador Hotel in downtown Los Angeles, publicly thanking Chavez—who had left early—along with Huerta, who stood by Kennedy's side in front of the lively crowd. He spoke of peace in Vietnam and progress at home, of uniting the country to combat poverty and hunger. People cheered and clapped and shouted out messages of adoration. Ross and Frances watched the televised speech from their home in San Francisco, while Ross spoke to Fred Jr. on the phone, who had skipped class at UC Berkeley to knock on doors in East Oakland for Kennedy. Ross tended to be cynical about most politicians, but he was a big supporter of Kennedy, excited by the prospect of having a president who was such a strong advocate for the UFW.

Whatever immediate impact the primary might have had on the union's fortunes was quickly erased. Kennedy walked off the stage and was shot three times, dying the next day. But for organizers like Ganz, the experience—his first in electoral politics—was formative. After leaving the union, Ganz would work for a number of candidates, and he would play a key role in designing the field campaign for Barack Obama in 2008. "That was my school," Ganz said of working under Ross in 1968. "That has always been my basic point of reference for how you do grassroots political work. Not by sending in a ton of canvassers, but by recruiting people from the community to do the work. It wasn't just canvassing—it was organizing."[12]

Ross retired after the election and returned to live with Frances, who had sold their home in Corte Madera and purchased a small three-bedroom house atop a steep hill in San Francisco's Bernal Heights neighborhood. At fifty-eight, the energy Ross usually poured into organizing was channeled, once again, into attempts at finishing his book, which had grown into a sprawling memoir. His office was cluttered with stacks of yellow notepads and binders of typed manuscripts, which sat alongside a growing collection of tapes filled with interviews of Chavez, Huerta, and other UFW leaders. Ross was as diligent in his research as he was in his organizing, at one point traveling to the archives of the *Fresno Bee* and reading four years' worth of union-related articles into his tape recorder (this was, remember, the precomputer era).

Despite his earlier frustrations, Ross still had not given up the hope of being published. That winter, in December 1968, he wrote to Peter Matthiessen, asking for advice and describing the book he had in mind:

It is about a guy (me) who gets out of college in the middle of the War in Spain and the Depression, and stumbles into the struggle against hunger and injustice, and only rarely comes up for air for the rest of his life. . . . The book is also the story of *the organizer,* the guy who makes it simply because he can't give up or let up in the drive to accomplish something meaningful in his life, and of the mess such a guy can make of his family life if he isn't very, very careful. Also, the book is about people working and suffering together. It is a record of how the organizer learned to work with them, of his pratfalls and tiny triumphs, of how these, together with everything else he learned from the people, gradually coalesced into what he pedantically referred to as his technique. It is an account of how they took on the big issues of their time and place and the destructive forces of the Police Dept., the Urban Renewal Agency, the Growers Ass. and all the purveyors of the Big Lie and Smear.[13]

If Matthiessen found the proposal intriguing, there were reasons to hesitate before introducing Ross to his friends in publishing. Ross had been working on a book for years, without seeming to get any closer to completion. Not making the task any easier on himself, he informed Matthiessen that he wanted to tell the story in a nonchronological fashion, using a three-day period in 1968, amid Chavez's famous fast, to unleash a "series of memories" that are presented as "here and there in the time stream" but somehow "follow a logical plan of progression." Ross wrote that he had completed fifteen hundred pages—not understanding that such an enormous output hinted more at problems than potential—but still needed to write up and fold in "the whole Grape Strike sequence."[14] Unmentioned was another structural problem with the book: parts of it were told from Ross's perspective, others from that of a young Cesar Chavez. It was, in short, a mess.

It's not clear whether Matthiessen replied, but Ross continued to write, interrupted only for a spell in the fall of 1969, when Chavez asked him to temporarily run the Los Angeles grape boycott. By the summer of 1970, Ross was working on his book's newest section, a chronicle of the DiGiorgio campaign, when Chavez called to announce the unthinkable. Five years after farmworkers had walked out of the fields, the grape growers were finally ready to concede defeat. The typically reserved Ross was overcome with joy. "I don't think I've ever seen him as happy," his son, Fred Jr., wrote to Chavez.[15]

Chavez invited Ross to Delano, where he spent two days observing the historic negotiations. By July 29, 1970, all the details had been ironed out, with the growers assembling for a press conference at Forty Acres. While cameras flashed, a smiling but defeated John Giumarra raised his arms in surrender. The "whole Grape Strike sequence" had ended in as glorious a fashion as Ross could have imagined.

SIXTEEN

The Battle of the Butcher Paper

THE GRAPE BOYCOTT VICTORY GAVE Ross a storybook ending, but his book would have to wait, for at the very moment that the union was gathering in Delano to celebrate its improbable triumph, a new threat was developing. Vegetable growers in the Salinas Valley had followed the grape saga with trepidation, well aware that they would be the next industry targeted by the upstart union. The valley had long been hostile territory for unions, dating back to the strike of 1936, which growers had violently crushed by drafting a citizens' army and deploying tear gas. This time they took a more subtle approach, entering into secret negotiations with the Teamsters Union and signing contracts after several days of rushed discussions. The Teamsters were more than happy to get tens of thousands of new members without having to expend any effort, and the growers were eager to have a pliant union as a partner. But from the perspective of a farmworker, the contracts were pitiful, providing just a half-cent raise per year.

In a pattern that would be repeated throughout the 1970s, Cesar Chavez recruited Ross out of semiretirement in San Francisco to help. Ross was familiar with the Salinas area, having organized the Monterey County Community Service Organization back in the 1950s. Still, he was taken aback—as was everyone in the United Farm Workers—by the militancy of the lettuce workers. They descended in droves upon the new union office in Salinas, wanting to become members and eager to strike in response to the maneuvering of the Teamsters and growers. Ross and Marshall Ganz told workers that a successful strike needed to be a mass action, and they handed out union membership cards to circulate among the crews. Workers returned with stacks of signed cards. A rally called by the UFW brought out three thousand workers, who interrupted speaker after speaker with chants of "¡Huelga!"—strike!

Such workers were a far cry from those in Delano, who often seemed fearful and resigned to their fate. Lettuce workers, or *lechugueros,* were skilled workers—and they knew it. Branding specialized knives, they slashed through the fields with incredible speed, working within tight-knit crews that came to feel like extended families. Many were immigrants from Mexico, filled with the optimism and confidence of people who had learned that taking risks often led to progress. Instead of instigating action, the UFW was rushing to catch up with the lettuce workers, and Ross and Ganz set to work preparing for the strike. Though Ross had spent years working with Spanish speakers, his grasp of Spanish was limited, as most CSO members also spoke English. So while Ross met daily with a team of union organizers, the Spanish-speaking Ganz oversaw the building of worker committees within ranches. Despite widening signs of worker unrest, most growers refused to budge, claiming they couldn't get involved in a jurisdictional dispute between two unions—the UFW and the Teamsters—a dispute they had, of course, orchestrated. Chavez gave the grower-Teamsters alliance a ten-day deadline to prevent a strike, which expired on August 24, 1970.

That morning, a foggy and cool Monday, farmworkers made history by staging one of the largest strikes to hit California's fields. Growers had criticized the grape strike in Delano as little more than a shrewd public relations move, with some justification: production was barely affected and most workers soon returned to the vineyards. But Salinas was different. Thousands of workers struck, with hardly a head of lettuce cut that day. Ross spent the next three weeks in motion—coordinating pickets, supervising organizers, strategizing with Chavez—as lettuce wilted in the fields. Two weeks into the strike, production had only recovered to a third of its typical levels, while the price of lettuce more than doubled. Nightly meetings, held in the parking lot next to the union's office, attracted up to a thousand workers, with people singing and dancing and kicking up dust.

Feeling the pressure, a number of growers canceled their contracts with the Teamsters and signed with the UFW; by the strike's conclusion, the union had made inroads into the lettuce, strawberry, and tomato industries. When a Salinas Superior Court judge sided with the growers and ruled that the strike was a dispute between two unions—the UFW and Teamsters—and therefore illegal, Chavez sent his volunteer staff back out to the nation's cities. The boycott shifted to lettuce.

One of the visitors to Salinas that summer of 1970 was Larry Tramutola, a young Stanford graduate who was transporting a load of donated food for strikers. He walked into the UFW headquarters, a former post office on Wood Street, where people bustled about while a large meeting was held in a mixture of English and Spanish. In the middle of the tumult stood Ross, apparently unaffected by the noise as he listened to each speaker intently. Tramutola was curious about this man who seemed terribly out of place. Ross was the person who had trained Chavez, someone said. By chance, Tramutola bumped into Ross later that evening at Fosters Freeze—Ross never could resist the fast-food chain's milk-shakes and ice cream—and mentioned that he was interested in organizing. Ross handed over his phone number and said to get in touch, adding some words of caution: "Most don't have it in them to be any good."[1]

Undeterred, Tramutola later called Ross and said he was available to briefly work on the lettuce boycott. In typical boycott fashion, Tramutola was thrown into a sink-or-swim assignment, given a few names and five dollars a week to organize a committee in Santa Clara County. Tramutola quickly sank. People who said they would show up to leaflet or picket stores never arrived, and his list of contacts was soon exhausted. He called Ross, explaining that he wasn't making much headway. Ross wasn't surprised and told Tramutola that he clearly had no idea how to organize. When Tramutola next stopped by Ross's house, he found one wall covered in butcher paper. Ross had drawn up a two-week calendar, and he told Tramutola to write down every task he would need to do each day. Two hours later, prodded along by Ross, the young organizer had filled the sheet of paper with activities: phone calls, meetings, reminder phone calls, church visits, another round of reminder phone calls, leafleting. To Tramutola, Ross seemed a bit maniacal in his demand for detail—the schedule even included time set aside for sleeping, as well as a slot each night from 9:00 to 11:00 P.M. marked "TALK TO FRED"—but he copied it down dutifully.

By far, the most challenging hours of the schedule were those evening calls with Ross, as Tramutola described three decades later:

I felt raw from Fred's nightly "Inquisition" where he sought to uncover every short cut and mistake I had made during the day. Not only did he call my attention to each flaw, but my admitting I had made a mistake was not enough for him. No, he wanted to know why and what I had learned from that failure.... His approach was tougher and more grueling than anything I had encountered before. When I attended Stanford University, I had taken courses from demanding instructors, and I had tough bosses in my various jobs through school. My own father was a hard taskmaster who required chores and homework to always be done before play. Even so, I was unprepared for Fred's driving intensity. He considered organizing the highest form of community activism. "You have to do it right," he told me. "If you don't, you'll always be blaming something or someone else. Excuses are for failures, and you don't want to fail. Do absolutely everything you can to keep from failing."[2]

Tramutola had initially told Ross he would be available to help the union for "a few months." But as frequently occurred with boycott volunteers, the farmworker cause quickly took over his life. It helped that under Ross's intense supervision, Tramutola's organizing was finally moving forward, and he had one of the key qualities—a refusal to quit—that Ross prized in an organizer. Tramutola found that the Santa Clara chapter was soon growing, with new people signing up to picket grocery stores. One of the people he recruited was Nancy Elliott, a fellow Stanford graduate. Elliott initially worked on the UFW's newspaper and then administered strike funds during a 1973 grape strike in the Coachella Valley. After the strike, she was assigned to Marin County to build a grape boycott operation. The union provided her with just one contact: Fred Ross. He and Frances had recently sold their San Francisco house and returned to Corte Madera. "I set up an appointment and knocked on his door," recalled Elliott, laughing. "Not a bad contact to have!"[3]

Ross was still hard at work on his book, but he put his materials aside to help Elliott—as he had with Tramutola—holding weekly meetings that could exceed four hours. Unlike some students, Elliott found Ross patient and relentlessly encouraging. The first picket she tried to organize was at a busy market. The only person who showed up was Ross, who hoisted a long pole attached to the UFW flag. "I took one entrance and he took the other," she said. "I felt totally discouraged, but I would look across the parking lot and see that little flag going back and forth, and it kept me going."[4] Ross told her to stay positive, that in time she would see progress, and within months she, like Tramutola, had built a strong committee.

Ross's close supervision of Tramutola and Elliott gave him valuable insights into how local boycott committees could be built. And just three years after celebrating the historic grape victory, the UFW needed a revitalized boycott.

After the original grape contracts expired in 1973, growers rebuffed the UFW to sign with the Teamsters. The conflict began in the Coachella Valley, with the Teamsters playing the role of cartoon villain to a tee: burly representatives stalked the vineyards carrying chains and bats, barking obscenities and spitting in Chavez's face. It was high drama, seemingly made for the cinema; a documentary about the campaign, *Fighting for Our Lives,* would be nominated for an Academy Award in 1975. Two UFW members were killed that summer, including Juan de la Cruz, shot to death while walking a picket line near Arvin. The violence helped convince Chavez to restart the grape boycott, where he felt the battle would ultimately be won.

In the spring of 1974, Ross headed south to relaunch an ambitious Los Angeles boycott with Jim Drake, where the pair recruited and trained one hundred new organizers. In the coming years, Chavez would continue to call on Ross for special projects, but the trip to Los Angeles represented a significant shift: for the rest of his working life, Ross's time would largely be dedicated to training new organizers—first with the UFW and later, once Chavez abandoned organizing, with a variety of peace and social-justice groups. It was in these trainings, which could last for more than a month, that thousands of people were introduced to Ross's rigorous method of organizing, in sessions he dubbed the "battle of the butcher paper."[5]

As an organizer, Ross was endlessly patient. As a *trainer* of organizers, however, he could be merciless, driving many people away with his demanding approach. Ross didn't consider high attrition rates a bad thing: from his perspective, only a select few were cut out to make it as organizers. He considered training someone who wasn't right for the job a waste of time. He was also suspicious of what he termed "Twinkieland" organizers—people who had sweet intentions but little substance. He didn't hesitate to throw such people out.

With the grape boycott relaunched, Ross spent much of his time traveling around the country—Los Angeles, Toronto, Ohio, New York, Florida, back to California—teaching UFW volunteers how to use house meetings to expand boycott chapters. Ross typically began his trainings by reviewing the history of agriculture in California, explaining the many failed efforts to organize farmworkers and then Chavez's rise from the dusty barrio of Sal Si Puedes to helm a movement that finally challenged the power of growers. For Ross, mastery of this history was critical. Organizers were storytellers, and

FIGURE 18. Ross training UFW boycotters, mid-1970s. Courtesy of Fred Ross Jr.

the story they told needed to be compelling and urgent, with the long history of oppression and struggle flowing into the point of the present moment, when the support of outsiders would decide whether farmworkers would live with dignity or once again suffer at the hands of greedy growers.

This urgent message demanded an urgent presentation, and much of the trainings were dedicated to analyzing people's delivery. Ross was an early adopter of video technology, using cameras to record people as they role-played and later dissecting the performance in front of the group. He also went into the field, sitting in on house meetings to observe a (usually nervous) trainee. Often, people mumbled through their house meetings; others spoke clearly but in a way that failed to light up a room. "I have a pretty good feel in my bones who's gonna make it and who isn't as an organizer," Ross told one Brooklyn group, "just by the amount of vitality that they are exuding when they're going through the simulated meetings here." Ross's feedback was almost always the same: people needed more *animo,* a Spanish word meaning energy and vitality. "Right from the very beginning," he instructed, "right from your very first contact with the person [you are organizing], if you are not naturally a vital person—in other words, if you are not loaded with vitality yourself—you've got to start loading yourself with it."[6]

Doing so was partly an act, and Ross had long enjoyed acting, going back to his theater experiences in high school and college. People don't always bubble over with emotion, especially when repeating a message they have delivered many times before. But it wasn't only an act. For Ross, the talk of vitality was also a reminder of the need to connect with the portion of oneself that felt deeply about the issue and that had led the person to sign up with the union in the first place. "To move people, which is what we're talking about, you've gotta be moved yourself," he told a group of boycotters in Brooklyn.[7] Keeping in touch with this feeling, and sharing it, would attract others far more effectively than blandly reciting a set of talking points.

Another common pitfall Ross identified was what he called the "loser psychology." In the transcript from a Brooklyn training he gave in 1977, a woman interrupts him while he's talking about recruiting volunteers; she "found it difficult to see people come out and do something for nothing." Ross underlined her comment in the transcript, writing "loser" next to it.[8] This was less meanspirited than it appears. After decades of organizing, Ross had identified a pattern: people often set out as organizers with the anticipation that they would fail and quickly proved themselves right, finding all sorts of explanations for why something had not worked. Ross's talk about loser psychology was meant to inoculate young organizers from their initial, and inevitable, failures, encouraging them to look inward instead of casting blame on others. If no one comes to a meeting, an organizer doesn't blame the people she invited for letting her down; an organizer takes the blame and redoubles her effort, seeking to uncover at what point she failed. Ross used the example of a young boycotter who was flourishing after a rocky beginning: "She stopped blaming other people—started taking blame for herself, and boy she was a thousand miles down the road right from that second on. . . . As soon as she got over the idea that she was going to be a failure she started being a success."[9]

People who met Ross through his trainings tended to either love or hate him. Tramutola, who would rise to become the UFW's national boycott director in 1976, found Ross to be an inspiring figure who transformed the direction of his life. Still, he was well aware that others felt differently.

"Probably more people didn't like Fred than did," he recalled.[10] Like the students in Syracuse, some felt that Ross's style was too strict, and they at times emerged from the training sessions in a daze. One woman, identified only as Mary in her written feedback, went through a six-week program with Ross and found the experience traumatic:

> Emotionally, survival was a key concern during the training session. I felt we had to block out all past experiences and start from nothing upwards learning how to organize. But throughout the entire session *you did the thinking*, we just responded and acted. When you left we were lost, we had abruptly lost our direction and had very little confidence in our ability to think and plan. I believe an important ingredient in organizing is confidence. The nightmare of the training program was the destruction of self-confidence. Heavily emphasized in the meetings were problems and mistakes. There was little balancing or recognizing what went right, of any good ideas. . . . I felt we were only taught how to focus on faults and what we should not have done.[11]

Ross underlined the phrase—*you did the thinking*—though it's not clear what he took from her message.

One of the coordinators of the New York boycott in the late 1970s was David Dyson, a graduate of the Pittsburgh Theological Seminary. The UFW had a campaign directed against Connecticut Mutual Life Insurance, which had invested in some citrus ranches in the Coachella Valley that were engaged in a contract fight with the union. A couple dozen volunteers were brought in and trained by Ross to work on the Connecticut Mutual boycott. Over several weeks, Ross sent several people home, believing they didn't have the ability to organize effectively. The breaking point came when Ross grew exasperated with a young volunteer who had skipped college to work with the union. He was "clumsy, dorky, but so sweet," as Dyson described the teenager, and someone who, despite his awkwardness, won people over with his sincerity.[12] Ross told the hopeful recruit that he was hurting the farmworker movement more than he was helping it.

"Fred just broke him down," Dyson recalled. After Dyson dropped the devastated man off at the bus station to return to his home in Michigan, he and the other two boycott coordinators decided they had to confront Ross. "I was elected to tell Fred that this was counterproductive, that morale among the group was being shattered," said Dyson. On a drive out to Long Island, Dyson broached the subject, gently suggesting to Ross that it wouldn't be a bad thing, from time to time, to encourage people, perhaps mention how much he appreciated their work. Ross didn't respond directly, but the following day everyone noticed a sea change. He began saying, "That's better," when someone showed progress. He led rounds of applause to acknowledge people's effort. He did not send anyone else home that summer. While Dyson thought that Ross could be overly rigid, he never felt that Ross enjoyed pointing out people's weaknesses or sending them on their way. "I think he felt, above all, that it was his duty," said Dyson.[13]

Hundreds of hours of the trainings Ross gave are preserved on audiotapes. Listening to even a small sampling—which in themselves only represent a sampling of the trainings he conducted over the last two decades of his life—is to more fully appreciate Ross's dedication to the craft of organizing. Despite having given the same workshops countless times, he brings his full attention to whatever topic is being discussed; typically, he's reviewing the sort of thoroughly unglamorous details that are easy to overlook. "He's got all this experience, he's seventy years old, and he's teaching [how to make] phone calls," said Paul Milne, who worked closely with Ross, first at the UFW in the 1970s and later on Central American peace issues in the 1980s. "And he's doing it because he believes that is what is important."[14]

As 1974 ended, Ross estimated that the UFW had a boycott staff of four hundred posted in cities across the country. This far-flung network held house meetings, picketed stores, and figured out any number of ways to publicize the cause and recruit new supporters. By 1975, the Harris Poll found that 12 percent of the country—seventeen million adults—had stopped buying grapes. Another fourteen million were refusing to purchase lettuce. The UFW had created the most successful consumer boycott in US history, with Ross playing an important role in training the union's new organizers.

But professional success for Ross was once again linked to personal difficulties. Frances had long waited for her husband to settle down and become a more dependable partner. For several years, from the late 1960s to the early 1970s, this looked like a possibility, as Ross mostly remained at home writing. His daughter, Julia, recalled this as one of the rare periods when her mother was happy in the relationship. "He was working on the DiGiorgio book and she was editing it," she said. "They seemed to be really hitting it off. She wasn't resenting whatever he was doing."[15]

His new role training boycott volunteers once again found him on the road. Nearly thirty years after having been left alone in Long Beach for weeks at a time, Frances realized that her husband would not—perhaps could not—change. And now she was no longer dependent on him, financially or physically. Years of dogged physical therapy were behind her. Unlike her husband, she had discovered a nose for business, amassing a fair amount of savings through the sale of the Bernal Heights home, as well as income from a few other real estate deals. And professionally she had come into her own. After returning from Syracuse, she had become the executive director of the Conard House, a pioneering halfway house in San Francisco that provided psychiatric services in a noninstitutional setting. She would hold this position for more than three decades, and she found it challenging and meaningful. By 1975, she was again seriously considering divorce.

"She would call and end up crying, talking about how she thought she had to divorce him," recalled Bob. Ross's oldest son had survived his rocky youth to earn a graduate degree in history from the University of California, Davis, and was teaching high school in Davis, where he would eventually retire. Although he admired his father's work—especially his early work with the CSO in East Los Angeles—Bob considered Ross a virtual stranger who had shown little interest in his life. "He was a very cold, austere person," he said. "He was an organizer, and organizing came first. I don't even think family came second. It was organizing—that was his life. It took all of his energy and all of his efforts and emotions."[16] So when Frances called, telling him that his father seemed emotionally uninvolved, Bob supported her decision to file for divorce.

So did Julia. After dropping out of University of California, Berkeley, where she was involved in the Free Speech Movement, she had returned to school. By 1975, she was earning her master's degree in clinical psychology at the University of San Francisco and would go on to design treatment programs for addicts and compulsive overeaters, as well as write a best-selling book, *The Diet Cure*. Julia was very close to her mother and sympathized with her situation. "She couldn't go on with it, because it was so depressing to her that there was nothing between them," she said. "She asked me to call him and tell him not to come home." At the time, Ross was conducting an organizing training in Arizona. Julia made the call. She thought her father sounded relieved when she delivered the news. Over the next few months, they had several long talks. "I remember asking, 'How can you give her up? Aren't you going to fight for this?'" said Julia. "I could see that my mom was right. The fire was out. He just wasn't interested."[17]

The only one who argued against the divorce was Fred Jr. "I was still holding out hope, but I think I was in denial," he remembered. "My mother had concluded that this was not going to work. He wasn't really going to significantly change his lifestyle."[18] Julia and Bob had a hard time understanding why their father had been absent for so much of their lives. Fred Jr. had followed his father into organizing and tended to be more sympathetic. At the time of the divorce, Fred Jr. was running the San Francisco boycott and had proposed a recent march to E. J. Gallo's headquarters, which had succeeded beyond all expectations. Father and son's shared passion for organizing helped forge a strong bond; Fred Jr.'s choice of career also meant that, unlike Julia or Bob, he was able to spend a significant amount of time with his father.

Ross and Frances divorced in June 1975 and would never be together again. Ross would receive some money through the settlement, which he would draw on during the next decade to cover his modest expenses, along with a small stipend from the UFW. But he was now, at sixty-five, without a home. He would spend the next few years bouncing from the Bay Area home of one UFW supporter to the next, living rent-free as he continued to train organizers and work on his writings. He wouldn't settle down until he reached his seventies—and then his home would be a refurbished woodshed, located on the grounds of a house owned by a longtime Quaker activist in Corte Madera. The one-room cabin was tiny, with little furniture save for the mattress on the floor. But Ross never felt sorry for himself. When people remarked on the sacrifices he had made, he had a frequent rejoinder: "I did everything I wanted to do."[19]

Speaking to a reporter a year after the divorce, Ross dismissed the notion that he had any regrets about the impact of his work on his family life. "In the eyes of other people it seems like a sacrifice, but if you're crazy enough to do this work you must love it," he said. "You put up with these conditions because they're part of what you accept to get what you want more than anything else."[20] It was his family who suffered from the life he had decided to live. He considered their sacrifices unavoidable, and so he wasn't particularly bothered by them.

SEVENTEEN

Blind Spot

THE HARRIS POLL DEMONSTRATED THE power of the United Farm Workers' boycott operation, but it didn't mean that all was well within the union. While the grape boycott had galvanized the nation's attention, thrusting Cesar Chavez onto the cover of *Time* magazine, the union struggled with its day-to-day business. The hiring halls were chaotic, with growers frequently unable to get sufficient workers for their fields. The union's medical plan, named after Robert F. Kennedy, was a mess. Grievances filed by workers could go ignored for months. Chavez, like Ross, wasn't particularly skilled in administrative details. But Chavez, unlike Ross, craved control and power and was unable to delegate authority, insisting that the tiniest of matters be brought to him for review. (At one point, when asked to name the people who reported directly to him, Chavez stopped counting at fifty-eight.) His aversion to what he once told Ross was "too much democracy" found its expression in the structure of the UFW, which, unlike traditional unions, had no locals.[1] The UFW's sole decision-making body was the executive board. Vigorous arguments frequently occurred between the board and Chavez, but when push came to shove, everyone knew who was in charge.

None of this was accidental. Chavez felt that he had been burned by the Community Service Organization. He had worked around the clock for years, only to watch, powerless, as the middle-class leadership, soft and complacent, let that work go to waste. As he told an audience in 1965, "If you organize a good group, pretty soon you find yourself hoping, 'I wish I had a vote in this outfit.'"[2] But a simple vote would no longer suffice: Chavez wanted control, and he felt he had earned it. It had been Chavez—and no one else—who had left a stable job to settle in Delano and embark upon an impossible dream, and he became more consumed by the search for people who he believed might get in the way of what he wanted to do. That innocent people might be sacrificed was of little concern, as long as the end result was to instill more loyalty among those who remained. "Following orders is a gift," he once said.[3] For a leader of any organization—much less one dedicated to building the power of others—such an orientation was, simply stated, a big problem.

By the second half of the 1970s, Chavez's need for control and his growing concerns about disloyalty began to cause a series of major crises within the union. Ironically, the first crisis grew out of the UFW's signal legislative achievement. In 1975, California governor Jerry Brown signed the state's Agricultural Labor Relations Act (ALRA), which had been drafted by Jerry Cohen, the union's brilliant and combative general counsel. With justification, Cohen later called it "the best labor law in the country." The ALRA granted California farmworkers the rights they were denied under federal law, including the right to form unions and the right to speedy elections, while also, incredibly, preserving the right to engage in secondary boycotts. Ross was brought in to train union election organizers, and a blitz of elections followed—329 in the first three months after the law was enacted—with the UFW posting a fairly strong showing, especially among lettuce and citrus workers, where Marshall Ganz and Eliseo Medina were leading the efforts.

But by the end of the growing season, a new problem had emerged. The law had created a five-member body, the Agricultural Labor Relations Board (ALRB), responsible for overseeing elections and enforcing rules. The agency, stretched thin by the massive wave of elections, blew through its annual funding and was forced to shut down in February 1976.

In an impressive showing, the union collected nearly 720,000 signatures—more than twice the amount required—to put a proposition on the fall ballot that would enshrine the law into the state constitution, guaranteeing sufficient funding for the ALRB. Ross helped oversee the month-long drive in the Bay Area, attending the morning meeting of volunteers and then heading out to his assigned grocery store—the now-defunct Berkeley Co-op on Shattuck Avenue—gathering signatures from 10:00 A.M. until 7:00 P.M. He'd return for the evening meeting and report his numbers, just like everybody else. His dedication impressed young volunteers like eighteen-year-old John Brown, who would later work closely with Ross. "He was sixty-five," recalled Brown, "and here he is going out alone and standing in a parking lot for nine hours a day, breathing exhaust and saying the same thing to people hundreds of times."[4]

The signatures were gathered in April, a show of strength that convinced growers to back down from attempts to weaken the law. More good news arrived in June: legislators had restored funding to the ALRB. Governor Brown called Chavez personally to urge him to retract his support for the fall ballot proposition, arguing that it was the very definition of a losing issue— both unneeded and likely to be defeated. Relations between the two men were good. Union staff had helped Brown in the recent presidential primary, with Chavez himself giving the nominating speech for Brown at the 1976 Democratic National Convention. (Jimmy Carter had ultimately been selected.) But Chavez rejected calls to back down from what became Proposition 14, convinced that the union could emerge victorious. Ross had lobbied Chavez hard on the matter, urging him to go forward. While not a member of the UFW executive board, at times Ross joined its meetings. Usually he sat back and listened, but in the board's June meeting he spoke forcefully against pulling back, lest opponents weaken the law, bit by bit, over the years. "Those growers are never going to give up," he said.[5] A month later, Chavez called all boycott staff to California. The UFW was mounting a full-fledged campaign to pass Prop 14.

It was an exhausting few months. It also proved to be a major setback for the union. Growers bought newspaper ads and television time, framing the proposition—which granted organizers access to ranches in order to talk with workers—as a threat to private-property rights. One of the most effective spokespersons for this cause was Harry Kubo, a Japanese American fruit farmer who had been interned during World War II at the Tule Lake Relocation Center. In a full-page newspaper ad, Kubo intoned, "34 years ago I gave up my personal rights without a fight ... IT WILL NEVER HAPPEN AGAIN."[6] Growers took their case to television, spending nearly $2.5 million to echo Kubo's message. This was a painful irony for Ross, who had witnessed the shameful role that big growers had played in pushing for the evacuation of the Japanese. But on election day, voters overwhelmingly rejected Prop 14, with the union losing every county in the state except the UFW strongholds of San Francisco and Alameda.

On election night, Ross gathered with hopeful union supporters at a hall in San Francisco's Mission District. Ross, like most of the volunteers, had poured his energy into the campaign. A week before the election, the *San Francisco Examiner and Chronicle* ran a rare profile of Ross, noting that "every waking moment of his life is going towards" passing Prop 14.[7] The article, titled "The Man Who Taught Chavez How to Organize," finds Ross training a group of volunteers in Sacramento, where he goes over the finer points of handing out pro–Prop 14 bumper stickers: make the pitch to passersby in nine seconds, deal with any questions in forty-five seconds, and move along, avoiding what Ross calls "verbal diarrhea," which a farmworker volunteer likens to a worker staying on a grape vine too long. After a day of monitoring their work, Ross prepares to head south, where he will address volunteers in Anaheim, Long Beach, Riverside, East Los Angeles, and the San Fernando Valley. The reporter, Henry Weinstein, catches Ross in a rare moment of rest at an airport restaurant, as he sips white wine and eats his favorite Chinese dish, shrimp with lobster sauce. Weinstein asks if he has ever become discouraged during his decade with the UFW. Over the years, various reporters would ask Ross the same question, and he always gave the same answer. No, he tells Weinstein. He's in it for the long haul.

So when the mood turned sour at the Mission District hall, Ross wasn't one to let the defeat keep him down. "We didn't win," he later said about the moment. "So? Thousands of times we haven't won." One of the union's stalwart supporters, an older woman named Betty Meredith, turned to Ross at the hall and asked, "Fred, what are we going to be doing tomorrow?" Ross would always remember her question, amid the lamentations going on around them, as the perfect response to any setback. "It isn't for us to come through with this great blinding triumph, but to keep coming back," he later said, speaking about an organizer's role. "So what do we do tomorrow?"[8]

Chavez didn't take the defeat so gently. He had suffered a spectacular public drubbing and needed someone to blame. His target was Nick Jones, the national boycott director. Chavez claimed that Jones, who was one of the rare people to argue against pursuing Prop 14, was aligned with left-wing elements seeking to disrupt the UFW. A decade earlier, Ross had criticized Jones for his bushy beard when he arrived in Delano. In subsequent years, however, Jones had proven himself in the field, and Ross had come to consider him a valuable part of the union.

But Ross was not one to question Chavez's judgment. After Chavez accused Jones of helping spies infiltrate the union, Jones and his wife, Virginia—who had been the first to set up a tent next to the fasting Chavez in 1968—resigned from the union, sending a letter of protest to members of the executive board. Boycotters were called back to La Paz, the union's headquarters, now nestled at the foot of the Tehachapi Mountains in an old tuberculosis sanitarium. At one meeting, advertised as a Prop 14 debriefing, people began sharing their thoughts about what had gone wrong. Suddenly, Chavez, who had been covertly listening outside, scrambled through an open window and angrily condemned the group for daring to criticize the union. "It was an ugly moment and a sad end to my full-time work as a UFW organizer," wrote one volunteer, Nancy Carleton, who had campaigned for Prop 14 while battling pneumonia.[9]

The period would mark the end for many dedicated UFW organizers. In the wake of the Prop 14 defeat, nearly a third of the boycott staff were fired, and many others were reassigned or took leaves of absence. During this process—the first of a series of purges that Chavez would direct—Ross played an active role. He and Ganz took groups of volunteers to Hart Park in Bakersfield where, over several days, what had been advertised as a barbeque for the volunteers provided cover for the two men to identify any "assholes," Chavez's catchall term for people he considered disloyal or troublesome. Many of the volunteers had left their boycott homes to travel to California, where they worked up to sixteen hours a day for just five dollars a week. Now they sat alone, across from Ross and Ganz—two key figures of authority within the union—and were interrogated. Whom did they know? How close were they to Nick Jones? What had they done during the proposition campaign? Looking for the "spies" and "agents" among them, Ross and Ganz made quick judgments at the end of each interview about an individual's loyalty. "It was shitty," Ganz recalled decades later. "I'm ashamed of it now. Those of us that should have stood up didn't."[10]

Ross never gave any indication that he regretted the role he played during this period. It's likely that he considered several of the fired individuals simply incompetent. Ross also had little sympathy or patience for members of groups like the Revolutionary Communist Party, a Maoist organization founded by Bob Avakian. "I don't even consider them left wing," he once said. "They're in kooksville."[11] But these groups were extremely marginal, and it's hard to believe that Ross, who had traveled extensively to train volunteers during the proposition campaign, actually believed that they had undermined the effort. Or that Nick Jones was a Communist with hidden motives: a year after Jones resigned, Ross described him, without mentioning his name, as "one of the outstanding leaders in the organization."[12]

What is less speculative is what the episode revealed about Ross. He would do what Chavez asked, and he considered it the duty of other union supporters to do the same. Ross was known for his methodical cross-examinations—"Well, why did you do *that?*" he loved to ask—and he stressed the need to treat everyone equally, a trait he had learned under Robert Hardie at the Visalia migrant labor camp. But he could never apply the same democratic standards to Chavez. "The fact that he couldn't challenge Cesar was a real problem," said Ganz, who later parted with the union and apologized for his role in the purges. "He might have been one of the few people that Cesar would actually pay some attention to."[13]

The boycott never recovered. Chavez replaced Jones with Larry Tramutola, Ross's former pupil, who visited the remaining boycott staff around the country and found them demoralized and suspicious. Ross accompanied Tramutola to a meeting in Los Angeles, trying to reassure people about what he called "the firings." But his attempts only highlighted just how lopsided decision making at the union had become. "Cesar is the only one that can fire anybody or hire anybody," Ross explained. His statement didn't reassure anyone. The *Los Angeles Times* had caught wind of the Joneses' resignations and printed an article outlining the internal turmoil. Chavez's only response had been, "No comment."[14] At the Los Angeles meeting, one woman bravely persisted: "Fred, there was some press recently in the *LA Times* about the purgings of leftists and arbitrary firings that they were complaining about. Was there any basis in reality or was that just a total fabrication?"[15] The man with a well-deserved reputation for straight talk and honesty passed the question to Tramutola.

"Disruption is the lowest form of organizational life." That was one of Ross's favorite lines, and he repeated it in the aftermath of the Prop 14 firings, which he characterized as principally targeting "disrupters." The following years, however, would bring only more disruption to the union, though Ross would play no direct role in future purges.

The most notorious incident occurred in the spring of 1977, in a public purge orchestrated by Chavez at La Paz. In what became known as the Monday Night Massacre, a number of individuals were blamed for attempting to destroy the union. Most of the accused left in tears. One exception was David McClure, a volunteer with a plumbing background who was charged with being a spy. He so loudly proclaimed his innocence that Chavez stepped out of his feigned role as disinterested observer—Chavez had in fact planned the entire spectacle—and triumphantly proclaimed that McClure had been caught red-handed: phone records showed that he regularly called a right-wing senator named Hayakawa. A flabbergasted McClure informed Chavez that the calls were to Ayers & Hayakawa Energy Management, a local company that was fixing a furnace at the union headquarters. McClure was arrested for trespassing after refusing to leave.

"We're prepared to lose anyone that wants to leave," Chavez told the assembled volunteers. "We're also prepared to have people here who, when I ask them to jump, they're going to say, 'How high?' That's how it's going to run."[16]

Judy Kahn was another casualty of the Monday Night Massacre. She had been with the union for six years and was accused of being the "master counter-organizer."[17] Kahn's only crime was complaining about the dilapidated grounds of La Paz. Thus far, Ross had little personal connection to the people being purged, but Kahn was different, as she also happened to be the girlfriend of Paul Milne.

Milne had directed the wildly successful signature-gathering campaign for Prop 14 in the East Bay. During the month-long blitz, Ross sat in on the daily staff meetings in Oakland, listening quietly and offering suggestions after everyone had cleared out. Some people were turned off by Ross's systematic approach to organizing, but Milne soaked it up. His father, Crosby, specialized in organizational management and was working with Chavez at La Paz to implement a more efficient decision-making structure within the union. Milne appreciated the attention Ross lavished on even the smallest of details. (Milne once calculated how much time an organizer would save by switching from a rotary to touch-tone phone.) Ross was an astute judge of organizers, and there could have been little doubt in his mind that Milne was both talented and fiercely loyal; the notion that his partner was directing a devious plot to undermine the union was ludicrous. But word came down from Chavez: Milne had to decide between his girlfriend and the union. Tramutola delivered the ultimatum; Ross called soon after. When Milne protested that his relationship was independent from his work, Ross told him he was too emotionally attached to make the right decision, referencing W. Somerset Maugham's *Of Human Bondage*. Despite Ross's urging, Milne left the union.

"Fred didn't protect anybody," said Milne. "He just stepped out of the way to let people deliver the message." The two men would work closely again, and Milne would later play a key role in helping Ross organize his writings, but for a time Ross refused to visit Milne in his home. "You would think I would have felt betrayed," recalled Milne. "I wouldn't use the word 'betrayed.'

We are all very limited—and this was one of Fred's limits. He had a history of real commitment to democratic principles, but when it came to Cesar he gave him a pass. His one blindness was Cesar."[18]

The UFW's slide, which began in 1976, gathered speed over the next several years. Chavez had developed a reputation for strategic genius, always seeking, as he put it, to "kill two birds with one stone and keep the stone."[19] But the Prop 14 defeat seemed to upset his equilibrium. He traveled to the Philippines as the guest of Ferdinand Marcos, praising the military dictatorship and sparking widespread criticism. He disbanded the union's brilliant legal department, insisting that the lawyers earn the same pay—$10 a week, plus room and board—as the rest of the staff. And at the precise moment that the Teamsters Union finally agreed to abandon its efforts to organize farmworkers, Chavez turned his focus to a group therapy exercise developed by a cult leader. Precious staff energy that could have been used to run elections in the fields was instead spent sitting in a circle, screaming obscenities at one another.

To understand Chavez's turn toward the cult called Synanon, one has to understand his complicated thoughts on labor unions. Chavez obviously believed in unions and wanted farmworkers to live with respect and dignity. But Chavez's ambitions went far beyond simply wanting to be a "union leader." The focus of unions—higher wages, more benefits—was too narrow and, in Chavez's mind, had a double edge. Unions had propelled people like Tony Rios into the middle class, and Chavez viewed the middle class as a sort of spiritual wasteland, where people forgot the values of sacrifice and suffering. So while the UFW was a union, he also wanted it to be the incubator of a more transformative societal project, and he had grown intrigued by the potential of intentional communities. One of the reasons he had moved the union's headquarters from Delano to the sprawling buildings of La Paz, located far from the fields, was to take the first steps in creating such a community.

An example of successful communal living, at least in Chavez's eyes, was Charles Dederich's Synanon. Dederich had turned the once highly regarded drug-treatment program into a community of fanatical followers. Members of Synanon lived together, shaved their heads, and wore orange overalls. They also played "the Game," a version of group therapy in which people "gamed" each other by trading nasty barbs of criticism while looking for sensitive spots and, once those spots had been found, pouncing ruthlessly. There was a rationale behind the Game: by "indicting" one another's flaws, participants would start on the path to self-awareness and personal growth. But Dederich had also found that the Game was a useful means of controlling his followers, and he extolled this virtue to Chavez.

Orange overalls and shaved heads were a step too far, but Chavez became fascinated by the Game, introducing it at an executive board meeting in February 1977. People were, to say the least, caught off guard. The Teamsters were leaving the fields, and Ganz and Medina were eager to launch new campaigns to exploit the opening. Instead, they sat back, perplexed, and watched as members of Synanon—whose men had recently been ordered by Dederich to undergo vasectomies—showed them how to play the Game. For the next year and a half, Chavez would insist that the Game be incorporated into the union, forcing staffers from as far away as Salinas to make the trek to La Paz each weekend, where they were "cursed and trashed for everything from personal hygiene to work habits."[20] The bizarre nature of the Game, and its connection to the huckster Dederich—who would later plead no contest to charges that he conspired to commit murder by placing a rattlesnake in an opposing lawyer's mailbox—has received much attention in chronicles of the union's decline, and for good reason. But it was more a symptom than a cause of internal problems, further evidence that once Chavez made a decision, people followed, whether it was against their better judgment or not.

While Ross never played the Game, he certainly knew about it. One boycotter he trained, Gary Guthman, quit the union after spending three months in La Paz, where he played the Game regularly and had watched as participants—including dedicated longtime supporters—were reduced to tears. When Guthman returned to the Bay Area, he brought up his experiences during a conversation with Ross. "I just wanted to say something to him, but he didn't want to engage," Guthman recalled.[21] It's hard to imagine Ross having anything kind to say about the Game, though in deference to Chavez he would keep his mouth shut. It's also unlikely that Ross felt particularly enthusiastic about Chavez's efforts to create a commune in La Paz. Ross was an agnostic and in spiritual matters more aligned with Saul Alinsky, content with the earthbound glories of organizing: leaders developed, legislation passed, politicians held accountable. Ross's idea of a "model" community was one in which poor people were organized and powerful.

Organized and powerful. Those two words described the lettuce workers who shuttled back and forth between the Imperial and Salinas Valleys each year. And when their union contracts expired at the end of 1978, they were also angry.

At first their anger centered on the UFW. The purges, the Game, and the effort to create an intentional community all had one thing in common: nothing to do with serving union members. Chavez had filled La Paz with true believers willing to work for pennies, but these volunteers had little idea how to effectively run a complex system like the health insurance plan. What was the point of a union, workers wondered, if nothing at the union ever seemed to work as promised? A routine visit to the doctor could land a farmworker in debt. Calls to UFW offices went ignored. The union that had criticized the Teamsters for being unresponsive to farmworker needs was now vulnerable to that very same criticism.

Into this charged environment stepped Ganz, who, in preparation for the contract expirations, had researched the vegetable industry. The news he brought back was good: lettuce growers were flush with cash, while the wages of lettuce workers had failed to keep pace. The farmworkers shifted their anger to the growers. On January 19, 1979, nearly two thousand workers in the Imperial Valley—the prime lettuce-growing region during the winter—walked out, shutting down four companies. Workers from another five companies soon followed. With numbers on their side, the strikers took to rushing into fields to chase out scabs, the same tactic Ross had witnessed during the cotton strike of 1939. It was while rushing a field that the twenty-eight-year-old Rufino Contreras was shot and killed. Four days later, ten thousand mourners attended his funeral.

By the time the harvest shifted north to Salinas, workers were eager to expand the strike. Chavez had other ideas. His ultimate faith was in the boycott as a tactic, which had brought the growers to their knees in 1970. And he had a fat target. While the lettuce boycott had never enjoyed the visibility or success of the grape boycott, one of the largest vegetable companies, Sun Harvest, was a subsidiary of United Brands, which also owned Chiquita bananas. Soon after the death of Contreras, Ross was put in charge of launching a Chiquita boycott. A Sun Harvest spokesperson expressed skepticism. "You need machinery for an effective boycott," he said. "We don't think Cesar has the machinery anymore."[22]

The spokesperson was right: the once-national network of boycott houses that had operated as campaign hubs had closed up long ago. The only "machinery" was now the home of Lois Pryor, an ex-volunteer who lived in the city of Alameda. After his divorce, Ross had mostly lived with Pryor and her husband in one of their extra rooms, using an office in the house for writing. This office became the headquarters of the Chiquita boycott, with Ross aided in the effort by John Brown.

Brown was something of an organizing prodigy: he had begun walking picket lines at the age of eleven and joined the full-time UFW staff at sixteen. For six months in 1979, he and Ross raced around in Ross's 1968 Ford Galaxy, organizing pickets and rallies and fund-raising events. Supporters who had long been dormant started calling, asking what they could do. "We were coordinating this spontaneous upsurge of support," recalled Brown. After the passage of the Agricultural Labor Relations Act in 1975, the boycotts had become relatively minor affairs, focused not on an entire industry but on individual growers who were dragging their feet during contract negotiations. These one-off campaigns had never penetrated the country's consciousness. But the new lettuce strike had galvanized the public—at least in the Bay Area—once again. "It was like going from an old bicycle to a motorcycle," said Brown. "You hit the gas and took off."[23] In August, Ross and Brown coordinated a small twelve-day march led by Chavez from San Francisco to Salinas, where they were joined by another march, thousands strong, of farm-workers. A massive rally was held the following day. "Go out and win," Governor Jerry Brown told the cheering crowd. "The victory is yours."[24]

But a conflict loomed beneath the surface. Chavez wanted to follow the template of 1965: send striking lettuce workers out on the boycott. The lettuce workers hadn't been interested in the boycott back in 1970, and their attitude was unchanged. They wanted to expand the strike, believing they could win in the fields. After the rally, Chavez and the executive board met privately with a delegation of the farmworkers. The strike was bleeding the union dry, Chavez told them. The only way to win was the boycott. It might take longer, he acknowledged, but it was a "sure win."[25]

The man who had been underestimated so many times before—because of his brown skin, because he spoke Spanish, because he had worked in the fields—had now underestimated the resolve of the farmworkers. They weren't interested in a boycott. They wanted to extend the strike to all vegetable workers. And they weren't going to back down. When Chavez balked, the workers told him to put it to a vote at the convention, which was to be held the following day. The meeting went into the early morning hours, ending with a general agreement: union officials would announce the support of both a boycott and strike at the convention. Details could be worked out later. Before they left, one of the leaders, Mario Bustamante, put in a parting shot: "If tomorrow there is a resolution from the executive board that there is going to be just a boycott, I'm going to oppose it." Chavez promised that nothing of the sort would happen.[26]

Bustamante was right to be suspicious. The next day, before the convention, he looked over the resolutions. One endorsed a boycott; none mentioned a strike. He grabbed a pen and revised the offending resolution, ending with a call to strike "in order to do the right thing as men and women and to set an example for our children."[27] When no one read the resolution during the convention, the burly *lechuguero* grabbed the microphone and made the announcement himself. As had been predicted, the motion to strike passed easily.

It was a direct challenge to Chavez's power. And it worked. Over the next several weeks, the strike spread to more and more fields. The growers dropped like dominoes, signing contracts that raised wages to five dollars an hour—a 35 percent increase—and paid for several workers to become union representatives, whose job it was to enforce the contracts and deal with grievances. "It's a scary situation," one grower told the press. "You have the feeling emanating out of the workers that 'What's mine is mine. What's yours is mine too.'"[28]

Back in Alameda, over dinner at the Pryors' house, Ross enthusiastically shared the news about events in Salinas. Because he had not been involved in the private meeting before the convention, Ross likely didn't realize that the union had won by going against Chavez's orders. As soon as the convention was over, Chavez had left for La Paz, where he would remain throughout the strike. He didn't even return to sign the contracts marking the historic victory, sending his brother Richard instead.

Two years later, on a September day in 1981, Ross filed into an auditorium in Fresno for the UFW's national convention. Since the victory in Salinas, tensions between Chavez and farmworker leaders in Salinas had only grown. The union reps stipulated by the contracts, and elected by the workers, were the very same leaders who had bucked Chavez. "Fred taught me in organizing never to go to the so-called leadership, but to go right down to the grass roots and develop leaders there," Chavez had once said.[29] But that was years earlier. For someone who tended to see threats to his power wherever he looked, the paid reps promised to be a problem.

It's unclear how much Ross knew about the developing conflict, but he certainly had plenty of reasons to be concerned. After the Chiquita boycott, Ross had spent several months in 1980 working on a campaign to organize workers at a large plant nursery in Southern California. During this period he lived with Scott Washburn and his family in La Verne, twenty miles east of Los Angeles. Washburn had previously directed the boycott in San Diego, and while the effort at the nursery eventually bogged down, he enjoyed getting to know the man who had become a legendary figure within the UFW. Ross was again laboring earnestly on his autobiography, and he took Washburn on several research trips, including a jaunt to Casa Blanca, where Ross was apparently able to identify the site of his first house meeting.

The rest of Ross's free time was dedicated to movies. *Raging Bull* was in the theaters that winter, and Ross was mesmerized by Robert De Niro's performance. Most nights, after Washburn and Ross had concluded their house meetings, they gathered in front of the family's tiny television set and watched whatever movie happened to be on. One night they were interrupted by a phone call. It was Gilbert Padilla, calling to tell Ross he was resigning from the union.

Padilla's roots with Chavez and Ross were deep. Chavez had recruited Padilla into the CSO, and Ross had worked closely with Padilla back in 1963, when they had made a final attempt to get the organization back on its feet. Like Dolores Huerta, Padilla had been with the UFW from the beginning; during the Monday Night Massacre, Padilla had helped launch the attack, lecturing volunteers on the need to unquestioningly follow Chavez's every command. But he had started having second thoughts about those commands. "Cesar's gone nuts," he had begun to tell people.[30] Padilla likely delivered the same message when Ross tried to convince him to reconsider. Ross hung up, obviously disturbed. "It was an odd conversation to witness," recalled Washburn. "Just very, very sad."[31]

There were other worrying signs for Ross. Tramutola was now out of the union, accused by Chavez of taking orders from Moscow. Ganz was gone too. Ganz had spent much of his time working with the paid union reps, and Chavez had grown convinced that Ganz was trying to use the reps to organize a challenge to his leadership. Another recently departed executive board member was Jessica Govea. Her connection to Ross dated back to the 1950s: her parents had been leaders in the CSO in Bakersfield. Govea had proven herself to be an extremely skilled organizer, having led the successful grape boycott in Toronto. But Govea also happened to be Ganz's partner, and so she was presumed to be disloyal.

And then, a week before the 1981 convention, Ross received another troubling phone call, this time from Jerry Cohen. There were three openings on the executive board, and the dissident farmworkers were running two candidates, both farmworkers. Cohen had just talked to Washburn, who, after the unsuccessful nursery campaign, was organizing in San Diego. A member of the executive board, Frank Ortiz, had visited San Diego to campaign against the paid union reps, claiming that "two Jews," Cohen and Ganz, were maneuvering to take over the union. (Like Ganz, Cohen had left the union.) When Cohen finished describing to Ross what had occurred, there was a long silence. "Even when you're on the phone, you can tell when somebody's been hit in the gut," he recalled.[32] Cohen had one question for Ross: was Ortiz the kind of person who acted on his own, or was he following orders when he pushed the anti-Semitic message? There was another long pause. Finally, Ross spoke. Ortiz, he said, was the kind of person who, if you gave him a paint-by-numbers picture, still needed someone to hold his hand.

"Fred was really upset," recalled Cohen.[33] Nearly fifty years earlier, Ross had participated in his first activist campaign, challenging the anti-Semitic policies of fraternities at the University of Southern California. Now it looked like Chavez had a hand in something just as ugly. Little wonder the news had momentarily taken his breath away. Cohen told Ross that Chavez might have to answer for this in the press. Ross replied that while loyalty was important, there were certain lines that shouldn't be crossed, and when they were, action had to be taken. Ross called Chavez to register his concern, though precisely what he said is unknown. It was one of the few times he challenged Chavez.

At the convention, Chavez took to the microphone and asked for a show of hands in support of an emergency measure. The "emergency" in this case was that farmworkers had proposed candidates independent of Chavez. The measure was an antidemocratic provision, created by Chavez, in support of his own candidates. If a small minority of workers at any one ranch—less than 10 percent—signed a petition endorsing Chavez's candidates, the votes of the entire ranch went to those candidates. In the run-up to the convention, Chavez had dispatched Huerta and others to the fields to collect the needed signatures.

The first vote was split; Chavez announced they would vote again after lunch. During the break, Chavez loyalists passed out leaflets that portrayed the paid union reps as being pawns of "the two Jews." The second vote clearly tilted in Chavez's favor. After the measure passed, dozens of outraged farmworkers stood up and marched out, greeted with shouts of "Down with the traitors" and "Death to the Bustamantes." On his way out, Mario Bustamante broke the staff of his union flag in half.

Nearly twenty years earlier, Chavez had walked out on the CSO, convinced that the group's leaders weren't willing to truly commit to building a union of farmworkers. Now farmworkers who wanted a true union were walking out on Chavez. Ross watched it all unfold. The hateful chants. The antidemocratic maneuvering that robbed farmworkers of their votes. But at the end of the convention, when the shouting died down and the protesting farmworkers left the building, Ross walked to the front and swore in the newest members of the executive board of the United Farm Workers, which had not a single farmworker on it.

If Ross was troubled by what he had witnessed, it was a feeling he would never express—either out loud or in his writings. Shortly after the convention, he had dinner with Fred Jr. at a San Francisco restaurant. Over the years, his Spanish-speaking son had worked closely with many of the Salinas workers, and he had no reason to doubt their sincerity, or militancy. "I told him, 'Dad, this is fucking wrong. You know it's wrong,'" Fred Jr. recalled. "But my dad had a hard time going there. His fallback position was that no one had made the sacrifices that Cesar had made. Except for the anti-Semitism, I don't think my father ever challenged Cesar."[34]

Why he didn't challenge Chavez is an open question. Perhaps Ross felt his legacy was too linked to Chavez, and to break with Chavez would undercut what he considered his greatest organizing achievement. Perhaps, as his son noted, Ross thought that Chavez's many sacrifices entitled him to run the union as he saw fit. Perhaps, in the end, he simply valued Chavez's friendship too much and couldn't bear the thought of being exiled: he knew by now that when Chavez turned on someone, the relationship was over.

There is also, of course, the possibility that he believed Chavez was right: that the people who were pushed out of the union really did have a covert agenda. But this seems highly unlikely. In the coming years, Ross would work on a number of campaigns with people like Jerry Cohen and Paul Milne. "He loved working with all the UFW vets," said Fred Jr. "As loyal as he was to Cesar, he didn't allow that loyalty to get in the way of continuing to work closely in the later years with folks who had left the UFW, or who had been forced out."[35]

And one shouldn't single out Ross unfairly. Almost no one spoke out publicly against Chavez; most simply left and remained quiet, not wanting to give ammunition to the growers or undercut the union. (Gilbert Padilla was one of the rare exceptions.) Whether Chavez would have listened to Ross is another matter entirely. As the person who had changed the trajectory of Chavez's life, Ross certainly held a privileged position; when Ross first went on the payroll of the union, Chavez—a notorious penny-pincher—told his assistant, LeRoy Chatfield, to pay whatever salary Ross requested. But it is also hard to imagine anyone stopping Chavez from implementing his vision, whether it was ridding himself of the threat posed by militant lettuce workers or building a commune in La Paz. In the end, the reason one lingers over Ross's inability to challenge Chavez's antidemocratic actions is precisely because of who Ross was: someone who had spent his long life in the service of building democracy and who, in any other situation, would have been walking alongside the dissident farmworkers as they exited the convention center.

EIGHTEEN

The Forever Project

IN THE SUMMER OF 1988, at the age of seventy-seven, Ross moved out of the cabin in Corte Madera. The man who had spent decades on the road—living in motels, sleeping on living room floors, moving between the homes of United Farm Workers supporters—was now settling in the Redwoods, an attractive retirement community nestled in nearby Mill Valley. Or not quite settling: immediately after checking in, he headed south to Ventura for six weeks, where he would participate in the final organizing campaign of his career.

As an organizer, Ross no longer had much to offer the UFW. After the tumultuous 1981 convention, the union shifted to other strategies of influence, such as direct-mail campaigns and political donations, which didn't pose a threat to Cesar Chavez's power. But other groups sought Ross out, usually connecting with him through Paul Milne, who arranged for his mentor to conduct a number of trainings. In Ohio, the Farm Labor Organizing Committee was organizing tomato workers and launching a corporate campaign against Campbell Soup Company. In San Diego, the United Domestic Workers Union needed to expand its base. Jobs for Peace, based in Los Angeles, sought to channel military funding into social programs. Chapters of Nuclear Freeze were trying to stop the nuclear arms race in its tracks. The diversity of the groups that Ross worked with in the 1980s spoke to one of the attributes of the house meeting tactic: with a few tweaks, it could be used to build support around virtually any issue.

The issue that brought Ross to Ventura was US intervention in Central America. His son Fred Jr. was now the director of Neighbor to Neighbor, a group organizing to stop the flow of military aid to El Salvador's right-wing government, which had been founded by a notorious death-

FIGURE 19. Ross and Fred Jr. in 1987, just before Ross set out to train organizers with Neighbor to Neighbor. Courtesy of Liz Hafalia/San Francisco Chronicle/Polaris.

squad leader. In Ventura, the target was US Representative Robert Lagomarsino, who was facing off against state senator Gary Hart (no relation to the two-time presidential candidate). Lagomarsino was a military hawk while Hart, who had protested against the Vietnam War, promised to vote for cutting off aid to the Contras in Nicaragua. Ross gathered with the team of organizers each morning, reviewing the previous evening's activities and offering suggestions. Though he worked six days a week, by his standards he was slowing down: Ross spent afternoons resting at the hotel; and on the nights when he wasn't observing house meetings, he feasted on salads at the local Sizzler.

Marc Dohan, a Neighbor to Neighbor staffer who had worked with Ross on earlier campaigns, noticed that Ross seemed softer and less intimidating in Ventura. "He would say the same thing, but in a different way," Dohan said. "He was more gentle, sort of like a wise man."[1] While Dohan led many of the group trainings, Ross would pull individuals aside who needed assistance on the finer points, the sort of painstaking work to which he had dedicated his life. The campaign went well: house meetings snowballed, voters were registered, money was raised. Just as Ross had done in East Los Angeles during the Edward Roybal and Robert F. Kennedy campaigns, volunteer precinct captains put in long hours to get out the vote. "We parachuted in with nothing and definitely had a lot of momentum," said Dohan.[2] But on election day, Hart was defeated by a narrow margin. One of the country's most dedicated and talented organizers lost his last campaign, an outcome that, given Ross's long view on history, somehow seemed appropriate. "It isn't for us to come through with this great blinding triumph, but to keep coming back," Ross had said. "So what do we do tomorrow?"

When he wasn't consulting for various organizations, Ross spent his final years trying to get his writings in publishable shape. It was a formidable task. For more than two decades, the stacks of yellow legal pads had continued to pile up, filled with sketches and notes and outlines. His handwriting often looked like chicken scratch; his papers were stuffed into boxes, filed in no particular order. Ross had shared some of his writings with Milne, who thought it was a shame that the material was hidden away. Milne contacted Gretchen Laue, another UFW alum, and asked if she would be interested in helping Ross organize his papers, to be paid out of Milne's group, the Institute for Effective Action. Laue was enthusiastic and began visiting Ross once a week, a pattern she continued for more than a year.

Laue and Ross had developed a close friendship over the years. In her twenties, Laue had left her home in Oregon eager to see the country. She got as far as Boston, where her truck broke down and she signed on for what she imagined would be a short stint with the UFW, living in the boycott house in the Dorchester neighborhood. When volunteers were called west to work on Proposition 14, she left behind her belongings, including a trunk that contained her journal from the period. Later, when Ross traveled to the East Coast to help rebuild the boycott after the purges, he stayed in Laue's old room, where he discovered the trunk and read through her writings: how she had set out from Oregon, how she had camped in the White Mountains while deciding whether or not to join the union, how she had learned to overcome her shyness to lead pickets and marches. Later that year, Ross met Laue in Los Angeles, where she was now directing the boycott. She'd left her things behind, he told her, and she needed to get her trunk. Laue didn't much care; her priority was the union. "Gretchen, you have your *writing* there," Ross insisted. He helped arrange for the trunk to be flown west.

"I always feel like I got an extra break from Fred, because he had read what I'd written," said Laue. "He was curious about this person. He's a realist and I'm a romantic—but he's also a romantic."[3]

As she helped Ross sift through his writings, Laue found free office space at a nearby Lutheran church, where they organized his folders in a large metal filing cabinet. She arrived in the morning and they reviewed what he had written during the week, breaking for lunch at the Good Earth, a health-food restaurant.* Milne was particularly interested in creating a document that would share Ross's approach and philosophy with young organizers, and much of Laue's time was spent typing what would become *Axioms for Organizers,* a series of pithy quotes that Neighbor to Neighbor published as a booklet in 1989. (Selected axioms are included in the appendix.) During lunch, though, the conversation frequently turned to Mario Bustamante, the ousted lettuce worker who also happened to be Laue's husband.

Early on, after Laue described Ross's living situation to her husband—the tiny cabin, the mattress on the floor—Bustamante grew upset. Though he wasn't close to Ross, he had long admired the man who had trained Chavez and always positioned himself at the back of the meeting. During the 1970 lettuce strike in Salinas, Bustamante was amazed when Ross had unveiled a map of the entire Salinas Valley that listed the crews of each company, expressing both the union's ambition and preparation. "He was very quiet; he almost never spoke," Bustamante recalled. "But the way he just did his work, it was impressive to me—very impressive."[4]

At first, Ross had little interest in discussing Bustamante. Soon, however, his curiosity won out. He asked why Bustamante, a legal resident, had never become a US citizen, stressing to Laue the importance of the vote. He also wanted to know what Bustamante was doing. After being fired by Chavez— firings that a judge eventually ruled illegal—Bustamante and a number of the ex–UFW representatives had formed their own organization, Campesinos Adelante. Laue updated Ross about their activities. Borrowing a page from the UFW, the lettuce workers stood outside grocery stores with ironing boards as portable tables and surveys, asking farmworkers about the changes they wished to see. After she described the latest news, Ross peppered her with questions. *Why are they doing that? Well, have they tried this? How about this other idea?*

"He went from not wanting to talk about Mario to giving advice," recalled Laue.[5] At the 1981 convention, Chavez had described the workers aligned

---

* By his late forties, Ross had become a serious health-food devotee. A number of people in the UFW recalled that Ross started many mornings by downing a foul-smelling concoction of wheat germ, nutritional yeast, and grapefruit juice.

FIGURE 20. Ross celebrating his seventy-fifth birthday with his three children, Julia, Fred Jr., and Bob, August 23, 1985. Courtesy of Fred Ross Jr.

with Bustamante as part of an "evil force" determined to "bury our beloved union."[6] While Ross could never bring himself to publicly criticize Chavez, he also couldn't help but offer suggestions for Bustamante. "It was just who he was," said Laue. "It was all right up Fred's alley."[7] The last time Ross saw Bustamante was during the Neighbor to Neighbor campaign in Ventura County: he and Laue had been invited up by Fred Jr. to help out during the last days of the effort. Ross greeted Bustamante warmly. At one point, during a meeting of Spanish-speaking supporters, an argument broke out, some sort of minor disagreement. Bustamante stepped in to intervene, and the group was once again on the same page. He looked up to see Ross in the back, giving him a thumbs-up.

In 1989, Fred Jr. traveled with a delegation to El Salvador to meet with local groups about the possibility of launching a boycott of Salvadoran coffee to increase pressure on the right-wing government. It proved to be a harrowing trip. Several meetings were held in secret, and at one point the delegation rushed to the home of a union leader in San Salvador to prevent the military from dragging him away. (Soon after they left, just a few miles from the union leader's house, military forces murdered six Jesuit priests, their housekeeper, and her daughter.) After the group's safe return, they held a report-back meeting, which Ross attended. "He's taking it all in, but I could tell there was a shift," Fred Jr. recalled.[8] While Ross was clearly proud of his son's work, he had trouble following exactly what was being said, which proved to be one of the first signs that he had Alzheimer's.

That same year, Ross became a published author. In the early 1960s, he had completed a long manuscript about his years with the Community Service Organization, which included a chronicle of Chavez's experiences organizing farmworkers in Oxnard. That section, edited by longtime UFW spokesperson Marc Grossman, became *Conquering Goliath: Cesar Chavez at the Beginning*. Published by the UFW's own print shop, El Taller Grafico, it's a thin and uneven book—blocks of uninterrupted dialogue can run for pages, and the action is hard to follow—but it does communicate Ross's enthusiasm for Chavez while shedding light on some of the pitfalls Chavez faced in challenging the bracero system.

By the following year, Ross had grown acutely aware of his disease, and he declined to attend social events, concerned that he would become confused or be unable to remember people's names. For his father's eightieth birthday, Fred Jr. organized a party at Neighbor to Neighbor's headquarters in San Francisco's Mission District. "He was worried," said Fred Jr., "but I told him that he didn't have to give a speech, or do anything. We just want to honor you." While Ross was initially hesitant, photos from the event show him smiling widely, his eyes beaming. As the disease progressed, it became an increasing struggle to recall the dates and times of appointments, though Ross would still have unexpected moments of lucidity and humor. "How's the food?" Fred Jr. once asked. "For shit," replied Ross, bringing a smile to his son's face.[9]

In the fall of 1992, as it became clear that Ross's health was rapidly deteriorating, Fred Jr. called Chavez to update him on his father's condition. Chavez quickly rearranged whatever appointments he had to travel up to Mill Valley. By now the Alzheimer's had reached an advanced state, and Fred Jr. warned Chavez that his father might not recognize him. But Ross would never forget Chavez. When he arrived, Ross opened his eyes wide, raised his arms, and said, "Ah, Cesar." They spent several hours meandering along the paths of the Redwoods, Chavez walking slowly next to Ross, who was being pushed in a wheelchair. The unlikely pair had met on a fateful evening forty years earlier, Ross attracting Chavez with his vision for the future. Now they talked about the past: the fights they had waged, the lessons Ross had taught, the memories they shared. When Chavez expressed his gratitude for everything Ross had done, he recalled that Ross shrugged it off, saying, "Come on, I haven't done anything for you guys—you did it all yourselves."[10]

Ross's health faded quickly after Chavez's visit, caused by his failing kidneys, and he was transferred to a hospital in San Rafael. Upon hearing the news, Herman Gallegos visited. Ross remained asleep during his stay, so he left behind a note. When Fred Jr. read the note to his father, he could see that he immediately perked up. "So I sent the word out: get messages in and I'll read to him every night."[11] The letters began to arrive, which buoyed Ross's spirits, as did the stream of visitors. But it was clear that his body was giving out, and after several days he closed his eyes and became unresponsive. His eldest son, Bob, suggested they play his favorite music, and a record player was brought into the intensive care unit. Among the records was a Pete Seeger album that included a cover of Woody Guthrie's "Union Maid." The song is about a militant female organizer, and when the song reached its chorus— "Oh, you can't scare me, I'm sticking to the union / I'm sticking to the union 'til the day I die"—Ross's eyes snapped open.[12] In what Fred Jr. called "a little miracle," his father remained alert for two more days, listening to songs and receiving visitors, before passing away in his sleep on September 27, 1992. A week later, the family gathered on Mount Tamalpais and buried his ashes under a bay tree overlooking the Pacific Ocean.

On a sunny October afternoon, four hundred people filed into a hall at the Delancey Street Foundation, on San Francisco's waterfront, to remember Ross. Many in the crowd had not spoken to each other in years, casualties of the UFW's internal fights and purges. Jerry Cohen, the union's former general counsel, served as the master of ceremonies. Several years earlier, Cohen had penned an op-ed for the *Los Angeles Times* critical of Chavez's turn away from the fields, writing that "junk mail does not organize people; people organize people."[13] But when Chavez and Cohen met before the service began, the men embraced warmly. The occasion provided an opportunity to put aside old grievances, if only for a day. This served, as many speakers noted, as a final testament to Ross. "Even in his death," Cohen said during his opening remarks, "Fred is a great organizer."

Luis Valdez and El Teatro Campesino performed, leading the audience in farmworker songs and a bilingual rendition of "Solidarity Forever." In his remarks, Valdez was characteristically eloquent, noting that he had met Ross "in the trenches" of the DiGiorgio campaign. "This was a century that exposed the ugly American," he said. "Fred Ross was the beautiful American, the human American, the American who came out to the barrios, who came out to the labor camps, and put himself on the line."

Many of the speakers described how they had first met Ross. Ann Saito Howden, who settled in Cleveland after being released from an internment camp in Arizona, was first struck by Ross's looks—"somewhere between Henry Fonda and Clint Eastwood"—but she soon came to appreciate his "matchless perseverance" in finding jobs and housing for Japanese Americans. Tony Rios was initially suspicious of Ross, who showed up at his door in Boyle Heights wearing cowboy boots. "I figured, what is this redneck doing in my house?" Rios said. But Rios loved to talk, and Ross loved to listen, and Rios was soon won over. Dolores Huerta remembered how, at that first house meeting in Stockton, Ross pulled out photos of hundreds of people attending CSO gatherings, sharing a vision that swept her away from her planned career in teaching.

Each of his children spoke. Bob Ross likened his father to Tom Joad in *The Grapes of Wrath*, who always fought on the side of the underdog. Julia focused on Ross's personal side: how he loved music, poetry, and acting and how once, during a six-month stretch when he was home, he had thrilled the kids by reading to them every night in his marvelous voice. Fred Jr. spoke about the immense pride he had in his father, recounting that as a youngster he had nearly gotten into a fight with Saul Alinsky's son over whose father was the better organizer. He recalled how a journalist had once described Ross as looking a bit like Gary Cooper in *High Noon*. That was how Ross approached life, Fred Jr. said, always ready to take on the biggest bullies, wherever they might be, but he never did it alone.

One of the most moving speakers was Jessica Govea, whose history with Ross dated back to her childhood. During the summer of 1956, her parents, Juan and Margaret, had invited Ross over for dinner at their tiny home in Bakersfield. Jessica was only nine, but she had clear memories of that night and its guest, "a tall man who wore plaid shirts and khaki pants," and whose presence was considered so special that Jessica's mother never forgot what she had cooked. From that night on, Govea's childhood memories were wrapped up in the CSO. She watched Ross encourage her mother, a shy farmworker and homemaker, to become an aggressive advocate. Jessica went door-to-door with her father, who would become a key leader in the CSO chapter. She joined living room meetings, listening as her parents and their neighbors debated issues and developed strategies. Govea had two siblings, and the entire family would attend the packed membership meetings each month. She had become a "CSO kid." Three years later, when her friend was hit and killed by a car while walking to the nearest playground—which was three miles away, arrived at by walking along a busy road—the twelve-year-old sprang into action. "I was grief stricken, but I had seen Fred teach people how to turn grief and anger into action," she said. She led a petition drive to demand a local playground, gathering her friends to collect signatures from every adult in the neighborhood. "Six years later, we got our park." After she finished speaking, she sang a haunting rendition of the Spanish song "La Paloma," one of Ross's favorites.

Finally, it was Chavez's turn to speak. He did not look well. Suffering from an awful cold, his voice frequently cracked and he had to pause several times to cough and wipe his nose. But he soldiered on, managing to capture the essence of Ross. Chavez told the assembled guests that he had a number of reasons to initially distrust the man who became his mentor, who was white and middle class. "I watched him at first very closely for the signs of paternalism and superiority," he said. "Never, ever did I see those signs in Fred. He never looked down on us. But he also never pitied us. He was a tough, unrelenting taskmaster." The first large meeting in East San Jose had seemed magical, but Chavez soon learned that behind the magic was old-fashioned effort. "The thing I liked most about Fred was there was no bullshit, no pretentions, no ego gimmicks; just plain hard work—at times grinding work."

When others grew impatient—when Chavez grew impatient—Ross was there to remind them that the struggle was long, that easy shortcuts never panned out. "Fred would say, '*Calma,*' have patience. It'll come."

Four years earlier, Ross had sat down for a rare media interview, one of the last he would give in his life. He spoke to a reporter about his improbable journey from a sheltered youth in Los Angeles to his work with Dust Bowl migrants and imprisoned Japanese Americans. He talked about his initial organizing attempts in the Citrus Belt, where he hung around and talked with whomever he encountered, tentatively feeling his way into what soon became a calling. He told of meeting Chavez and how they later divided up the state to organize the CSO. "I took one valley," he explained, "and Cesar took another."[14]

And he recounted how, soon after getting involved, Chavez had asked him just how long this organizing project was going to last.

"I had to tell him," Ross said, chuckling. "I said, 'It's going to last forever.'"[15]

Axioms for Organizers

In the fall of 2014, Fred Ross was posthumously inducted into the California Hall of Fame, joining such luminaries as Amelia Earhart, Jackie Robinson, and John Steinbeck (along with his former students Dolores Huerta and Cesar Chavez). To honor the occasion, and to continue to share the legacy of his father, Fred Jr. republished a bilingual version of *Axioms for Organizers*. The selected axioms below reflect Ross's thoughts on the organizing craft, arrived at through more than four decades in the field.

Social Arsonist: A good organizer is a social arsonist who goes around setting people on fire.

Lead by Pushing: An organizer is a leader who does not lead but gets behind the people and pushes.

Duty of Organizer: The duty of the organizer is to provide people with the opportunity to work for what they believe in.

Hope: To inspire hope, you have to have hope yourself.

Winning Hearts & Minds: To win the hearts and minds of people, forget the dry facts and statistics; tell them the stories that won you to the cause.

Willpower: There is no substitute for willpower in an organizer.

Fast Talkers: Look out for the fast talkers.

The Incidentals: The incidentals make up the fundamentals.

Follow-Up: Ninety percent of organizing is follow-up.

Little Things: If you are able to achieve anything big in life, it's because you paid attention to the "little" things.

Short-Cuts: Short-cuts usually end in detours, which lead to dead-ends.

Half-Assed Job: In any kind of work if you do a half-assed job at least you get some of the work done; in organizing you don't get anything done.

People: It's the way people are that counts, not the way you'd like them to be.

Do It Now: If you wait until you have all the time, people and resources to go ahead, you may still never get there because you didn't fill the interval with the action needed to get you there.

Live Wires: When you find "live wires" put them to work immediately. Find something they can do—any little thing—to get them started and ready to do more, or you'll lose them for the cause.

Questions: When you are tempted to make a statement, ask a question.

Maybe: "Maybe" is a double, triple "No!"

Reminding: Reminding is the essence of organizing.

Burn-Out: Organizers don't "burn-out," they just give up and cease being organizers.

Pressure: It's not the quantity of pressure we exert that counts, it's the quality.

Messages: Rare is the delivered message. There is no substitute for face-to-face communication.

Doing It "for" People: If you think you can do it for people, you've stopped understanding what it means to be an organizer.

Losers: Losers are loaded with alibis.

Blame: When you are able to take the blame for failure, you are on the way to becoming a good organizer.

If You Don't Know: If you don't know the answer, don't pretend you do.

People Power: People power must be visible to have an impact.

Concentration: When you are pushing a big drive or issue, you stay on it to the total exclusion of everything else—until it is done.

Leadership: You don't develop new leaders, you push people into taking action by refusing to do it yourself. You are then providing them the opportunity to become aware of their own capabilities.

Hardest Choice: The hardest choice is usually the correct one.

Vacations: Injustice never takes a vacation.

Monotony: The way to break monotony is with motion and emotion.

Put People to Work: Don't talk at people—put them to work.

The Disrupter: The disrupter is the lowest form of organizational life.

Organize: The only way to organize is to organize, not sit around and jaw about it.

NOTES

INTRODUCTION

1. Vern Partlow, "Bypassed 'Islands' of L.A. Experience Awakening," *Los Angeles Daily News,* December 27, 1950.

2. Quoted in Jacques E. Levy, *Cesar Chavez: Autobiography of La Causa* (Minneapolis: University of Minnesota Press, 2007), 97.

3. Ibid., 99.

4. Quoted in *Cesar Chavez: An Organizer's Tale,* ed. Ilan Stavans (New York: Penguin, 2008), 225.

5. This is one of Ross's organizing "axioms"; the full collection is available online at the Farmworker Movement Documentation Project, https://libraries.ucsd.edu/farmworkermovement/essays/essays/MillerArchive/064%20Axioms%20For%20Organizers.pdf (accessed September 22, 2014). I have included selected axioms in the book's appendix.

6. This is another of his axioms.

7. Box 20, Folder 10, Ross Papers.

8. Box 37, Folder 101, Ross Papers.

9. Alinsky to Ross, November 3, 1960, Fred Ross Jr. papers.

10. Box 37, Folder 101, Ross Papers.

CHAPTER ONE

1. Audiotape, April 27, 1985, Box 41, Folder 329, Ross Papers.

2. "Boyhood and College," audiotape, November 13, 1979, Bob Ross audiotapes.

3. "Workbook of a Wayfaring Organizer," n.d., Box 20, Folder 1, Ross Papers.

4. Quoted in Robert Fitch, *Solidarity for Sale: How Corruption Destroyed the Labor Movement and Undermined America's Promise* (New York: Public Affairs, 2006), 98.

5. "Boyhood and College," audiotape, November 13, 1979, Bob Ross audiotapes.

6. "Workbook of a Wayfaring Organizer," n.d., Box 20, Folder 1, Ross Papers.

7. Alinsky to Ross, January 4, 1962, Fred Ross Jr. papers.

8. "Boyhood and College," audiotape, November 13, 1979, Bob Ross audiotapes.

9. Poem in author's possession.

10. "Workbook of a Wayfaring Organizer," n.d., Box 20, Folder 1, Ross Papers.

11. Ibid.

12. Ibid.

13. "Draft Ross Wrote for Carey McWilliams," n.d., Box 21, Folder 9, Ross Papers.

14. Quoted in George J. Sánchez, *Becoming Mexican American: Ethnicity, Culture and Identity in Chicano Los Angeles, 1900–1945* (New York: Oxford University Press, 1993), 83.

15. Kevin Starr, *Material Dreams: Southern California through the 1920s* (New York: Oxford University Press, 1990), 69.

16. Quoted in Sánchez, *Becoming Mexican American*, 96.

17. "LA River," n.d., Box 21, Folder 17, Ross Papers.

18. Fred Ross report cards, 1928–29, Fred Ross Jr. papers.

CHAPTER TWO

1. Roosevelt's "The Forgotten Man" speech is at the New Deal Network, http://newdeal.feri.org/speeches/1932c.htm (accessed April 21, 2015).

2. "Book Drafts, Beginning," n.d., Box 20, Folder 9, Ross Papers.

3. "Draft Ross Wrote for Carey McWilliams," n.d., Box 21, Folder 9, Ross Papers.

4. Quoted in Starr, *Material Dreams*, 154.

5. Mario T. García, *Memories of Chicano History: The Life and Narrative of Bert Corona* (Berkeley: University of California Press, 1994), 78.

6. "Boyhood and College," audiotape, November 13, 1979, Bob Ross audiotapes.

7. "Book Drafts, Beginning," n.d., Box 20, Folder 9, Ross Papers.

8. "Boyhood and College," audiotape, November 13, 1979, Bob Ross audiotapes.

9. Ibid.

10. FBI file on Fred Ross, in author's possession.

11. "State Relief Administration," n.d., Box 22, Folder 21, Ross Papers.

12. Ibid.

13. Carey McWilliams, *Southern California: An Island on the Land* (Layton, UT: Gibbs Smith, 1973), 220.

14. "Boyhood and College," audiotape, November 13, 1979, Bob Ross audiotapes.

15. "Book Drafts, Beginning," n.d., Box 20, Folder 9, Ross Papers.

16. "Boyhood and College," audiotape, November 13, 1979, Bob Ross audiotapes.

17. Eugene Wolman to his father, March 13, 1937, Carton 3, Folder 8, VALB–Bay Area.

18. *Daily Trojan,* October 23, 1935.

19. Eugene Wolman to his father, July 15, 1937, Carton 3, Folder 8, VALB–Bay Area.

20. "Trojan Graduate Killed in Spain," *Daily Trojan,* November 3, 1937.

21. "Boyhood and College," audiotape, November 13, 1979, Bob Ross audiotapes.

22. Untitled manuscript, n.d., Box 25, Folder 15, Ross Papers.

23. "State Relief Administration," n.d., Box 22, Folder 21, Ross Papers.

24. Untitled manuscript, n.d., Box 25, Folder 15, Ross Papers.

25. "SRA," n.d., Box 22, Folder 20, Ross Papers.

26. Quoted in Devra Weber, *Dark Sweat, White Gold: California Farm Workers, Cotton, and the New Deal* (Berkeley: University of California Press, 1994), 168.

27. Ibid., 167.

28. "State Relief Administration," n.d., Box 22, Folder 21, Ross Papers.

29. Ibid.

30. Quoted in Elaine Steinbeck and Robert Wallsten, eds., *Steinbeck: A Life in Letters* (New York: Penguin, 1989), 161.

31. Robert DeMott, introduction to John Steinbeck, *The Grapes of Wrath* (New York: Penguin, 2006), xxxii.

32. "State Relief Administration," n.d., Box 22, Folder 21, Ross Papers.

33. Miscellaneous manuscript pages, n.d., Box 25, Folder 17, Ross Papers.

CHAPTER THREE

1. Untitled manuscript, n.d., Box 25, Folder 15, Ross Papers.

2. "Weekly Council Meeting Minutes, 5–24–38," Box 3, FSA San Bruno.

3. "Bob Hardie," n.d., Box 20, Folder 7, Ross Papers.

4. Quoted in Brian Q. Cannon, "Keep On A-Goin: Life and Social Interaction in a New Deal Farm Labor Camp," *Agricultural History* 70, no. 1 (Winter 1996): 13.

5. For migration figures, I have relied on James N. Gregory, *American Exodus: The Dust Bowl Migration and Okie Culture in California* (New York: Oxford University Press, 1989), 9–10.

6. Ibid., 20.

7. Cecilia Rasmussen, "LAPD Blocked Dust Bowl Migrants at State Borders," *Los Angeles Times,* March 9, 2003.

8. Quoted in Gregory, *American Exodus,* 96.

9. Ibid., 96.

10. Ibid., 100.

11. Ibid., 101.

12. Quoted in Will Kaufman, *Woody Guthrie: American Radical* (Chicago: University of Illinois, 2011), 25.

13. Petition dated May 26, 1939, Box 5, FSA San Bruno.

14. Letter from Eric H. Thomsen, n.d., Box 7, FSA San Bruno.

15. Quoted in Jay Parini, *John Steinbeck: A Biography* (New York: Henry Holt and Company, 1995), 181.

16. John Steinbeck, *The Grapes of Wrath* (New York: Penguin, 1976), 369.

17. Narrative Report for May 31, 1939, Box 5, FSA San Bruno.

18. "Feinstein Training Session," 1983, Box 16, Folder 7, Ross Papers.

19. Weedpatch Report for October 24, 1936, Box 6, FSA San Bruno.

20. Quoted in Gregory, *American Exodus,* 108.

21. Untitled manuscript, n.d., part 3 of 7, Box 24, Folder 4, Ross Papers.

22. Quoted in Gregory, *American Exodus,* 151.

23. David Kinkead to R. W. Hollenberg, July 10, 1939, Box 5, FSA San Bruno.

24. Carey McWilliams, *The Education of Carey McWilliams* (New York: Simon & Schuster, 1978), 78.

25. Peter Richardson, *American Prophet: The Life and Work of Carey McWilliams* (Ann Arbor: University of Michigan Press, 2005), ix.

26. Strike notice printed in *Tow Sack Tattler,* October 6, 1939. The *Tow Sack Tattler,* and the other newspapers published at FSA camps are on microfilm at the Doe Library at the University of California, Berkeley.

27. Quoted in Anne Loftis, *Witnesses to the Struggle: Imaging the 1930s California Labor Movement* (Reno: University of Nevada Press, 1998), 185.

28. Ibid., 221.

29. *Tow Sack Tattler,* October 28, 1939, Doe Library, UC Berkeley.

30. *Tow Sack Tattler,* October 6, 1939, Doe Library, UC Berkeley.

31. James H. Ward to Earl Beckner, June 18, 1940, Box 5, FSA San Bruno.

32. Laurence Hewes, *Boxcar in the Sand* (New York: Knopf, 1957), 123.

33. For information about the strike, see Weber, *Dark Sweat, White Gold,* 189–99.

34. "Farm Worker Association," November 1939, Folder 8, Carton 6, Hollenberg Collection.

35. Loftis, *Witnesses to the Struggle,* 7.

36. *Tow Sack Tattler,* May 1, 1940, Doe Library, UC Berkeley.

37. *Tow Sack Tattler,* October 20, 1939, Doe Library, UC Berkeley.

38. Report, April 29, 1940, Box 5, FSA San Bruno.

39. *Tow Sack Tattler,* October 20, 1939, Doe Library, UC Berkeley.

40. Audiotape, April 27, 1985, Box 41, Folder 329, Ross Papers.

41. Loftis, *Witnesses to the Struggle,* 175

42. Quotes from Todd and Sonkin come from their field notes, available online at the Library of Congress, www.loc.gov/resource/afc1985001.afc1985001_fn001. Selected audio files, including Ross reciting "Cotton Fever," are at Voices of the Dust Bowl, http://hearingvoices.com/news/webworks/dust-bowl (both accessed April 21, 2015).

43. "Joseph DiGiorgio," *Fortune,* August 1946.

44. "Weedpatch," audiotape, n.d., Bob Ross audiotapes.

45. Untitled manuscript, n.d., part 3 of 7, Box 24, Folder 4, Ross Papers.

46. Yvonne Gregg notebook, courtesy of Bob Ross.

47. Hewes, *Boxcars in the Sand,* 127.

48. Marysville migrant camp newspaper, January 20, 1942, Doe Library, UC Berkeley.

CHAPTER FOUR

1. Quoted in Richard Drinnon, *Keeper of Concentration Camps: Dillon S. Myer and American Racism* (Berkeley: University of California Press, 1987), 32.

2. In fact, as noted in *Personal Justice Denied,* a publication of the US Commission on Wartime Relocation and Internment of Civilians (Seattle: University of Washington Press, 1997), there was never a single documented instance of sabotage or espionage committed by Japanese Americans in the Pacific states.

3. Quoted in ibid., 64.

4. Ibid.

5. Ibid., 82.

6. Quoted in H. L. Pohlman, *Constitutional Debate in Action: Civil Rights and Liberties* (Lanham, MD: Rowman & Littlefield, 2005), 151.

7. John DeWitt to Laurence Hewes, March 15, 1942. This letter and many other documents pertaining to the FSA's role in evacuating Japanese Americans are housed at UC Berkeley's Bancroft Library and available at the Online Archive of California, "Farm Security Administration Reports and Miscellaneous Documents, 1942–1943," www.oac.cdlib.org/view?docId=hb009n99p1&query=&brand=oac4 (accessed February 3, 2014).

8. Roger Daniels, *Concentration Camps, North America: Japanese in the United States and Canada during World War II* (Malabar, FL: Krieger Publishing Co., 1993), xxii.

9. Quoted in Greg Robinson, *A Tragedy of Democracy: Japanese Confinement in North America* (New York: Columbia University Press, 2009), 72.

10. Figures for Japanese farmers and acreage come from a June 5, 1942, letter from Laurence Hewes, available at the Online Archive of California. On the value of land, see Audrie Girdner and Anne Loftis, *The Great Betrayal: The Evacuation of the Japanese-Americans during World War II* (Toronto: Macmillan, 1969), 128.

11. Fred Ross oral history with Bob Ross, July 16, 1972, Fred Ross Jr. papers.

12. Alison Bell, "Santa Anita Racetrack Played a Role in WWII Internment," *Los Angeles Times,* November 8, 2009.

13. Quoted in Gerald Schlenker, "The Japanese of San Diego County during the Second World War," *Journal of San Diego History* 18, no. 1 (Winter 1972), available online at www.sandiegohistory.org/journal/72winter/internment.htm (accessed February 8, 2014).

14. Fred Ross oral history with Bob Ross, July 16, 1972, Fred Ross Jr. papers.

15. Ibid.

16. Quoted in Girdner and Loftis, *Great Betrayal,* 115.

17. Quoted in Coleen Lye, *America's Asia: Racial Form and American Literature, 1893–1945* (Princeton, NJ: Princeton University Press, 2005), 162.

18. Quoted in Girdner and Loftis, *Great Betrayal,* 115.

19. That the WRA called internees "colonists" is noted in Reel 313 of the Japanese American Evacuation and Resettlement Records (JAERR), located at UC Berkeley's Bancroft Library. This collection, preserved on microfilm, is the primary archival source for Ross's time at Minidoka, along with his future assignments in Cleveland and, later, San Francisco.

20. Descriptions of the camp are principally drawn from National Park Service, General Management Plan, "Background of the Monument," and Girdner and Loftis, *Great Betrayal.* Details on daily life in the camp—including the death of the man who became lost while searching for wood—is from *Minidoka Interlude: September 1942–October 1943,* a yearbook of sorts published by residents of the camp in 1990 and edited by Thomas Takeuchi.

21. Quoted in US Commission on Wartime Relocation, *Personal Justice Denied,* 161.

22. US Commission on Wartime Relocation and Internment of Civilians, August 11, 1981, San Francisco, transcript, p. 262, in author's possession.

23. Fred Ross oral history with Bob Ross, July 16, 1972, Fred Ross Jr. papers.

24. Reel 313, JAERR.

25. Audiotape, April 27, 1985, Box 41, Folder 329, Ross Papers.

26. Fred Ross oral history with Bob Ross, July 16, 1972, Fred Ross Jr. papers.

27. Girdner and Loftis, *Great Betrayal,* 248.

28. *Minidoka Interlude,* calendar, n.p.

29. "Japanese Americans," audiotape, n.d. (likely July 16, 1972), Bob Ross audiotapes.

30. Ibid.

31. Census data are available at the US Census Bureau, www.census.gov/population/www/documentation/twps0027/tab17.txt (accessed May 12, 2015).

32. Reel 60, JAERR.

33. Fred Ross oral history with Bob Ross, July 16, 1972, Fred Ross Jr. papers.

34. Audiotape, April 27, 1985, Box 41, Folder 329, Ross Papers.

35. Reel 64, JAERR.

36. Audiotape, April 27, 1985, Box 41, Folder 329, Ross Papers.

37. Audiotape, August 29, 1985, Box 37, Folder 116, Ross Papers.

38. Reel 61, JAERR.

39. "Japanese Americans," audiotape, n.d. (likely July 16, 1972), Bob Ross audiotapes.

40. Ibid.

41. Audiotape, August 29, 1985, Box 37, Folder 116, Ross Papers.

42. Ibid.

43. Reel 64, JAERR.

44. Ibid.

45. Ibid.

46. Quoted in Girdner and Loftis, *Great Betrayal,* 390.

47. The description of Bridges and Ross in Petaluma comes from Kay Uweda, audiotape, August 29, 1985, Box 37, Folder 116, Ross Papers.

48. *San Jose Evening News,* August 28, 1945.

49. Ibid.

50. Quoted in Gary Kamiya, *Cool Gray City of Love: 49 Views of San Francisco* (New York: Bloomsbury, 2013), 303.

51. Audiotape, April 27, 1985, Box 41, Folder 329, Ross Papers.

52. Luis Alvarez, *The Power of the Zoot: Youth Culture and Resistance during World War II* (Berkeley: University of California Press, 2009), 200.

CHAPTER FIVE

1. For background on Short, see Mike Davis, *City of Quartz: Evacuating the Future in Los Angeles* (New York: Verso, 2006), 397–401.

2. "San Bernardino: Ruth and Ignacio," n.d., Box 22, Folder 17, Ross Papers.

3. "Community Organization in Mexican American Colonies, 1946–47," Box 20, Folder 19, Ross Papers.

4. For more information on Ignacio Lopez, see Mario T. García, *Mexican Americans: Leadership, Ideology, and Identity, 1930–1960* (New Haven: Yale University Press, 1989), 84–112.

5. Quoted in Matthew Garcia, *A World of Its Own: Race, Labor, and Citrus in the Making of Greater Los Angeles, 1900–1970* (Chapel Hill: University of North Carolina Press, 2001), 231.

6. Ruth Tuck to Ross, September 10, 1946, Box 11, Folder 12, Ross Papers. Colonias are typically unincorporated rural communities of ethnic Mexicans, as opposed to an ethnic Mexican community within a city, which is often referred to as a barrio.

7. "Community Organization in Mexican American Colonies, 1946–47," Box 20, Folder 19, Ross Papers.

8. Ruth Tuck, *Not with the Fist: Mexican Americans in a Southwest City* (New York: Harcourt, Brace and Co., 1946), 162.

9. McWilliams, *Southern California,* 207.

10. Garcia, *A World of Its Own,* 23–24.

11. The evocative phrase "orange curtain" is used by Matt Garcia in his penetrating analysis of the Citrus Belt, *A World of Its Own.*

12. Gilbert G. Gonzales, "Segregation of Mexican Children in a Southern California City," *Western Historical Quarterly* 16, no. 1 (January 1985): 57.

13. Quoted in Philippa Strum, *Mendez v. Westminster: School Desegregation and Mexican-American Rights* (Lawrence: University Press of Kansas, 2010), 17–18.

14. "Bell Town Unity League," n.d., Box 20, Folder 4, Ross Papers.
15. Ibid.
16. For background on David Marcus, see Strum, *Mendez v. Westminster,* 39–41.
17. Quoted in ibid., 64.
18. Ibid., 83.
19. Mark Brilliant, *The Color of America Has Changed: How Racial Diversity Shaped Civil Rights Reform in California, 1941–1978* (New York: Oxford University Press, 2010), 73.
20. "Community Organization in Mexican American Colonies, 1946–47," Box 20, Folder 19, Ross Papers.
21. "Council Rejects Sign Ordinance of NAACP," *Riverside Daily Press,* August 13, 1946.
22. "'KKK' Note Received," *Riverside Daily Press,* August 14, 1946.
23. "Transcript—Training, Florida UFW, 1974–75," Box 34, Folder 15, Ross Papers.
24. *Riverside Daily Press,* September 16, 1946.
25. *Riverside Daily Press,* September 25, 1947.

CHAPTER SIX

1. Carey McWilliams, *Factories in the Field* (Santa Barbara: Peregrine Smith, 1971), 233.
2. Audiotape, April 27, 1985, Box 41, Folder 330, Ross Papers.
3. Santa Ana School Board of Education meeting minutes, September 12, 1946, available online at Chapman University Digital Commons, http://digitalcommons. chapman.edu/mendez_v_westminster/12 (accessed October 1, 2015).
4. Quoted in Strum, *Mendez v. Westminster,* 130.
5. "Manuscript about LULAC," n.d., Box 22, Folder 3, Ross Papers.
6. FBI file of Fred Ross, in author's possession.
7. Associated Farmers of Orange County to Isadore Gonzales, May 5, 1947, in author's possession.
8. Interview with Hector Tarango, available online at Community Service Organization, www.csoproject.org/Histories.html (accessed January 8, 2014).
9. Ibid.
10. Ross to Laurence Hewes, February 2, 1947, Box 5, Folder 50, CFCU.
11. Ibid.
12. Ross to Alinsky, September 26, 1947, Box 2, Folder 1, Ross Papers.
13. Ross to Laurence Hewes, January 12, 1947, Box 5, Folder 50, CFCU.
14. Louis Wirth to ACRR Board of Directors, March 7, 1947, Box 6, Folder 19, CFCU.
15. Author interview with Bill Pastreich, June 29, 2011.
16. Quoted in Sanford D. Horwitt, *Let Them Call Me Rebel: Saul Alinsky, His Life and Legacy* (New York: Random House, 1992), 223.

17. "Community Organization in Mexican American Colonies, 1946–47," Box 20, Folder 19, Ross Papers.

18. Ibid.

19. Ibid.

CHAPTER SEVEN

1. Quoted in Kenneth Burt, *The Search for a Civic Voice: California Latino Politics* (Claremont, CA: Regina Books, 2007), 57.

2. Ibid., 228.

3. Untitled manuscript, Box 23, Folder 8, Ross Papers.

4. Ross to Alinsky, September 26, 1947, Box 2, Folder 1, Ross Papers.

5. Ibid.

6. Ross to Alinsky, November 16, 1947, Box 2, Folder 1, Ross Papers.

7. Quoted in George J. Sanchez, "What's Good for Boyle Heights Is Good for the Jews: Creating Multiracialism on the Eastside during the 1950s," *American Quarterly* 56, no. 3 (September 2004): 637.

8. Ross to Alinsky, September 26, 1947, Box 2, Folder 1, Ross Papers.

9. Ross to Alinsky, November 3, 1947, Box 2, Folder 1, Ross Papers.

10. Kenneth Burt, "The Fight for Fair Employment and the Shifting Alliances among Latinos and Labor in Cold War Los Angeles," in *Labor's Cold War: Local Politics in a Global Context,* ed. Shelton Stromquist (Chicago: University of Illinois Press, 2008), 89.

11. "CSO—Executive Committee, Minutes, 1951," Box 5, Folder 6, Ross Papers.

12. "CSO," September 5, 1950, Box 10, Folder 12, Ross Papers.

13. "Notebooks, 1957," Box 30, Folder 5, Ross Papers.

14. Untitled manuscript, n.d., Box 25, Folder 12, Ross Papers.

15. Burt, *Search for a Civic Voice,* 71.

16. Quoted in Horwitt, *Let Them Call Me Rebel,* 212.

17. Frances Ross to May Gibson, June 8, 1947, Julia Ross papers.

18. Frances Ross to May Gibson, June 26, 1946, Julia Ross papers.

19. Author interview with Julia Ross, November 18, 2011.

20. Frances Ross to May Gibson, January 20, 1947, Julia Ross papers.

21. Frances Ross to May Gibson, November 15, 1946, Julia Ross papers.

22. Author interview with Julia Ross, November 18, 2011.

23. Audiotape, April 24, 1978, Box 39, Folder 259, Ross Papers.

24. Index card kept on Ross by California Un-American Activities Committee, in author's possession.

25. "News of the CSO," *El Pueblo,* March 6, 1948, Box 14, Folder 2, Ross Papers.

26. CSO flyer, in author's possession.

27. For background on the campaign, see Beatrice W. Griffith, "Viva Roybal—Viva America," *Common Ground,* September 1949.

28. Katherine Underwood, "Pioneering Minority Representation: Edward Roybal and the Los Angeles City Council, 1949–1962," *Pacific Historical Review* 66, no. 3 (August 1997): 412.

29. "CSO," September 5, 1950, Box 10, Folder 12, Ross Papers.

30. Audiotape, August 24, 1985, Box 37, Folder 105, Ross Papers.

31. Audiotape, April 27, 1985, Box 41, Folder 330, Ross Papers.

32. Ibid.

33. Ibid.

34. Ibid.

CHAPTER EIGHT

1. Frances Ross to May Gibson, November 11, 1949, courtesy of Bob Ross (emphasis in original).

2. Frances Ross to May Gibson, February 4, 1950, Julia Ross papers.

3. Box 2, Folder 1, Ross Papers.

4. For background on these cases, see Don Parson, "Injustice for Salcido: The Left Response to Police Brutality in Cold War Los Angeles," *Southern California Quarterly* 86, no. 2 (Summer 2004): 145–68.

5. Audiotape, August 24, 1985, Box 37, Folder 105, Ross Papers.

6. "Bloody Xmas," n.d., Box 20, Folder 6, Ross Papers.

7. Edward J. Escobar, *Race, Police, and the Making of a Political Identity: Mexican Americans and the Los Angeles Police Department, 1940–1945* (Berkeley: University of California Press, 1999), 286.

8. "The Last Round/Tony Rios/Bloody Xmas," n.d., Box 21, Folder 18, Ross Papers.

9. Edward J. Escobar, "Bloody Christmas and the Irony of Police Professionalism: The Los Angeles Police Department, Mexican Americans, and Police Reform in the 1950s," *Pacific Historical Review* 72, no. 2 (May 2003): 184.

10. "Officer Beaten in Bar Brawl; Seven Men Jailed," *Los Angeles Times,* December 26, 1951.

11. Quoted in Burt, *Search for a Civic Voice,* 120.

12. "Bloody Xmas," n.d., Box 20, Folder 6, Ross Papers.

13. "Jury Vindicates Rios and Ulloa," *Los Angeles Daily News,* March 11, 1952, in Box 4, Folder 23, Ross Papers.

14. Escobar, "Bloody Christmas and the Irony of Police Professionalism," 187.

15. "Jurors Hear Account of Police Beating," *Los Angeles Times,* March 20, 1952.

16. Roger Baldwin to Ross, December 12, 1950, Box 10, Folder 12, Ross Papers.

17. Ross to Roger Baldwin, January 4, 1951, Box 6, Folder 1, Ross Papers.

18. Quoted in Neil Foley, *Quest for Equality: The Failed Promise of Black-Brown Solidarity* (Cambridge, MA: Harvard University Press, 2010), 132.

19. Roger Baldwin to Ross, December 17, 1951, Box 6, Folder 1, Ross Papers.

20. Audiotape, September 25, 1979, Box 40, Folder 285, Ross Papers.

21. Frances Ross to May Gibson, August 22, 1951, Julia Ross papers.

22. "CSO—Executive Committee, Minutes, 1949–50," Box 5, Folder 5, Ross Papers.

23. Frances Ross to May Gibson, June 28, 1949, Julia Ross papers.

24. Frances Ross to May Gibson, February 19, 1951, Julia Ross papers (emphasis added).

25. Author interview with Julia Ross, November 18, 2011.

26. Board meeting minutes, June 14, 1952, Box 7, Folder 7, CFCU.

CHAPTER NINE

1. Board meeting minutes, March 28, 1952, Box 7, Folder 7, CFCU.

2. Josephine Duveneck to Sacramento Council, April 22, 1952, Box 3, Folder 9, CFCU.

3. "Breaking into the Community," n.d., Box 17, Folder 9, Ross Papers.

4. Ibid.

5. Father McDonnell to Archbishop Mitty, February 15, 1951, Mission Band.

6. "Breaking into the Community," n.d., Box 17, Folder 9, Ross Papers.

7. Josephine Duveneck, *Life on Two Levels* (Los Altos, CA: William Kaufman, 1978), 255.

8. Box 31, Folder 8, Ross Papers.

9. Work journal, Box 31, Folder 8, Ross Papers.

10. Quoted in Levy, *Cesar Chavez,* 98.

11. Author interview with Richard Chavez, July 6, 2011.

12. Quoted in Levy, *Cesar Chavez,* 93.

13. Board meeting minutes, June 14, 1952, Box 7, Folder 7, CFCU.

14. In 1913, workers in Ludlow, Colorado, went on strike against Colorado Fuel & Iron, owned by David Rockefeller. During the strike, the National Guard engaged in a shootout with the workers and set fire to the tents of their camp, killing eleven children and two women.

15. Author interview with Herman Gallegos, December 11, 2010.

16. Ibid.

17. "GOP Ballot Watch Plan Draws Fire," *San Jose Mercury News,* October 1952, Box 11, Folder 12, Ross Papers.

18. Thurgood Marshall's speech is listed in the CFCU convention program, 1952, Box 10, Folder 8, Ross Papers. Unfortunately, it doesn't appear that notes or a transcript of Marshall's speech were kept.

19. Duveneck, *Life on Two Levels,* front jacket.

20. Quoted in Carl Tjerandsen, *Education for Citizenship,* available online at COMM-ORG: The On-Line Conference on Community Organizing, http://comm-org.wisc.edu/papers2003/tjerandsen/contentsd.htm (accessed March 22, 2014).

21. Ross to Alinsky, August 3, 1953, Box 47, Folder 659, IAF Chicago.

22. Alinsky to Ross, August 5, 1953, Box 47, Folder 659, IAF Chicago.

CHAPTER TEN

1. Ross to Alinsky, October 7, 1953, Box 3, Folder 12, CFCU.
2. *San Bernardino Sun,* September 15, 1954.
3. *San Bernardino Sun,* November 18, 1954.
4. Ross to Alinsky, January 3, 1954, Fred Ross Jr. papers.
5. "Citizenship Report of Eugene Lowery," June 21, 1954, Box 25, Folder 20, Ross Papers.
6. Ibid.
7. Ross to Alinsky, January 3, 1955, Fred Ross Jr. papers.
8. Ross to Alinsky, April 13, 1955, Fred Ross Jr. papers.
9. Quoted in William Deverell, *Whitewashed Adobe: The Rise of Los Angeles and the Remaking of Its Mexican Past* (Berkeley: University of California Press, 2004), 45.
10. Ross to Alinsky, April 13, 1955, Fred Ross Jr. papers.
11. Author interview with Bob Ross, June 25, 2011.
12. Ross to Alinsky, January 21, 1955, Fred Ross Jr. papers.
13. Ibid.
14. Quoted in Levy, *Cesar Chavez,* 104.
15. Ibid., 112
16. Ibid., 99.
17. Ibid., 113.
18. Chavez to Ross, July 16, 1954 , Box 1, Folder 2, Ross—Wayne State.
19. Ross to Alinsky, January 19, 1955, Fred Ross Jr. papers.
20. Ross interview of Dolores Huerta, audiotape, 1961, Box 35, Folder 7, Ross Papers.
21. Ibid.
22. Ross to Alinsky, March 10, 1960, Box 2, Folder 3, Ross Papers.
23. Author interview with Dolores Huerta, April 18, 2008.
24. "Work Diary, 1957," Box 1, Folder 19, Ross Papers.
25. Ibid
26. Lawrence Goodwyn, *The Populist Moment: A Short History of the Agrarian Revolt in America* (New York: Oxford University Press, 1978), xix.
27. Roybal speech from 1954 conference, Fred Ross Jr. papers.
28. Ross to Alinsky, June 7, 1955, Fred Ross Jr. papers.

CHAPTER ELEVEN

1. Annual meeting minutes, February 15–16, 1947, Box 7, Folder 1, CFCU.
2. Ross to Cruz Nevarez, September 30, 1953, Box 6, Folder 2, Ross Papers.
3. Ross to Alinsky, n.d. (end of 1954), Fred Ross Jr. papers.
4. Ross to Alinsky, March 16, 1955, Fred Ross Jr. papers.
5. Box 11, Folder 10, Ross Papers.
6. 1958 consolidation report, Fred Ross Jr. papers.
7. Ibid.

8. Quoted in Tjerandsen, *Education for Citizenship.*
9. Ibid.
10. "Notebooks, 1957," Box 30, Folder 5, Ross Papers.
11. Tjerandsen, *Education for Citizenship.*
12. Ross to Alinsky, undated report (likely mid-December 1954), Fred Ross Jr. papers.
13. Alinsky to Ross, June 24, 1958, Fred Ross Jr. papers.
14. Ross to Alinsky, May 25, 1959, Fred Ross Jr. papers.
15. Ibid.
16. Chavez to Ross, June 28, 1960, Fred Ross Jr. papers.
17. Ibid.
18. Chavez to Ross, May 7, 1959, Box 3, Folder 3, Ross—Wayne State.

CHAPTER TWELVE

1. Box 1, Folder 13, Ross Papers.
2. Box 30, Folder 6, Ross Papers.
3. Box 10, Folder 14, Ross Papers.
4. Alinsky to Ross, November 3, 1960, Fred Ross Jr. papers.
5. Quoted from Ross's manuscript on the CSO, Box 21, Folder 4, Ross Papers.
6. Alinsky to Ross, January 16, 1961, Fred Ross Jr. papers.
7. Alinsky to Ross, April 6, 1961, Fred Ross Jr. papers.
8. Alinsky to Ross, December 31, 1962, Fred Ross Jr. papers.
9. Alinsky to Ross, April 23, 1962, Fred Ross Jr. papers.
10. Box 30, Folder 1, ESF.
11. Ibid.
12. Ibid.
13. Chavez to Alinsky, n.d. (likely late 1961/early 1962), Fred Ross Jr. papers.
14. Summary of educational meeting held January 24, 1962, Box 11, Folder 7, Ross Papers.
15. Nicholas von Hoffman, *Radical: A Portrait of Saul Alinsky* (New York: Nation Books, 2011), 171.
16. Alinsky to Ross, March 27, 1962, Fred Ross Jr. papers.
17. Ross to Chavez, May 2, 1962, Box 48, Folder 18, OPC—Wayne State.
18. Ross to Alinsky, April 4, 1962, Box 2, Folder 3, Ross Papers.
19. Alinsky to Ross, May 28, 1962, Fred Ross Jr. papers.
20. Chavez to Ross, May 10, 1962, Box 3, Folder 6, Ross—Wayne State.
21. Ross to Chavez, May 27, 1962, Box 48, Folder 18, OPC—Wayne State.
22. Chavez to Huerta, n.d. (likely 1962), Box 18, Folder 378, Levy Collection.
23. Chavez to Ross, May 22, 1962, Box 3, Folder 6, Ross—Wayne State.
24. Ross to Chavez, September 1, 1962, Box 48, Folder 18, OPC—Wayne State.
25. Ross to Chavez, September 25, 1962, Box 48, Folder 18, OPC—Wayne State.
26. Ross to Chavez, October 3, 1962, Box 48, Folder 18, OPC—Wayne State.

27. Alinsky to Ross, November 20, 1962, Box 4Zd559, Folder 1, IAF Austin.
28. Horwitt, *Let Them Call Me Rebel,* 398.
29. Quoted in ibid., 399.
30. Ross to Alinsky, November 28, 1962, Fred Ross Jr. papers.
31. Ross report to Carl Tjerandsen, October 7–November 30, 1963, Fred Ross Jr. papers.
32. Carl Tjerandsen to Ross, May 1, 1963, Box 29, Folder 17, ESF.
33. Author interview with Gilbert Padilla, June 23, 2009.
34. Ross to Carl Tjerandsen, October 15, 1963, Box 29, Folder 17, ESF.
35. Ibid.
36. Ross to Alinsky, April 5, 1964, Box 4Zd527, IAF Austin.

CHAPTER THIRTEEN

1. "Guadalupe," n.d., Box 21, Folder 16, Ross Papers.
2. "Memorandum on Guadalupe," June 20, 1964, Box 4Zd527, IAF Austin.
3. Margaret Mead and Muriel Brown, *The Wagon and the Star: A Study of American Community Initiative* (Chicago: Rand McNally, 1966), 96, 97.
4. Author interview with Fred Ross Jr., August 14, 2014.
5. For more on the Guadalupe Organization's work, see Octaviana V. Truillo, "Yaqui Cultural and Linguistic Evolution through a History of Urbanization," in *American Indians and the Urban Experience,* ed. Susan Lobo and Kurt Peters (Lanham, MD: Rowman & Littlefield, 2001), 63–64.
6. "Workbook of a Wayfaring Organizer," n.d., Box 20, Folder 1, Ross Papers.
7. "Memorandum on Guadalupe," June 20, 1964, Box 4Zd527, IAF Austin.
8. Noel A. Cazenave, *The Urban Racial State: Managing Race Relations in American Cities* (Lanham, MD: Rowman & Littlefield, 2011), 71.
9. Interview of Ross, audiotape, August 26, 1965, Box 15375, CATC.
10. Ibid.
11. "The Genesis of the Community Action Training Center of Syracuse University," February 1967, by Robert S. Pickett, in author's possession.
12. Author interview with Danny Schechter, August 20, 2011.
13. Warren C. Haggstrom, "The Power Bind," n.d. (likely 1966), p. 4, available at Gather the People: Creative Tools for Congregational Community Development and Organizing, www.gatherthepeople.org/Downloads/WCH_POWER_BIND.pdf (accessed May 5, 2015).
14. Author interview with Bill Pastreich, June 29, 2011.
15. Ibid.
16. *Syracuse Post-Standard,* June 11, 1965.
17. *Syracuse Post-Standard,* June 22, 1965.
18. *Syracuse Post-Standard,* June 11, 1965.
19. *Syracuse Herald-American,* August 8, 1965.
20. Author interview with Bill Pastreich, June 29, 2011.

21. Ibid.

22. Author interview with Danny Schechter, August 20, 2011.

23. Wini Breines, *Community and Organization in the New Left, 1962–1968: The Great Refusal* (New Brunswick, NJ: Rutgers University Press, 1989), 126.

24. Ibid., 142.

25. "Brooklyn 1977," n.d., Box 20, Folder 14, Ross Papers.

26. Breines, *Great Refusal*, 137.

27. "A Professional Radical Moves In on Rochester," interview with Saul Alinsky, part 2, *Harper's*, July 1965.

28. "The War on Poverty within Syracuse University, January–February 1965," January 1967, by Robert S. Pickett, in author's possession.

29. Frances Fox Piven and Richard Cloward, *Poor People's Movements: Why They Succeed, How They Fail* (New York: Vintage, 1979), xxi–xxii.

30. Danny Schechter, "Reveille for Reformers: Report from Syracuse," *Studies on the Left* 5, no. 4 (Fall 1965): 84.

31. Ibid., 87.

32. Danny Schechter, "Reveille for Reformers II," *Studies on the Left* 6, no. 1 (January–February 1966): 26–27.

33. Quoted in Scott Stossel, *Sarge: The Life and Times of Sargent Shriver* (New York: Smithsonian, 2004), 405.

34. Quoted in "Antipoverty Program Funds Doubled," *Congressional Quarterly Almanac, 1965*, available online at http://library.cqpress.com/cqalmanac/document.php?id=cqal65-1259400 (accessed May 13, 2015).

35. "House Panel Hails Antipoverty Efforts," *New York Times*, April 13, 1965.

36. Staff meeting minutes, September 16, 1965, CATC.

37. *Syracuse Post-Standard*, December 9, 1965.

38. *Salinas Californian*, June 5, 1976.

39. *Chicago Tribune*, July 14, 1987.

40. Strangely, Ross apparently never spoke or wrote about the trip publicly; the few details I have were provided to me by his son and Jeff Miller, a professor who found documents related to the trip in Syracuse University's archives.

41. Guest lecturer notes, August 20, 1965, CATC.

42. Charles Payne, *I've Got the Light of Freedom: The Organizing Tradition and the Mississippi Freedom Struggle* (Berkeley: University of California Press, 1995), 367.

43. Barbara Ransby, *Ella Baker and the Black Freedom Movement: A Radical Democratic Vision* (Chapel Hill: University of North Carolina Press, 2003), 241.

44. Payne, *I've Got the Light of Freedom*, 97.

45. Ross to Chavez, n.d. (likely 1965), Box 48, Folder 18, OPC—Wayne State.

46. Fred Ross, "The DiGiorgio Story," n.d., Fred Ross Jr. papers.

CHAPTER FOURTEEN

1. Chavez to Ross, May 10, 1962, Box 3, Folder 6, Ross—Wayne State.

2. Ronald B. Taylor, *Chavez and the Farm Workers* (Boston: Beacon Press, 1975), 127.

3. Miriam Pawel, *The Crusades of Cesar Chavez* (New York: Bloomsbury, 2014), 118.

4. Frances to Ross, February 18, 1965, Julia Ross papers.

5. Alinsky to Frances Ross, May 3, 1965, Box 4Zd559, IAF Austin.

6. Author interview with Julia Ross, November 18, 2011.

7. Jacques Levy interview of Ross, April 4, 1969, Box 6, Folder 196, Levy Collection.

8. Fred Ross, "The DiGiorgio Story," n.d., Fred Ross Jr. papers.

9. Ibid.

10. "Grape Strikers Score Gov. Brown as March Ends," *New York Times,* April 11, 1966.

11. Marshall Ganz, *Why David Sometimes Wins: Leadership, Organization, and Strategy in the California Farm Worker Movement* (New York: Oxford University Press, 2009), viii.

12. Fred Ross, "The DiGiorgio Story," n.d., Fred Ross Jr. papers.

13. Quoted in Levy, *Cesar Chavez,* 234.

14. Fred Ross, "The DiGiorgio Story," n.d., Fred Ross Jr. papers.

15. Ibid.

16. Box 12, Folder 1, Ross Papers.

17. Author interview with Eliseo Medina, December 7, 2014.

18. Author interview with Ida Cousino, May 13, 2013.

19. Quoted in Horwitt, *Let Them Call Me Rebel,* 522.

20. Quoted in John Gregory Dunne, *Delano: The Story of the California Grape Strike* (New York: Farrar, Strauss & Giroux, 1967), 170.

21. Author interview with Dolores Huerta, March 18, 2008.

22. Taylor, *Chavez and the Farm Workers,* 201.

23. Levy, *Cesar Chavez,* 235.

24. Quoted in Taylor, *Chavez and the Farm Workers,* 195.

CHAPTER FIFTEEN

1. Fred Ross, "The DiGiorgio Story," n.d., Fred Ross Jr. papers.

2. Ganz, *Why David Sometimes Wins,* 211.

3. Author interview with Marshall Ganz, October 18, 2014.

4. Ibid.

5. Ed Chiera personal essay, FMDP.

6. Boycott planning, January 1969, recording courtesy of LeRoy Chatfield.

7. Quoted in Levy, *Cesar Chavez,* 277.

8. Ibid., 278.

9. Quoted in Peter Matthiessen, *Sal Si Puedes: Cesar Chavez and the New American Revolution* (New York: Dell Publishing, 1969), 321.

10. Box 6, File 24, Levy Collection.

11. Fred Ross Jr. to Julia Ross, April 8, 1968, in author's possession.
12. Author interview with Marshall Ganz, October 18, 2014.
13. Ross to Peter Matthiessen, December 8, 1968, Box 2, Folder 3, Ross Papers.
14. Ibid.
15. Quoted in Pawel, *Crusades of Cesar Chavez,* 206.

CHAPTER SIXTEEN

1. Larry Tramutola, *Sidewalk Strategies: Seven Winning Steps for Candidates, Causes and Communities* (Austin, TX: TurnKey Press, 2003), 19.
2. Ibid., 40.
3. Author interview with Nancy Elliott, October 9, 2014.
4. Ibid.
5. Todd Eisenstadt, "41 Years in the Grassroots, Organizer Fred Ross, 76, Still Has Work to Do," *Chicago Tribune,* July 14, 1987.
6. "Brooklyn, 1977," Box 20, Folder 14, Ross Papers.
7. Ibid.
8. Ibid.
9. Ibid.
10. Author interview with Larry Tramutola, May 2, 2014.
11. Box 17, Folder 41, Ross Papers.
12. Author interview with David Dyson, August 27, 2013.
13. Ibid.
14. Author interview with Paul Milne, June 6, 2013.
15. Author interview with Julia Ross, November 18, 2011.
16. Author interview with Bob Ross, June 25, 2011.
17. Author interview with Julia Ross, April 24, 2015.
18. Author interview with Fred Ross Jr., January 6, 2015.
19. A number of people relayed this to me, including Bob Ross and Larry Tramutola in their interviews with me, June 25, 2011, and May 2, 2014, respectively.
20. Henry Weinstein, "The Man Who Taught Chavez How to Organize," *San Francisco Examiner and Chronicle,* October 31, 1976.

CHAPTER SEVENTEEN

1. Quoted in Pawel, *Crusades of Cesar Chavez,* 104.
2. "Cesar Chavez Talks about Organizing and the History of the NFWA," December 1965, FMDP.
3. Quoted in Pawel, *Crusades of Cesar Chavez,* 342.
4. Author interview with John Brown, December 27, 2014.
5. Pawel, *Crusades of Cesar Chavez,* 330.

6. Matthew Garcia, *From the Jaws of Victory: The Triumph and Tragedy of Cesar Chavez and the Farm Worker Movement* (Berkeley: University of California Press, 2012), 175.

7. Henry Weinstein, "The Man Who Taught Chavez How to Organize," *San Francisco Examiner and Chronicle,* October 31, 1976.

8. Audiotape, September 24, 1979, Box 40, Folder 286, Ross Papers.

9. Nancy Grimley Carleton personal essay, FMDP.

10. Author interview with Marshall Ganz, October 18, 2014.

11. Box 34, Folder 15, Ross Papers.

12. "Brooklyn, 1977," Box 20, Folder 14, Ross Papers.

13. Author interview with Marshall Ganz, October 18, 2014.

14. "UFW Aide Quits, Alleges Chavez Antileftist Bias," *Los Angeles Times,* December 22, 1976.

15. Audiotape, Box 39, Folder 207, Fred Ross Papers.

16. Quoted in Pawel, *Crusades of Cesar Chavez,* 345.

17. Miriam Pawel, *The Union of Their Dreams: Power, Hope, and Struggle in Cesar Chavez's Farm Worker Movement* (New York: Bloomsbury Press, 2009), 214.

18. Author interview with Paul Milne, June 6, 2013.

19. Ganz, *Why David Sometimes Wins,* 159.

20. Pawel, *Crusades of Cesar Chavez,* 365.

21. Author interview with Gary Guthman, December 5, 2014.

22. Quoted in Frank Bardacke, *Trampling Out the Vintage: Cesar Chavez and the Two Souls of the United Farm Workers* (New York: Verso, 2011), 615.

23. Author interview with John Brown, December 27, 2014.

24. Quoted in Bardacke, *Trampling Out the Vintage,* 639.

25. Quoted in Pawel, *Union of Their Dreams,* 280.

26. Ibid, 281.

27. Pawel, *Union of Their Dreams,* 281.

28. Bardacke, *Trampling Out the Vintage,* 653.

29. Quoted in Levy, *Cesar Chavez,* 117.

30. Pawel, *Crusades of Cesar Chavez,* 431.

31. Author interview with Scott Washburn, January 18, 2015.

32. Author interview with Jerry Cohen, December 10, 2014.

33. Ibid.

34. Author interview with Fred Ross Jr., January 6, 2015.

35. Ibid.

CHAPTER EIGHTEEN

1. Author interview with Marc Dohan, January 20, 2015.

2. Ibid.

3. Author interview with Gretchen Laue, March 22, 2012.

4. Author interview with Mario Bustamante, March 22, 2012.

5. Author interview with Gretchen Laue, March 22, 2012.

6. Pawel, *Crusades of Cesar Chavez,* 426.

7. Author interview with Gretchen Laue, March 22, 2012.

8. Author interview with Fred Ross Jr., January 6, 2015.

9. Ibid.

10. This recollection comes from Chavez, who included it in his eulogy of Ross, a video of which is posted at the Farmworker Movement Documentary Project. All other quotes from speakers at the memorial service are also at the site, https://libraries.ucsd.edu/farmworkermovement/media/video/index.shtml (accessed September 2, 2014).

11. Author interview with Fred Ross Jr., January 6, 2015.

12. Woody Guthrie, "Union Maid," © copyright 1960 (renewed) and 1963 (renewed) by Woody Guthrie Publications, Inc. & TRO-Ludlow Music, Inc. (BMI), www.woodyguthrie.org/Lyrics/Union_Maid.htm.

13. Jerry Cohen, "UFW Must Get Back to Organizing," *Los Angeles Times,* January 15, 1986.

14. "An Organizer's Organizer," *Progressive,* December 1988.

15. Ibid.

SELECTED BIBLIOGRAPHY

ARCHIVES

CATC
Community Action Training Center Records, Special Collections Research Center, Syracuse University Libraries

CFCU
California Federation for Civic Unity Records, Bancroft Library, University of California, Berkeley

ESF
Emil Schwarzhaupt Foundation Papers, Special Collections Research Center, University of Chicago Library

FMDP
Farmworker Movement Documentation Project, https://libraries.ucsd.edu/farmworkermovement

FSA San Bruno
Farm Security Administration Records, Record Group 96, Federal Archives and Regional Center, San Bruno, CA

Hollenberg Collection
Ralph W. Hollenberg collection of materials relating to the Farm Security Administration, Region IX, Bancroft Library, University of California, Berkeley

IAF Austin
Industrial Areas Foundation Records, Dolph Briscoe Center for American History, University of Texas, Austin

IAF Chicago
Industrial Areas Foundation Records, Special Collections and University Archives, University of Illinois, Chicago

JAERR
Japanese American Evacuation and Resettlement Records, Bancroft Library, University of California, Berkeley

Levy Collection
Jacques E. Levy Research Collection on Cesar Chavez, Yale Collection of Western Americana, Beinecke Rare Book and Manuscript Library, New Haven, CT

Mission Band
Donald McDonnell/Spanish Mission Band Papers, Archives of the Archdiocese of San Francisco, Menlo Park, CA

OPC—Wayne State	Office of the President Collection, Walter P. Reuther Library, Wayne State University, Detroit
Ross Papers	Fred Ross Papers, Special Collections and University Archives, Stanford University, Stanford, CA
Ross—Wayne State	Fred Ross Sr. Papers, Walter P. Reuther Library, Wayne State University, Detroit
SCDA	Syracuse Community Development Association Records, Special Collections Research Center, Syracuse University Libraries, Syracuse, NY
VALB—Bay Area	Veterans of the Abraham Lincoln Brigade, Bay Area Post Records, Bancroft Library, University of California, Berkeley

PRIVATE COLLECTIONS

These three private collections proved critical for filling in details about Ross's professional and personal life.

Bob Ross audiotapes	This collection, held by Ross's son Bob Ross, consists of several lengthy interviews with Ross that focus on his youth and work with Japanese Americans.
Fred Ross Jr. papers	This collection, held by Ross's son Fred Ross Jr., primarily consists of letters between Ross and Saul Alinsky. A few of these documents can be found in the Ross Papers at Stanford or at IAF Chicago and IAF Austin, but most are not available elsewhere. Fred Ross Jr. will be adding this valuable collection to his father's papers at Stanford.
Julia Ross papers	This collection, held by Ross's daughter, Julia Ross, consists of hundreds of letters written by Ross's second wife, Frances, to her mother, mostly between 1946 and 1951.

INTERVIEWS

Jorge Acuña	June 23, 2009
John Brown	December 27, 2014
Mario Bustamante	March 22, 2012, and January 26, 2015
LeRoy Chatfield	April 25, 2013
Jerry Cohen	December 10, 2014
Ida Cousino	May 13, 2013
Richard Chavez	July 6, 2011
Suzanne Darweesh	July 13, 2011

Marc Dohan	January 20, 2015
David Dyson	August 27, 2013
Nancy Elliott	October 9, 2014
Herman Gallegos	December 11, 2010
Marshall Ganz	October 18, 2014
Margie Garcia	February 16, 2011
Louis Gonzales	June 24, 2009
Margaret Govea	July 7, 2011
Gary Guthman	December 5, 2014
Chris Hartmire	July 9, 2011
Craig Heverly	April 16, 2015
Edward Howden	December 13, 2011
Dolores Huerta	March 18, 2008
Gretchen Laue	March 22, 2012, and January 26, 2015
Frank Ledesma	June 22, 2009
Juan Marcoida	December 30, 2008
Eliseo Medina	December 7, 2014
Paul Milne	June 6, 2013
Gilbert Padilla	June 23, 2009
Bill Pastreich	June 29, 2011
Lois Pryor	June 7, 2013
Bob Ross	June 25, 2011
Fred Ross Jr.	August 14, 2014, and January 6, 2015
Julia Ross	November 18, 2011, and April 24, 2015
Susan Sachen	June 18, 2015
Gilbert Salazar	July 7, 2011
Danny Schechter	August 20, 2011
Larry Tramutola	May 2, 2014
Scott Washburn	January 8, 2015

BOOKS

Alinsky, Saul. *Reveille for Radicals.* New York: Random House, 1969.
———. *Rules for Radicals.* New York: Random House, 1972.
Bardacke, Frank. *Trampling Out the Vintage: Cesar Chavez and the Two Souls of the United Farm Workers.* New York: Verso, 2011.
Bernstein, Shana. *Bridges of Reform: Interracial Civil Rights Activism in Twentieth-Century Los Angeles.* New York: Oxford University Press, 2011.
Brilliant, Mark. *The Color of America Has Changed: How Racial Diversity Shaped Civil Rights Reform in California, 1941–1978.* New York: Oxford University Press, 2010.
Burt, Kenneth. *The Search for a Civic Voice: California Latino Politics.* Claremont, CA: Regina Books, 2007.

Cazenave, Noel A. *The Urban Racial State: Managing Race Relations in American Cities*. Lanham, MD: Rowman & Littlefield, 2011.

Daniel, Cletus E. *Bitter Harvest: A History of California Farmworkers, 1870–1941*. Ithaca, NY: Cornell University Press, 1981.

Davis, Mike. *City of Quartz: Evacuating the Future in Los Angeles*. New York: Verso, 2006.

Dunne, Gregory John. *Delano: The Story of the California Grape Strike*. New York: Farrar, Strauss & Giroux, 1967.

Escobar, Edward J. *Race, Police, and the Making of a Political Identity: Mexican Americans and the Los Angeles Police Department, 1940–1945*. Berkeley: University of California Press, 1999.

Ganz, Marshall. *Why David Sometimes Wins: Leadership, Organization, and Strategy in the California Farm Worker Movement*. New York: Oxford University Press, 2009.

García, Mario T. *Mexican Americans: Leadership, Ideology, and Identity, 1930—1960*. New Haven, CT: Yale University Press, 1989.

Garcia, Matthew. *From the Jaws of Victory: The Triumph and Tragedy of Cesar Chavez and the Farm Worker Movement*. Berkeley: University of California Press, 2012.

———. *A World of Its Own: Race, Labor, and Citrus in the Making of Greater Los Angeles, 1900–1970*. Chapel Hill: University of North Carolina Press, 2001.

González, Gilbert G. *Labor and Community: Mexican Citrus Worker Villages in a Southern California Country, 1900–1950*. Chicago: University of Illinois Press, 1994.

Gregory, James N. *American Exodus: The Dust Bowl Migration and Okie Culture in California*. New York: Oxford University Press, 1989.

Hewes, Laurence. *Boxcar in the Sand*. New York: Knopf, 1957.

Horwitt, Sanford D. *Let Them Call Me Rebel: Saul Alinsky, His Life and Legacy*. 1989. New York: Random House, 1992.

Levy, Jacques E. *Cesar Chavez: Autobiography of La Causa*. Minneapolis: University of Minnesota Press, 2007.

Loftis, Anne. *Witnesses to the Struggle: Imaging the 1930s California Labor Movement*. Reno: University of Nevada Press, 1998.

Matthiessen, Peter. *Sal Si Puedes: Cesar Chavez and the New American Revolution*. New York: Dell Publishing, 1969.

McWilliams, Carey. *Factories in the Field: The Story of Migratory Farm Labor in California*. Santa Barbara: Peregrine Smith, 1935.

———. *Southern California: An Island on the Land*. Layton, UT: Gibbs Smith, 1973.

Pawel, Miriam. *The Crusades of Cesar Chavez*. New York: Bloomsbury, 2014.

———. *The Union of Their Dreams: Power, Hope, and Struggle in Cesar Chavez's Farm Worker Movement*. New York: Bloomsbury Press, 2009.

Payne, Charles. *I've Got the Light of Freedom: The Organizing Tradition and the Mississippi Freedom Struggle*. Berkeley: University of California Press, 1995.

Pitti, Stephen J. *The Devil in Silicon Valley: Northern California, Race, and Mexican Americans*. Princeton, NJ: Princeton University Press, 2003.

Ransby, Barbara. *Ella Baker and the Black Freedom Movement: A Radical Democratic Vision*. Chapel Hill: University of North Carolina Press, 2003

Richardson, Peter. *American Prophet: The Life and Work of Carey McWilliams*. Ann Arbor: University of Michigan Press, 2005.

Robinson, Greg. *By Order of the President: FDR and the Internment of Japanese Americans*. Cambridge, MA: Harvard University Press, 2001.

———. *A Tragedy of Democracy: Japanese Confinement in North America*. New York: Columbia University Press, 2009.

Ross, Fred. *Conquering Goliath: Cesar Chavez at the Beginning*. Keene, CA: El Taller Grafico Press, 1989.

Sánchez, George J. *Becoming Mexican American: Ethnicity, Culture, and Identity in Chicano Los Angeles, 1900–1945*. New York: Oxford University Press, 1993.

Shaw, Randy. *Beyond the Fields: Cesar Chavez, the UFW, and the Struggle for Justice in the 21st Century*. Berkeley: University of California Press, 2008.

Starr, Kevin. *Endangered Dreams: The Great Depression in California*. New York: Oxford University Press, 1996.

———. *Material Dreams: Southern California through the 1920s*. New York: Oxford University Press, 1990.

Steinbeck, John. *The Grapes of Wrath*. 1939. New York: Penguin, 1976.

Strum, Philippa. *Mendez v. Westminster: School Desegregation and Mexican-American Rights*. Lawrence: University Press of Kansas, 2010.

Taylor, Ronald B. *Chavez and the Farm Workers*. Boston: Beacon Press, 1975.

Tuck, Ruth. *Not with the Fist: Mexican-Americans in a Southwest City*. New York: Harcourt, Brace and Co., 1946.

US Commission on Wartime Relocation and Internment of Civilians. *Personal Justice Denied: Report of the Commission on Wartime Relocation and Internment of Civilians*. Seattle: University of Washington Press, 1997. Originally published in 2 vols. by the US Government Printing Office in 1982 and 1983.

von Hoffman, Nicholas. *Radical: A Portrait of Saul Alinsky*. New York: Nation Books, 2011

Weber, Devra. *Dark Sweat, White Gold: California Farm Workers, Cotton, and the New Deal*. Berkeley: University of California Press, 1994.

INDEX

Labor Youth League, 90
Lagomarsino, Robert, 227–28
Lakewood Experiment, 58–59
Lange, Dorothea, 41
Lapham, Roger, 60–61
Laue, Gretchen, 228
League of United Latin American Citizens (LULAC), 76–77, 78, 81, 106, 149
Library of Congress Archive of American Folk Song, 42–43
Long Beach, Ross family in, 62, 92–93, 122–23
Lopez, Ignacio, 64–66, 67, 81, 189
Lopez, Joaquin, 100
Los Angeles: anti-Mexican American sentiment in, 15; CSO founding and early activities in, 1–2, 86–91; Ross's childhood in, 9–11; Ross's work in East L.A., 1, 81, 86–91; Roybal City Council campaigns, 85–88, 94, 95–97; UFW organizing for the Robert Kennedy campaign, 195–96; Watts riots, 166; Zoot Suit Riots, 61
Los Angeles Central Labor Council, 91, 113
Los Angeles Daily News, 85, 92fig., 95, 104
Los Angeles Police Department, 22, 27, 99–104
Los Angeles Times: coverage of UFW internal conflict, 215; on Japanese Americans after Pearl Harbor, 48; 1910 bombing at, 11; and police brutality cases, 102, 104; Ross Sr.'s job with, 10–11
Lowrey, Eugene, 119, 120
LULAC (League of United Latin American Citizens), 76–77, 78, 81, 106, 149

Madera CSO chapter, 125–26
Maldonado, Claudia, 67–68, 69, 70
Marcos, Ferdinand, 217
Marcus, David, 68–69, 70
Marin County, Ross family in, 108, 123–24
Marshall, Thurgood, 70n, 114
Martinez, Frank, 72, 74
Matthiessen, Peter, 194, 197
McCarran-Walter Act, 119
McCarthy, Eugene, 195
McCarthy, Joseph, 79
McClure, David, 215–16

McCormick, Paul, 69, 76
McCullough, Thomas, 110
McDonnell, Donald, 109–10, 136
McGarrey, William, 163
McGucken, Joseph, 87
McWilliams, Carey, 22, 41, 66, 75; as California immigration and housing commissioner, 38, 50; and the CSO, 88–89; on immigrant assimilation, 121; and Ross, 38, 50
Mead, Margaret, 154–55
Medina, Eliseo, 182–83, 192, 218
Mencken, H. L., 35
Mendez v. Westminster, 69, 70n, 76–77
Meredith, Betty, 213
Merriam, Frank, 28
Mexican American communities: Casa Blanca, 71–74; community organizing in the 1940s Citrus Belt, 64–67; Guadalupe (Arizona) organizing project, 153–57; police brutality in, 99–104; Roybal City Council campaigns (Los Angeles), 85–88, 94, 95–97; in San Bernardino, 119–20; school desegregation efforts, 67–71, 76–77. See also Community Service Organization; individual CSO chapters
Mexican American organizations, 90, 105–6; Mexican American Political Association, 90–91, 179–80
Mexicans and Mexican Americans: anti-immigrant programs and legislation, 22, 119, 120, 121–22; anti–Mexican American sentiment and discrimination, 15, 20, 41, 64, 66–67; the bracero program, 50–51, 136–38; CSO citizenship education, 119–22, 132; deportations, 22, 29, 50, 120; as farm laborers, 66, 67; in 1920s–1930s Southern California, 15, 22; Ross's earliest contacts with, 16; Ross's work in East L.A., 1, 81, 86–91; stereotyped views of, 15, 66–67, 69, 70; Zoot Suit Riots, 61. See also United Farm Workers
Milligan (migrant acquaintance of Ross's), 30–31
Milne, Crosby, 216
Milne, Paul, 207, 216–17, 224, 226, 228

United Packinghouse Workers of America (UPWA), 135, 136–39
United Peanut Shelling Workers of America, 191*n*
U.S. Military Intelligence Service, 56
U.S. Office of Economic Opportunity (OEO), 155, 160, 163, 168–69, 171
unity councils, 65, 108, 131; Bell Town Improvement League, 68, 69–71; Casa Blanca Unity League, 71–74; Ross's feelings about, 108, 149; Ross's San Diego organizing, 78–79. *See also* California Federation for Civic Unity
University of Chicago, and TWO activism, 147
University of Southern California (USC), 20, 68; Ross at, 19–25
UPWA (United Packinghouse Workers of America), 135, 136–39
USC. *See* University of Southern California
Uweda, Kay, 57–58

Vagrancy Penal Camps, 28
Valdez, Luis, 189, 233
Ventura: Neighbor to Neighbor campaign supporting Gary Hart, 226–28
Ventura County Farm Labor Association, 136
Viega, Manuel, 76, 77, 78
Vietnam War, 165
vigilantism and violence, 60, 61, 63, 71, 203, 219
Visalia Migrant Labor Camp, 32–33, 42
Von Hoffman, Nicholas, 147
voter registration and get-out-the-vote efforts, 64, 65, 73, 73*n*; in Bell Town, 68, 69, 70; in Casa Blanca, 72, 73–74; CSO support for the John F. Kennedy campaign, 140–41; in El Modena, 77; in Guadalupe, Arizona, 154; in Los Angeles, 91, 92*fig.*, 94–95; Roybal City Council campaigns, 85–88, 94, 95–97; in San Bernardino, 119; in San Diego, 78; in San José, 112–16, 124–25; in Stockton, 127; in Syracuse, 159, 162; UFW support for the Robert F. Kennedy campaign, 195–96

Walker, Charles A., 163
Walsh, William, 158, 159, 160, 163, 164, 169, 171
war industry: African American migration and, 60; Japanese American relocation programs and, 55–56
War Manpower Commission, 55
Warner, James, 102, 104
War on Poverty, 158, 160, 169; federal Community Action project, 160, 168–69. *See also* Syracuse University antipoverty project
War Relocation Authority (WRA): Ross's Cleveland position, 5, 54–59; Ross's position at Minidoka camp, 51–54; Ross's San Francisco position, 59–61
Washburn, Scott, 222
Watts riots, 166
Weber, Devra, 29
Weinstein, Henry, 213
Western Reserve University, 57
West Riverside School District, Bell Town school desegregation efforts, 67–68, 69–71
Wiley, George, 170
Wirth, Louis, 79–80, 81
Wolman, Elmer, 24
Wolman, Eugene, 20–23, 24, 25*fig.*
women, as organizers, 70–71, 94*n*. *See also* specific individuals
Woodward, Marcus, 91
World War II: Japanese Americans as U.S. servicemen, 5, 54, 59; the Pearl Harbor attack and its aftermath, 46–47, 48–50. *See also* Japanese Americans; war industry
WRA. *See* War Relocation Authority

Yaqui Indians: the Guadalupe (Arizona) organizing project, 153–57
Yorty, Sam, 168, 180
Young, Newton, 98

Zamora, Hector, 136
Zimmerman, Ben, 158, 159
Zoot Suit Riots, 61